CATHOLICS IN THE
AMERICAN CENTURY

CATHOLICS IN THE AMERICAN CENTURY

RECASTING NARRATIVES OF U.S. HISTORY

R. SCOTT APPLEBY *and*
KATHLEEN SPROWS CUMMINGS,
EDITORS

CORNELL UNIVERSITY PRESS
Ithaca and London

First published 2012 by Cornell University Press

First printing, Cornell Paperbacks, 2012
Printed in the United States of America

Library of Congress Cataloging-in-Publication Data

Catholics in the American century : Recasting narratives
of U.S. history / R. Scott Appleby and Kathleen Sprows
Cummings, editors.
    p. cm.
  Includes bibliographical references and index.
  ISBN 978-0-8014-5140-9 (cloth : alk. paper) —
  ISBN 978-0-8014-7820-8 (pbk. : alk. paper)
  1. Catholics—United States—History—20th century.
2. Catholic Church—United States—History—20th
century. I. Appleby, R. Scott, 1956- II. Cummings,
Kathleen Sprows.

  E184.C3I5 2012
  305.6'82730904—dc23
                                        2012019700

Cornell University Press strives to use environmentally
responsible suppliers and materials to the fullest extent
possible in the publishing of its books. Such materials
include vegetable-based, low-VOC inks and acid-free
papers that are recycled, totally chlorine-free, or partly
composed of nonwood fibers. For further information,
visit our website at www.cornellpress.cornell.edu.

Cloth printing 10 9 8 7 6 5 4 3 2 1
Paperback printing 10 9 8 7 6 5 4 3 2 1

∾ CONTENTS

Introduction: The American Catholic Century

JOHN T. MCGREEVY

Time magazine's founding editor Henry Luce used to enjoy cocktails with his friend, the Jesuit priest John Courtney Murray. Almost exact contemporaries—Murray was born in 1896, Luce in 1898—the two men would relax at one of Luce's residences in Manhattan, Connecticut, or Phoenix and assess the state of the world. The urbane Murray's ease in this milieu—he once reportedly quipped that the Jesuit vow of poverty was "less a sacred promise than a regrettable fact"—made him a congenial house guest. Luce's gratitude was also personal because Murray counseled Henry and his wife, Clare Boothe Luce, on the state of their troubled marriage. In 1952 Luce whimsically drafted a "declaration of intent" (never acted on) to convert to Catholicism; his wife actually had converted a few years earlier.[1]

In December 1960 Luce placed Murray on the cover of *Time*, as visible a perch as was then available in U.S. life. The editors of *Time* conceded that Murray was little known outside Catholic circles except "among the co gnoscenti" but praised his "lucid, well-modulated concern for the United States."[2] The immediate impetus was the election just weeks earlier of John F. Kennedy, the nation's first Catholic president, and both Murray, indirectly through advice to Kennedy's aides, and Luce, a Kennedy admirer despite his longtime allegiance to the Republican Party, had assisted in the dismantling of a once seemingly ironclad prejudice against a Catholic as president.[3]

But Luce had other motives. He knew that Murray worked under a cloud of suspicion, and that the Vatican had asked the Jesuits to forbid Murray from writing on church-state issues in 1955.[4] Murray's offense was to question traditional Catholic teaching advocating unity of church and state and to insist that the U.S. experiment in religious freedom offered a worthy, even superior, alternative. The practical wisdom of Murray's approach was self-evident to the overwhelming majority of U.S. Catholics, who had neither the desire nor the capacity to make theirs a state church. But the practical challenge was significant for a global institution accustomed to confessional privileges in Spain, Italy, South America, and the Philippines.

The theological problem was trickier. What would doctrinal development on the question of religious freedom mean for other Catholic doctrines? Even in the United States traditional teaching on the union of church and state had defenders, including two prominent priest-professors at the Catholic University of America who helped persuade the Vatican to ask the Jesuits to silence Murray, and who continued to lobby for more restrictions on his activities. These priests saw alteration of church teaching on religious freedom as trading doctrinal coherence for U.S. mores. They knew that their views were unpopular. One of the priests predicted after meeting with a *Time* correspondent working on the Murray profile, "The [traditional] view which Cardinal Ottaviani and you and myself have championed will be held up to ridicule by some clever writer."[5]

Luce also appreciated Murray's more philosophical writings. Tightly linked to Murray's appreciation for the U.S. experiment in religious freedom was a fear that Americans would not be able to sustain constitutional democracy absent a greater consensus on first principles. Modern barbarians do not wear a bearskin or carry an axe, Murray explained. Instead, they "may wear a Brooks Brothers suit and carry a ballpoint pen." Catholics' concern with perennial principles and their suspicion of relativism made them more like the founders of the United States than most contemporary philosophers. "Where this kind of language is talked," Murray asserted, "the Catholic joins the conversation with complete ease. It is his language. The ideas expressed are native to his own universe of discourse. Even the accent, being American, suits his tongue."[6] Luce passed through an autodidact phase of fascination with natural-law theory and, like Murray, came to see a deeper Catholic natural-law tradition complementing a U.S. one. The *Time* cover story quoted Reinhold Niebuhr: "What makes Murray significant is that he thinks in terms of Catholic theology and the American tradition at the same time. He rejoices in being in the American tradition."[7]

This American tradition had been Henry Luce's primary concern. Luce's description of the twentieth century as one of "passionate devotion to great American ideals . . . a feeling for the equality of opportunity, a tradition of self-reliance and independence," did as much as any other statement to articulate a new confidence that the United States must "exert upon the world the full impact of our influence."[8] Luce's convictions about the global importance of U.S. civilization began during his boyhood as the son of Chinese missionaries and extended to his vigorous support for an activist U.S. foreign policy during the Cold War.

Luce carried his vision of America and its endless opportunity and abundance into the pages of the nation's most influential magazines, *Time, Life, Fortune,* and even *Sports Illustrated.* Murray carried an American vision of religious freedom, what he called "a new problem . . . put to the universal Church," into the debates of the Second Vatican Council. After considerable to and fro, the Council emerged in 1965 with a Declaration on Religious Liberty affirming Murray's vision of religious freedom as residing not in the forbearance of the state but in the inherent dignity of the individual.[9]

Luce and Murray's friendship helps orient our understanding of the American Catholic century. Already by 1900 Catholics were the nation's single largest religious group. Most of these Catholics were immigrants, and many of these immigrants, perhaps more than half, spoke a language other than English in the home. Priests, nuns, and bishops saw their task as simply to absorb or, more optimistically, catechize these immigrants, building in the process the world's most multilingual and multicultural Catholicism. In 1916, 4,475 parishes conducted services in a language other than English. As late as 1933 Catholics in Detroit heard the gospel preached in twenty-two languages.[10]

By this time the foreign-born priests, nuns, and bishops—Germans in the Midwest, French in Louisiana, Italians in much of the West, Irish everywhere—who had built the infrastructure of the Catholic Church in the nineteenth century had passed from the scene. Appreciating the freedom in the United States to build Catholic institutions, these Catholics, like their counterparts across Europe and South America, had resisted what seemed to them almost tyrannical demands for national, as opposed to Catholic, self-identification. As one Italian Jesuit, trained in Turin but living in California, sarcastically explained in 1874, "You know the State is every thing & every thing should be for the benefit of the State, cost what it may. Thanks to heaven, we have succeeded in this glorious 19th century in getting rid of that old-fogish maxim that the State is made for men."[11]

Their successors more fully absorbed a patriotic ethos, and Catholics on both sides of the North Atlantic, especially after the sacrifices made by

Catholic soldiers in all armies during World War I, made their peace with a nationalism once thought too ready to substitute the nation-state for religious loyalties.[12] Baltimore's Cardinal Gibbons, the prelate widely perceived as the leader of the U.S. bishops and a man who cultivated associations with Theodore Roosevelt, William Howard Taft, and other political leaders, proclaimed his pride in belonging to "a country where the civil government holds over us the aegis of its protection, without interfering with us in the legitimate exercise of our sublime mission as ministers of the Gospel of Christ. Our country has liberty without license, and authority without despotism."[13] This more sympathetic understanding of the U.S. national project was reinforced by a diminishment of religious prejudice, a pattern interrupted by the rise of the second Ku Klux Klan and anti-Catholicism during the 1928 presidential campaign of Al Smith but consolidated during the shared experience of the Depression and service during World War II.

By then the contours of the Catholic response to a U.S. modernity—happily in the United States but not quite of it—had been established. Catholics pledged their loyalty to the U.S. nation-state, but they also assumed that the Catholic faith could not flourish absent a Catholic milieu. To that end they built a vast network of institutions and associations that limited contact with what they understood as a potentially subversive U.S. society. The most important of these institutions were parochial schools, a system that at its height enrolled up to half and in some cities well over half of Catholic schoolchildren and constituted the largest private school system in the world. And this parochial school system lay nestled within an archipelago of Catholic beliefs and groups, from Marian apparitions to the Knights of Columbus, from rosary crusades to Catholic hospitals.

How these Catholic ideas and institutions at once inhibited and facilitated assimilation into U.S. society is the central drama of twentieth-century U.S. Catholic history. The assimilation accelerated in the crucial first decades after World War II, when the children of immigrants were now a generation past the restrictive laws of the 1920s, and when Catholics were moving into white-collar jobs during the postwar economic boom, purchasing suburban homes, and sending children to college. The Jesuit sociologist John Thomas worried in the 1950s that the newly affluent, suburban landscape of U.S. Catholicism might shatter the "time- and space-ignoring solidarity" of the Catholic milieu.[14]

Robert Orsi's chapter sketches assimilation's limits. Orsi's Henry Luce, rightly, is less the friend of John Courtney Murray than the descendant of a long line of Protestants conceiving the nation in direct antithesis to Catholicism, merging American and Protestant tropes about the United States as a "providential nation."[15]

Orsi stresses that the Catholic route to full status as U.S. citizens traveled through a distinctively Catholic focus on suffering and sacrifice, from the Jesuit martyrs of the seventeenth and eighteenth centuries to Tom Dooley working in Vietnam in the 1950s. Just as Dooley refused pain medication in his unsuccessful bout with cancer, to the cheers of the Catholic press, so did a theological vision of suffering as productive, necessary work inform narratives of Catholic patriotism. The consumer society celebrated in Henry Luce's magazines—"How does one prepare for an Age of Plenty?" asked *Life* cheerfully in 1954—worried Catholics accustomed to denouncing the "chronic social sickness" brought on by "economic liberalism."[16] By the 1960s, Orsi demonstrates, Catholics had become fully American, but they had done so through a circuitous, peculiar set of beliefs and institutions that they and some of their historians tried to repress in the immediate aftermath of the Second Vatican Council.

R. Marie Griffith's chapter points to another area of assimilation and distinctiveness, gender and sexuality. That Catholics made up roughly a quarter of the nation's population during the twentieth century, that their leaders held to a particular, well-developed view of sexuality and gender, and that contemporary historians of sexuality and gender have neglected to integrate Catholicism into their accounts are Griffith's starting points. She draws on Leslie Woodcock Tentler's study of Catholics and birth control to survey the ways in which disparate reformers, including Margaret Sanger, Alfred Kinsey, and Mary Steichen Calderone, managed their interactions with Catholic leaders and ideas.[17]

Here too there was assimilation. Catholics by the 1980s were slightly less supportive of legal abortion than other Americans but otherwise virtually identical in their use of contraceptives, approval of divorce and remarriage, and support for rights for gays and lesbians.

But assimilation is again not the only story. If reformers such as Kinsey viewed celibacy as pathological, Catholics saw it as an exalted state. If reformers saw the spacing of children as common sense, some of the most idealistic Catholics of the 1950s welcomed large families as an implicit challenge to a focus on consumption and material goods.

This Catholic sexual ethic became visible in surprising ways. In 1948 Catholic voters in Massachusetts decisively rejected a proposal to ease the distribution of birth-control devices for married couples. As late as the 1950s Catholic college-educated women, when polled on the question of how many children they judged would make an ideal family, calmly answered "five." (With their response, these women destroyed the almost universal demographic truth that women's fertility diminishes with increased women's education.) In the 1970s Catholics took the lead in the pro-life movement, one of the most sustained social protest movements of the late twentieth and early twenty-first centuries.

The same dynamic of assimilation and distinctiveness informs Thomas Sugrue's chapter on Catholics and the politics of the 1960s. The extant literature on Catholics and twentieth-century politics is currently anchored at the local level, with Evelyn Sterne and Mary Wingerd demonstrating the ways in which Catholicism shaped political machines in Providence and St. Paul.[18] That Catholics, unlike their confessional counterparts in much of Europe and South America, did not form a political party seems to leave little room for religious actors to exert political influence.

Sugrue demonstrates the opposite. He concedes that the numerous Catholic political figures of the 1960s—ranging from William F. Buckley to Robert Kennedy, Eugene McCarthy, Cesar Chavez, and Daniel Patrick Moynihan—did not share a common political vision, but he also suggests how Catholic principles of social justice, ideas of the family, and reaction against an overbearing state inform this disparate group. Sugrue draws on the work of Joshua Zeitz to note that Catholics and Jews located in the same suburbs might arrive at entirely different policy preferences, and he argues that the Catholic flight to the suburbs helped reorient the spatial contours of U.S. public life.[19] Sugrue even suggests how artifacts of the Catholic nineteenth century, notably the existence of a massive parochial school system that effectively taxed parents sending children to parochial schools twice, once for the local public school and once for the Catholic school, helped fuel the tax revolt of the 1970s.

Wilfred McClay, too, is intrigued by the political consequences of Catholic ideas. His outline of the role played by Catholic social thought in the contemporary alliance between Protestant and Catholic social conservatives illuminates one of the most important and unanticipated developments in U.S. politics. McClay's Catholic moment—drawing on Richard John Neuhaus's hope that Catholicism might serve as a guiding public philosophy in a public sphere bereft of sophisticated reflection on the common good—is brief, disabled by the sexual-abuse crisis, a Democratic Party irrevocably committed to a pro-choice position on abortion, and a powerful libertarian strain within the Republican Party. Still, the fate of the most important piece of social legislation since the 1960s, President Obama's health-care bill, seemed for a time to lie in the hands of Catholics, with Speaker of the House Nancy Pelosi and Michigan congressman Bart Stupak deciding how to balance competing claims about the bill's effect on public funding of abortions.

David Gutiérrez returns us to the topic of immigration, where the American Catholic century began. When Murray and Luce first began chatting about the fate of the U.S. experiment, they could understandably view the immigrant era as part of Catholic and U.S. history, not its present.

Now we know better. Just before Murray and Luce died, Senator Edward Kennedy led the reform of the nation's immigration laws, little imagining that the rate of immigration (legal and illegal) to the United States would soon rival that of the late nineteenth century. Latino Catholic immigrants, in particular, now make up at least one-third of the U.S. Catholic population, and their importance for both church and society will only increase. Roughly seven of ten of these Latinos identify as Catholic, and a pitched effort is under way to sustain the allegiance of Latino Catholics against the twin competitors of secularization and Protestant evangelicalism.

Gutiérrez might add that the rapid secularization of Euro-American Catholics makes the role of Latinos even more pivotal for Catholicism's future. The fastest-growing group within U.S. society, according to the Pew Religious Landscape Survey of 2008, is those claiming no affiliation with any church or religious tradition, a full 16.1 percent of the population, more than double the percentage of twenty years ago. Fully one-third of U.S. Catholics are lapsed or at least not regular churchgoers, and one in ten U.S. citizens is a lapsed Catholic. The sharpest declines are in once heavily Catholic areas such as New England, where detachment from the institutional church, a pattern evident for a generation but accelerated by the sexual-abuse crisis, is transforming the religious ethos of the region.[20]

The end of the American Catholic century, then, resembles its beginning. Once again an immigrant church with a fragile institutional structure attempts to navigate an uncertain environment. The atmosphere, in sharp contrast to 1960 and even 1900, is one of fractious Catholic decline, not growth, with Catholics divided on ideological grounds from one another and a clergy considerably more conservative than even active Catholics within a shrinking laity. But Catholicism remains the single largest institution in the United States beyond the federal government, encompassing thousands of parishes, schools, social service agencies, and associations with a reach extending to all corners of U.S. society.

Writing its history is not a simple task. Lizabeth Cohen anticipates a "broadband" history able to take advantage of the gains made by social historians since the 1970s but also attuned to new global emphases. She urges practitioners to move from San Antonio—perhaps the Boston of the twenty-first century, with Catholicism shaping civic, cultural, and religious life—to Mexico to Rome and back again. She joins Vincent Viaene and other historians in placing Catholicism, at the center of the more global and transatlantic currents so powerfully shaping the historical profession.[21]

This advice, too, takes historians of U.S. Catholicism full circle. Early twentieth-century historians of Catholicism, usually priests and nuns, knew that theirs was an international church with direct ties to Roman authorities. Laypeople, especially women, appeared only in the margins of their narratives, organized around episcopal appointments made, churches founded, and schools begun. The next generation of scholars of Catholicism focused more on the laity (although still insufficiently on women) and pondered whether and how the U.S. experience produced a U.S. Catholicism.

Now the current has again reversed, with Catholicism in the United States more likely to be understood as one setting for dilemmas besetting the universal church. Peter D'Agostino's history of Italian immigrants, Vatican officials, and U.S. bishops, all shifting their attention back and forth between Rome and the United States, set a new standard for integration. We see this new global emphasis in books not especially concerned with U.S. history, such as John Connelly's powerful new history of European Catholics and race, where a U.S. haven for Catholic refugees from Nazism permits breathtaking changes in official church teaching on Judaism and the Jews, or in Matthew Connelly's study of global efforts to control population, where Catholics and their opponents in the United States play significant roles.[22] We see it in new histories of seemingly narrow theological quarrels over modernism during the nineteenth century, newly illuminated and broadened when they are viewed from beyond the United States.[23] We see it too in the international history of the Second Vatican Council, the single most important religious event of the twentieth century, with John O'Malley's survey offering a clear, if contested, intellectual history.[24]

I could list even more excellent new books with a global or international emphasis on topics as diverse as the parish trustee controversies of the early nineteenth century, the Catholic response to antebellum slavery, Italian Jesuits in the Southwest, and the migration of French Catholic intellectuals to the United States in the 1930s and 1940s. These scholars, unusually for U.S. history, write in German, French, and Italian, as well as English, and often make use of Roman archives, shedding a more cosmopolitan light on what were once understood as strictly U.S. problems.[25]

Certainly there is more work to do. The sheer scope of Catholic influence in U.S. history on topics insufficiently treated in this volume, ranging from prayer to popular culture to foreign policy, remains daunting. Scott Appleby's conclusion to this volume effectively summarizes this literature while also pointing to new directions. Luce and Murray, the most important U.S. journalist and the most important U.S. Catholic intellectual of the twentieth century, also understood this. Both men had a feel for the nature of global institutions—in the mass media and religion—and the unpredictable qualities of their histories.

The two men died in 1967, a few months apart, just before the dissolution of the liberal consensus they had shaped and the U.S. establishment they had joined. Their last exchange of letters expressed puzzlement about growing student radicalism. For Luce's generation of U.S. leaders, the quagmire in Vietnam sabotaged the hope of remaking the world in a democratic, pluralist image. (They never guessed that these hopes would resurface almost forty years later, in an even more utopian mode, as policymakers sent U.S. troops into the Middle East.) For Murray's generation of Catholics, the trauma of dissent on the topic of birth control, the movement away from natural-law philosophy as an architectonic discipline, and the entrance of U.S. Catholics into all sectors of U.S. life made discussion of a coherent Catholic complement to mainstream U.S. society less plausible.

Of course, the end of Luce and Murray's worlds is not the end of ours. Rather, the challenge is to better understand their experience as one chapter in a still-unfinished story of engagement between the world's most powerful nation and the world's most important global institution.

∞ CHAPTER 1

U.S. Catholics between Memory and Modernity

How Catholics Are American

ROBERT A. ORSI

> The first explorers of our coasts were Catholic, and when they landed they planted the symbol of the Cross, and so studded their maps with names from the Church calendar, that we can trace their course by them.
>
> John Gilmary Shea

> We are perhaps about to give our blood and our lives in the cause of our Master, Jesus Christ. . . . Blessed be His Name forever, that He has chosen us, among so many better than we, to aid Him to bear His cross in this land.
>
> Jean De Brébeuf

By the 1960s and 1970s Catholics in the United States seemed to have become indistinguishable from their fellow Americans. By every measure—where they lived and whom they married, their levels of education, professional achievements (which included a Catholic president), how much money they made, and even, after the reforms mandated by the Second Vatican Council, how they worshipped—Catholics looked more like other Americans than their parents and grandparents had. They had "come of age" (a much-used phrase among Catholics in these years). Two prominent Catholic writers argued in a popular 1966 volume that this was the age of the "de-Romanization of the American Catholic Church," by which they meant the passage of U.S. Catholics from "authoritarianism" to "freedom," from privilege" to "achievement," from "corporate" to "personal responsibility," and from "other" to "this-world valuation." Catholics had become fully American, and in becoming fully American, they had become thoroughly modern. Articles in Catholic family magazines endlessly drew a stark contrast between a living and hopeful modern religious present and the dead religious inheritance of the past. This antithesis became the framework for assessing everything from the clothes nuns wore to the sounds of the liturgy and to the kinds of conversations Catholic parents might have with their children. (The title of a 1972 Catholic guide for the parents of teenagers was *We Were Never Their Age*.) So confidently American were Catholics now that they even had the courage of public political dissent. Among the enduring images of the era, which had the force of revelation at the time, were those of nuns and priests marching in Selma and of Fathers Daniel Berrigan (a Jesuit) and Philip Berrigan (a Josephite) bending together in prayer over a flaming pile of draft files they had removed from the Selective Service Office in Catonsville, Maryland, and set aflame with napalm in a protest against the Vietnam War.[1]

In the very evidence of how contemporary U.S. Catholics had ostensibly become in the 1960s and 1970s, however, there were hints that the break between the ancient and the modern was not as sharp as the change from the Latin to the English Mass made it seem or that some Catholics in these years were hoping. The stories that circulated among Catholic progressives of Father Philip Berrigan repeatedly stabbing himself in the arm to get more and more of his blood to pour on draft files at a political action before Catonsville had less to do with U.S. modernity and Catholic arrival than with inherited traditions of sainthood, martyrdom, and bodily mortification. The same was true of Cesar Chavez marching on a dusty road behind an image of La Señora de Guadalupe and of priests and nuns leading public rosaries and processions against slum landlords and drug dealers on inner-city streets, two other instances of Catholic action in the public sphere in this era. Other Americans did not always fully comprehend what Catholics were doing at such times and found aspects of these political rituals repugnant. Fire, chant, ashes, pilgrimage, blood, sacrifice, discipline, and surrender—these were the idioms of Catholic civic protest in the period (on the right too, in early Catholic actions against abortion, for example). Catholics might have become like other Americans, but they remained different too, although this was not how it seemed to Catholics at the time (or since).[2]

When they reflected on this new moment in their history, Catholics in the 1960s and 1970s proposed two inconsistent ways of relating the present to the past, both charged with deep feelings and contemporary aspirations and needs. The present represented, they said, a radical break with the past (there was disagreement over whether this was good or bad), by which they meant with the world of their own childhoods, in particular the devotional culture of late nineteenth- and mid-twentieth-century American Catholicism. Devotionalism refers to the extensive repertoire of things and practices by which Catholics interacted with the supernatural, which they took to be present to them in the circumstances of their everyday lives. Now this world of novenas and rosaries, graphic crucifixes, relics and holy cards, endless rounds of prayers and pains offered up for the souls in purgatory, and other practices was said to belong to a distant past.

But chroniclers of the history of the U.S. church also created a new overarching narrative of U.S. Catholicism in which Catholics in the United States, or at least the best and most forward looking of them, had always been modern and American, if only in anticipation, despite the impediments of immigration, working-class obstinacy, devotional culture, and "Rome." Catholic otherness, in other words, had coexisted with another way of being Catholic in the United States that was from the very beginning American, republican, and modern. It was overwhelmed at the end of the nineteenth century by the new European immigration and then by the devotional ethos of the early twentieth century, but this was the true inheritance of American Catholicism. A study of U.S. Catholic "spiritual life" from the colonial era to the 1960s, for example, written during the bicentennial of the Catholic Church in America with the approval of the National Conference of Catholic Bishops, argued that the American church's first bishop had established in the eighteenth century the template for the "synthesis" of American and Catholic identities, which stood as an "ideal for his own and future generations." The past of Catholicism in the United States had become at once completely alien (in its devotional life) and completely familiar (in being once and forever American).[3]

In remembering their past in the United States in this way, Catholics were forgetting and denying it. This was obviously so in one respect. Catholics in the age of de-Romanization threw away in great trash heaps the old statues that had filled their churches, the special instruments needed for various rituals (often made of precious metals), vestments and other religious garments, holy pictures, and pieces of church architecture, such as old wooden confessional boxes, making this time a chapter in the history of Western iconoclasm. I recently purchased a sacrarium on E-Bay. A sacrarium was the special sink in the sacristy behind the altar that led into the ground rather than into sewer lines, as ordinary sinks do. It was intended for the disposal of liquids that had been in contact with the real body of Christ, such as the water used to clean golden chalices of residue of the consecrated wine at Mass, which Catholics believed to be literally God's blood. A church in Washington State had disposed of this one. I paid about $200 for it, as a piece of archaeological evidence to show my students. But memory and history proved to be just as effective media for disposing of the past.

Historians of modern Western culture maintain that forgetting is a fundamental requirement of being modern for persons and nations. To be modern is to be liberated from the past, which is understood to be at best irrelevant and at worst an obstacle to happiness, success, and fulfillment. Modern liberal democratic nationalism requires amnesia about the racism, intolerance, violence, and religious exclusions of its foundations (which includes for Western liberal states the persecution and exile of Catholics, especially Catholic priests and vowed women religious, many of whom fled from Europe to the United States, where they became the founders of the U.S. church). Religiously speaking, being modern entails forgetting that the supernatural—gods, spirits, demons, and ancestors—had once upon a time, and not that long ago, been free of the limits imposed on it by the modern world and had regularly intruded on the natural, in miracles, for instance, or apparitions, or as God's body and blood under the priest's hands on the altar. It also means denying that in many parts of the modern world, the supernatural continues to so impinge on everyday life. Theorist Bruno Latour calls the processes of modern forgetting "purification," by which he means the creation in experience, imagination, and the law of modern nation-states of two "zones," one human (or natural), the other nonhuman (and supernatural), with the boundary between them strictly monitored and enforced.[4] Catholics came late to the discipline of modern forgetting, as late as the very end of the modern era, but they came at last. The onset of amnesia was for a time, in the 1960s and 1970s, a topic in Catholic popular periodicals. Then even the fact of forgetting was lost.[5]

But throughout the nineteenth century and well into the twentieth, Catholics in the United States and around the world specialized precisely in the mingling of the human and the nonhuman. Modern Catholics in the United States addressed their needs to images and statues. They anointed their homes, their bodies, and, later, their automobiles with holy water and oil. In the early twentieth century they prayed along with radio rosaries. They accepted and even welcomed pain in their bodies, going so far as to eschew painkillers when these became more common in twentieth-century medicine, taking their pain as an intimate and privileged connection to the redemptive suffering of Jesus on the cross and with the company of saints in their martyrdom. Until the 1960s and 1970s priests and nuns in the United States, as elsewhere in the Catholic world, inflicted pain on themselves with chains and whips in penitential disciplines required by their communities. U.S. Catholics waited with great excitement for news of the intervention of the nonhuman in the zone of the human, and they were not disappointed: the supernatural broke into the natural in Necedah, Wisconsin, in Bayside, Queens, and on the Grand Concourse in the Bronx, among other places, in the mid-twentieth century. Given this divergent ontology (meaning the understanding of what exists and how things exist) and metaphysics (the nature of the reality underlying what exists), modernity has not been especially hospitable to Catholics. Catholics have lived fully in the modern world, but modern Catholics were not always purified. It is not necessary to accept Max Weber's thesis entirely to see that there was a deep congruence between Protestantism and the various spirits of the modern world or that Catholicism was essentially out of alignment with these spirits. Catholics engaged modernity actively and fiercely and set their own terms in the confrontation. They lived robustly in the modern world—among other places, in the United States—but at an angle askew to the dominant culture.[6]

So it not true that the relationship between the identities "American" and "Catholic" was without problems and tensions, however successfully at different times particular Catholic writers and editors negotiated the two. (The most successful of such translators were American Protestant converts to Catholicism, such as Orestes Brownson and Isaac Hecker, in the nineteenth century.) The specific practices of the Catholic faith were alien and out of place in American culture. Well into the 1950s the cult of the saints, Catholic penitential idioms, the celibacy of vowed religious, or the way Catholics used holy oils and waters were the objects of morbid and sometimes pornographic fascination, of contempt, and, from time to time, of religious desire for other Americans. Moreover, from the colonial era forward, what the phrases "America" and "the New World" meant to Americans who were not Catholic derived their most emotionally compelling and politically consequential meanings from being cast in bitter and intractable opposition to Catholicism. America did not have anti-Catholic movements, Yale American religious historian Sydney E. Ahlstrom once said; America *is* an anti-Catholic movement. Throughout the nineteenth and early twentieth centuries Catholics in the United States understood that they would have to find a way into American public memory and civic culture that were imagined against them.[7]

How Catholics Are American

Catholics did so—to anticipate the argument that follows—in two ways. They took hold of the American story, as it was told by others, for Catholicism, going so far as to claim that what is best about the American nation, including its republican heritage, is rooted in the Catholic tradition.

Catholics in the United States also elaborated a powerfully evocative story about the church in the New World in the tropes and figures of Catholic hagiography and devotion that posited a different origin and destiny for Catholics and for the nation than those proposed by the dominant U.S. Protestant traditions of public memory and national identification. These two Catholic expressions of national memory, the civic and the sacred (as I will call them), were intertwined, but they were also different and often in tension with each other. (One of the things that happened in the 1960s and 1970s was that the civic traditions eclipsed the sacred story in U.S. Catholic consciousness.) The fact that Catholics in the United States possessed their own traditions of national myth and memory has been consequential for how they have acted in the U.S. public sphere. Philip Berrigan had more in common with Saint Isaac Jogues, to look ahead to a figure who appears later in this chapter, than he did with his fellow antiwar activists Benjamin Spock and William Sloane Coffin. Coming to national participation, memory, and identity by different routes, Catholics became other kinds of citizens.

These are the questions of this chapter, then: What stories and memories have grounded Catholic citizenship in the United States, and what kinds of citizens have Catholics been as a result? I will be concerned with what is forgotten about the meaning of "America" and with how Catholics lived with and against "American" national memory before they also forgot what others had forgotten. At issue too is the meaning and nature of modern nationalism. The case of U.S. Catholics, who were never anything other than the most loyal citizens but who were also excluded and estranged from the nation's sanctioned collective public languages, shows that the stories, images, and memories that went into the making of the public in the modern nation-state and its citizens were plural and incommensurate and included ways of being in the world that were at odds with the modern. I am talking about Catholics here, but similar arguments might be made about Muslims in Hosni Mubarak's Egypt, for example, and in other places where discrepant religious imaginaries intersected with the modern as it was authorized and normalized by various political economies. This pluralism of imaginaries may or may not have made for a more robust public sphere, but it means that the nationalism of modern states, which is commonly presented as univocal, universal, and inclusive, is seamed and fractured with divergent ontologies. Men and women of ancient faiths such as Catholicism have found their own ways of being modern citizens.

∽Catholics and the American Century

The most influential twentieth-century expression of the providential identity and mission of the United States was the notion of "the American Century" propounded by the founder of *Time, Life,* and *Fortune* magazines, Henry R. Luce, in 1941. Luce maintained that the ever-darkening world of his time had two choices: to embark under the leadership of the United States on an American Century, taking American values and virtues as its destiny, or to descend to its final terrible doom. Luce was drawing deeply here from the wellsprings of American political culture. The belief that the new world of America was, in Luce's words, "a special dispensation— under Providence," was first voiced in 1630 aboard the *Arbella* by John Winthrop in an address to the small, huddled cohort of English Puritans he was leading across the icy North Atlantic toward New England and religious freedom (for themselves, not for others, as Catholic historians would later emphasize).

Luce's connection to this ancient source of American nationalism was genetic as well as ideological. The first Henry Luce came to New England's shores just thirteen years after Winthrop's landing. Luce himself was born in China in 1898 to Presbyterian missionaries who had passionately embraced the late nineteenth-century American version of Winthrop's vision of the city on the hill, the evangelical summons to go forth and claim the world for Christ. This was a Christian calling, but a specifically American one too. Luce's parents, writes his biographer, "saw America as a providential land, selected [by God] to bring about the conversion of all peoples, perhaps in this generation." The United States, deemed "essentially good" by evangelicals like Luce's parents, was responsible for fulfilling its destiny "by doing unto others what God had done for the United States," an anticipation of Henry's later idea that the Bill of Rights was "our free gift to all peoples." A family friend who wrote to Luce's mother after the publication of "The American Century" noted the resonances of her son's idea with her and her husband's determination to go forth and save China, and Luce himself received a note of congratulation on his talk from the Presbyterian Board of Foreign Missions.[8]

But who is included in the designation "American" in the "American Century"? Luce was an ardent foe of isolationism. He fretted that his contemporaries were naïve in their determination not to go to war again, and he was anxious to mobilize the country in 1941 for the vast military and humanitarian campaign against tyranny, totalitarianism, and poverty he thought it was the United States' historical destiny to undertake in the near future.

To be effective, nationalism must have at least the pretense of universality and inclusivity, and certainly Luce understood himself to be talking about the responsibility of all Americans. As it turned out, U.S. citizens of all religious faiths loyally and doggedly assumed the burden of destiny Luce identified as America's by serving in the armed forces in the long years of World War II and in later campaigns of the American Century in Korea and Vietnam. By rising to the challenges of war, Catholic immigrants and migrants around the country, relative newcomers to the idea of "America" as Luce meant it, proved to others that they were Americans as they discovered this for themselves. Then, amid eventual postwar economic prosperity, a celebratory public culture of national religious harmony and inclusion took shape, and the United States was declared in all the media of modern communication a single nation of three religions. This spirit was exemplified for the wartime generation by the gripping story and imagery of the Four Chaplains (two Protestant ministers, a rabbi, and a Catholic priest) who surrendered their life jackets and went to their deaths with their heads bowed in common prayer on the USS *Dorchester*, torpedoed by a German U-boat in February 1943. The "American" in "American Century" appeared to mean all the men and women of the faiths represented by the four chaplains. Catholics in these years and later who identified Catholicism and "America" partook of this relatively recent ethos of national harmony and unity.[9]

There is a sleight of hand here, however, or a sleight of memory. Like all constructions of modernity, the American Century entailed forgetting—among other things, forgetting the racist savagery of the country's first imperial enterprises, campaigns that hardly exemplified Luce's reckoning of the country's core values as "a love of freedom, a feeling for the equality of opportunity, a tradition of self-reliance and independence, and also of cooperation." The idea of the American Century also entailed forgetting the necessary relationship between such assertions of the moral and political superiority of the United States and the nation's ingrained and formative anti-Catholicism. Whatever Luce meant, the "America" that would save the world as he envisioned it had been constructed from the start around the necessary exclusion of Catholicism. Winthrop's new world was meant to be the religious, ecclesiastical, and political antithesis to Catholicism. God willed it to be planted in New England's soil precisely in order to save the world in due time from Catholicism. The beginning made here was defined by being free of Catholicism. In this way Catholicism as the necessary oppositional figure to the idea of "America" was built right into the nation's myth and memory. The Puritans were well aware, moreover, that not only had they not come to a land free of Catholics but that Catholics, who had arrived here first and enjoyed more stable relationships with Native allies, surrounded the fragile British colonies on the north and south. This drove a spike of terror and paranoia into American memory. The long tradition of American exceptionalism, the idea of America's godly mission, explicitly—and anxiously—set the redemptive hope of the Atlantic settlements against the decadence and corruption of Europe and of Catholics, real and imaginary, closer to home.

This was true of the revolutionary generation too. As political theorist and historian Anthony Marx writes about John Locke, by the time the British philosopher was advocating religious toleration—exempting Catholics (and Muslims)—violence against Catholics in England had already successfully killed them off, driven them underground, or sent them into exile. "Nations drink at the fountains of Lethe," Marx writes, "clearing their memories, before their rebirth in the Hades of modernity." By the mid-1700s the view that England's "prosperity was associated with Protestantism and democracy" had become axiomatic to its national identity; "by the following century, justifications for England's profitable imperial rule over others included the image of spreading Protestant prosperity and of 'scientific racism' evocative of earlier anti-Catholicism. . . . Thus the legacies of intolerance were carried forward." American Anglo-Saxonism inherited this legacy and this cast of mind, which Marx calls "purposeful forgetting." Catholic historians at the turn of the twentieth century, who had not forgotten, pointed out how slowly religious toleration was introduced in the American nation.[10]

The new United States lacked an established church, but Protestant historian and diplomat Robert Baird affirmed America's identity as Protestant Christian in his 1844 work *Religion in America*. "Like many others of his generation," historian Daniel Walker Howe writes, "Baird saw evangelical Protestantism as the legatee of Puritanism, the core of American culture, the source of American democratic institutions, the primary engine of economic and political progress, and ultimately the hope of the world." Baird was writing amid a national storm over slavery, but the fears of the country's citizens had also been aroused by, and displaced onto, Catholic immigrants arriving in this period from Germany and Ireland. This was the start of a demographic revolution that would forever change the religious landscape of the country. Prominent Protestant figures worried that Catholics were taking over the American West, with good reason: the 1830s and 1840s witnessed the explosive institutional growth of the church in the United States as dioceses were founded in rapid succession across the frontier in anticipation of the great American church that still did not exist other than as Catholic ambition. The response to the visibility of Catholics in the Protestant nation was a season of anti-Catholic violence. In the year Baird's work came out (it was published first in Europe, where he worked as an agent to secure Protestant rights in Catholic nations), deadly riots against Irish Catholics engulfed Philadelphia, resulting in the destruction of several Catholic churches and religious houses and the burning of a major Catholic library of precious volumes.[11]

The Anglo-Saxon core of the belief in American moral superiority became ever more strident as the country's foreign policy became more ambitious and militant after the Civil War, Public support for war against Spain in Cuba was whipped up by anti-Catholic hysteria, although there were more than 150 Catholic crewmen on the USS *Maine*, and on the night it was sunk the only chaplain on board was a Catholic priest. Protestant preachers and U.S. journalists promoted the subsequent U.S. engagement in the Philippines in great measure because it was aimed at rescuing the islands from a Catholic power. The behavior of U.S. soldiers in the guerrilla war in the Philippines was marked by crude and blatant anti-Catholicism. Stories appeared in the Catholic press of U.S. troops digging up the graves of dead priests for buried treasure. One of the most lionized heroes of the war, Brigadier General Frederick N. Funston, was accused of "personally desecrating" a Catholic church and "leading a mock mass in ecclesiastic garb." It was in the Catholic Philippines that the custom arose of U.S. soldiers sending home photographs of the bodies of tortured and mutilated insurgents for their sweethearts' scrapbooks.[12]

Catholics in the United States had been supportive of the war against Spain, although they were anxious about church property and wary of the ambitions of Protestant missionaries who would follow the soldiers. But their enthusiasm for U.S. imperial adventures waned as the stories of atrocities and desecration mounted and soldiers came back from the islands with relics looted from churches as souvenirs. Taking up the cause of Filipino insurgents, the U.S. Catholic press denounced U.S. imperialism as anti-Catholic. "From this time forth," the *New York Freeman's Journal* concluded its protest against the ban on religious (meaning Catholic) instruction in the newly organized public schools of the U.S. empire, "wherever imperialism casts its black shadow there will be a systematized and energetic anti-Catholic campaign, backed by limitless financial resources." American prelates eventually added their voices to Catholic anti-imperialism.[13] A wedge had been driven between U.S. Catholicism and the nation's confidence and certainty in its providential global mission.

Catholics often found themselves out of step with U.S. foreign policy in the twentieth century, especially when its imperatives and exigencies were framed, as they often were, in the language of Anglo-Saxon superiority and global mission. Catholics served in the U.S. armed forces, but this does not mean that they or their loved ones on the home front understood their commitment and sacrifice in the same terms as other Americans did theirs. War seems to erase all divisions in a spirit of national unity, but Catholics remained anxious about what U.S. actions abroad meant for the church and for their families overseas, understandably so since many of the military conflicts of the American Century took place in Catholic lands. During World War II Catholics feared that U.S. forces would not make it a priority to protect Catholic holy sites in the Italian campaign, especially in Rome. Characteristically of the ambiguous place of Catholics in the United States, they also worried that if they were too vocal in their concerns, other Americans would accuse them of disregarding the lives of U.S. soldiers.

The postwar ideology of national harmony, made still more urgent and demanding by the anxieties of the Cold War, along with the changing social fortunes of Catholics in the United States, contributed to the forgetting of the historical and foundational connection between U.S. nationalism and anti-Catholicism. But in the middle of World War II, when their patriotism could not have been clearer, U.S. Catholics fretted that other Americans doubted their loyalties. President Truman's nomination of General Mark Clark in 1951 as ambassador to the Vatican sparked a miniepisode of renewed national Protestant hysteria. The fact is that Catholics never completely shared the traditions of memory and identity that went into the making of the "American Century."[14]

∞ "How Catholic America Was"/"Loyalty of Catholics Futile"

The nation's centennial in 1876 and the Columbian celebrations later in the century fostered a public appetite for American history that Catholics shared. They had their own reasons as well for wanting to tell the story of Catholicism's development in the United States for their generation. Because Columbus was Catholic, Catholics felt a special connection to the story of the New World's founding. Columbus sailed under the aegis of Catholic monarchs on a ship named after the Blessed Mother. "One of the primary objects in his voyage westward," a popular Catholic textbook reminded readers in

1928, "was to propagate the Catholic faith." Catholic publications aimed at a new market of Catholic readers flourished amid growing national prosperity in the 1880s; the rapidly expanding Catholic parochial school system needed classroom texts on American history suitable for Catholic youngsters. Modern U.S. Catholic historiography commences in this period in the career of New Yorker John Gilmary Shea (1824–92), an indefatigable writer and promoter of the study of the history of Catholics in the United States. Shea was possessed by a grand poetic vision of Catholic destiny in North America, which he saw as beginning before the Protestant settlements in New England and stretching across the American frontiers well in advance of Protestant easterners. Of special interest to him were the intimate ties between Catholic missionaries and Native Americans from the sixteenth century up to his own time. It was Shea's thesis that "the tribes evangelized by the French and Spanish subsist to this day, except where brought into contact with the colonists of England and their allies or descendants[,] while it is notorious that the tribes in the territories colonized by England, have in many cases entirely disappeared, and perished without ever having the gospel preached to them." What was most enduring of ancient America in the present, in other words, existed in relation to Catholicism, proof of the faith's longevity and priority on these shores. Shea's works, in particular his monumental *History of the Catholic Church in the United States* (in four volumes, 1886–92), were widely influential among Catholics and contributed to the rise of U.S. Catholic historical consciousness at the turn of the twentieth century.[15]

Catholic popular historians were responding as well to more threatening currents in the nation in the turbulent decades from the end of the Civil War through the 1920s. Anti-Catholicism was on the rise again, provoked, as in the early nineteenth century, by Catholic immigration and migration, this time from terrifying stiletto-wielding southern Italy, in the perfervid fantasies of Americans, as well as from eastern Europe, Ireland, and Mexico. The United States was becoming an urban nation—the 1920 census revealed for the first time a majority of Americans living in cities—and manufacture and industry were replacing farms and small shops as U.S. workplaces. These changes occasioned a crisis of national identity, and yet again Catholics, who were associated with all the things that Americans feared most about their time, became the necessary foil for the reassertion of the real meaning of America. The nation's anti-Catholicism was most extreme and politically effective in the period shortly before Luce's summons to common national sacrifice and destiny, culminating in the imposition of national Prohibition (Catholics opposed it, not surprisingly to the movement's supporters, who had long associated alcohol abuse with working-class Catholics), immigration restriction in 1924, the revival of the Ku Klux Klan, and the humiliation of Alfred E. Smith Jr. in the presidential election of 1928.

It was in these convulsive decades that Catholics in the United States generated the traditions of national memory I identified earlier as the civic and the sacred. Shea's work provided the sources, arguments, and plots. The civic narratives aimed to show how Catholics fit into the American story. The impulse of the civic narratives was assimilative, as assimilative as Catholics could be in the United States. American Catholic sacred memory, on the other hand, was deeply imbued with a Catholic religious sensibility, grounded in the tropes and images of devotional culture, of liturgy, and of Catholic theology, which put it most at odds with the dominant story of the modern American nation. The two traditions of Catholic national narrative were intertwined. Sacred memory more or less followed the plot of the civic narrative; the spirit of the sacred memory burned within even the most anxiously American versions of the Catholic civic narrative. It is possible to view the two as public history and sacred memory, with the caveat that until the end of the twentieth century the traditions and spirit of American Catholic sacred memory profoundly informed those of the civic narrative. Perhaps another way of putting this is that Catholic civic traditions were American in their aspirations, whereas the sacred narrative sought to transform the United States into a Catholic reality. It is the uneasy synthesis of the two over time that constitutes American Catholic historical consciousness and civic motivation.

Writers of U.S. history textbooks for parochial schools beginning in the 1870s stressed the "role of Church members and ideas in the nation's past," according to historian Joseph Moreau's review of the textbook literature of the period. This effort to demonstrate the harmony between Catholicism and U.S. civic life continued into the twentieth century as Catholic educators labored to bring parochial schools into line with the curriculum standards and academic expectations of public schools. It became even more exigent in seasons of national crisis, when Catholics inevitably found their loyalties and commitments questioned. During official times of national patriotic celebration and on public holidays, Catholics eagerly sought to take possession of the key symbols of national identity as other Americans were doing. The Commission on American Citizenship was established at Catholic University in 1938 to produce written materials highlighting the Catholic contribution to American democracy. This work of demonstrating Catholic loyalty continued through World War II.[16]

The proof of the Catholic church's place in U.S. history and memory in such accounts was Catholics' participation in the major events of the

American epic, the War of Independence, when Maryland's Charles Carroll put his huge fortune on the line for the patriots' cause, and the Civil War, when the U.S. Catholic Church was said to have preserved a national unity the nation itself had lost. On days of national and local commemorations the children of Catholic immigrants and migrants in communities around the country dressed up in the costumes of exemplary figures of the American past and arranged themselves into heroic tableaux of an American identity that did not always include their parents or grandparents and often explicitly denied them. In these ways Catholics sought to "unite Catholicism and status quo 'Americanism,'" as Moreau writes, to take hold of the traditions that went into the making of the American Century.[17]

But Catholics in these years did not forget that the American narrative was made against them, as they were continually reminded. According to the author of *The Church in United States History*, a popular textbook published in 1937–38 under the imprimatur of the robustly isolationist and widely influential Bishop John Francis Noll of Fort Wayne, Indiana, "An unbroken record of a century and a half of Catholic patriotism should by this time lay low this ghost of political bigotry," but, the author solemnly notes, it had not. The section of the introduction where this judgment appears is titled "Loyalty of Catholics Futile." This consciousness contributed to the making of a more assertive variant of the American Catholic "Americanist" civic narrative tradition.[18]

"Compared with the Catholic part in the history of America," Catholic scholar and poet Maurice Francis Egan (who also served as the envoy extraordinary and minister plenipotentiary to Denmark under Theodore Roosevelt), "the coming of the Mayflower is but an episode." In this Catholic retelling of American history, the lineaments of which first appeared in the early nineteenth century at the time when Baird was identifying the United States with evangelical Protestantism, "the discovery of America was preeminently a Catholic enterprise" since at the time obviously "Protestantism did not yet exist." (This resonant historical fact is pointed out by the author of the Catholic textbook *Sadlier's Excelsior Studies in the History of the United States for Schools*, 1879.) The country's political ideals are said to have developed out of the Catholic tradition, not the Reformation, and Catholics are represented as the most uncompromising and loyal defenders of these ideals, in comparison with American Protestants who betrayed them by their intolerance. This history is proof of "how Catholic America is," in the words of another Catholic textbook author, Sister Mary Celeste.[19]

⏣American Catholic Sacred Memory

Catholic sacred memory went beyond the civic narratives and reframed the American narrative as a recognizably Catholic drama of heroic holiness, suffering, and sacrifice. The American landscape was taken up by this vision of the American Catholic past into Catholic sacred geography, as if the United States were contiguous with the deserts of the ancient world, the forests of pre-Christian Europe, and the killing fields of early modern Europe. Diverging in spirit and aim both from the Catholic civic narratives and from American Protestant providential histories, American Catholic sacred memory sanctified Catholic difference in the United States while maintaining Catholic prominence in the saga of the American past. It introduced elements even into the most determinedly "Americanist" version of the American Catholic civic narrative that were incongruous and disruptive. Catholic sacred memory absorbed the stories that immigrants and migrants brought with them to this country, their sense of what life was about, and what their journey to America had meant for themselves and their children. Catholics encountered the sacred narrative of the American Catholic past everywhere—in the lives and writings of American Catholic martyrs and missionaries; in accounts of the founding of religious orders in the United States; in the stories told by immigrants and migrants; in the stained-glass windows of their churches; and in popular literature. The long inheritance of American Catholic sacred memory brought Catholics to a place after World War II that despite similarities (such as Catholics' fervent participation in anticommunism) was not completely congruent with the nation's broader and ostensibly inclusive postwar culture or with its cultures of history and memory.

The interplay and tension between the civic narratives and sacred memory can be seen in the destiny of a figure who was central to both, Kateri Tekakwitha, "Lily of the Mohawks," who lived from 1656 to 1680. Meeting in plenary council in Baltimore in 1884, U.S. prelates decided to petition Rome to initiate a cause for Kateri's canonization. Their aim, writes historian Allan Greer, was "to solidify the church's position in a predominantly Protestant society with pronounced anti-Papist traditions" with an "American saint that could symbolically root the church in American soil." The bishops were imagining the Lily of the Mohawks within the frame of the American Catholic civic narrative, in other words. But they chose to accomplish this Americanist aim with a figure who embodied and exemplified Catholic traditions most deeply at odds with the modern world and with the American story.[20]

Kateri Tekakwitha was one of the most popular early modern Catholic holy persons in Europe and in the New World. A widely read life of this Native American woman, published in 1744, depicts in detail her tremendous physical suffering, near rape, and ferocious self-imposed mortifications, the least of which was her custom of mixing dirt into her food. Describing her difficult life at the mission of Sault St. Louis, where she lived with other native Christian converts in daily expectation of being tortured to death by Iroquois, her hagiographer, the Jesuit father Pierre François Xavier Charlevoix, writes, "They thought only of preparing for martyrdom by all the means that austerity can suggest for chastising the flesh," specifically by fasting, flagellation, exposure to the cold, and burning themselves. As Kateri's cult moved forward in the early years of the new century with the support of her ardent U.S. (and Canadian) Catholic devout, it did so, says Greer, "under the sign of primitivism," meaning that in these later accounts, which built on earlier traditions, Kateri is presented as "belonging to another age, outside the forward march of history." So Kateri was an odd choice for a civic hero. Greer understands the late nineteenth- and early twentieth-century biographies of the saint as having the contradictory ambitions both of assimilating Kateri to the contemporary world—as an exemplary Catholic American, a fusion of the two cultures, indigenous and European—and of having her stand for "the antithesis of modernity."[21] Given the fraught nature of the engagement of Catholicism generally, and U.S. Catholics in particular, to modernity and the modern world, it could hardly have been otherwise.

Kateri Tekakwitha's biographers at the turn of the century inherited the language and imagery used by early modern hagiographers to describe her, with their devotional and hagiographical emphasis on her fierce self-inflicted corporal disciplines as the expression of her piety and sanctity, and these inevitably shaped how Kateri entered the American Century. The story of Kateri's journey to American sainthood shows how sacred memory intruded on civic ambition, disrupting and reframing it or, in Latour's word again, impurifying it with a divergent ontology. The making of Kateri Tekakwitha as an American saint is an instance of the uneasy convergence of civic and sacred traditions of American Catholic memory and history, the knotting of the two threads of memory. It has been such knots, expressive of the simultaneity of realities that are not simultaneous, that have provided the creative source of Catholic citizenship in the United States.

∞ Before the Founding of the Republic, Consecrating America with Catholic Blood

Separating and nonseparating members of the Church of England fled what they saw as a corrupt popish church to establish, in the latter case, a godly community that might be transplanted back in the Old World in God's due time. This is the germ of the American notion of global moral preeminence, national innocence, and good intentions, as noted, but it is not how Catholic national memory begins. As the traditions associated with the Lily of the Mohawks suggest, the divergence of Catholic memory from the story that underwrites the American Century originates in profoundly discrepant constructions of Catholic experience in the colonial period. Catholics came to the New World not to be liberated from the past in order to make a new and more perfect community that would be a light to the rest of the world, but to suffer and die in the cruel northern forests and scorched southern deserts at the hands of "savages" whom they loved even as they were tortured and mutilated by them. The main themes of American Catholic sacred memory have to do with persecution, pain, and sacrifice. Even the Jesuit father Jacques Marquette, who died a relatively normal death in the woods, is transformed by Catholic narrative into a martyr.[22]

American Catholic sacred memory takes its cues here from the self-understanding of the first nuns and priests in what would become the United States. These men and women saw their destinies and defined their ambitions in the New World in the figures of the ancient Christian martyrs, not in terms of the Puritan idea of corporate providential revival. Even before they left Europe, Catholic missionaries anticipated what lay ahead with all the sensuous and erotic fervor of early modern piety. As the Jesuit superior of New France, Père Jérôme Lalement, records in his 1647 account of the passion of Isaac Jogues in New France, "Sometime before his departure from the Hurons in order to come to Quebec, finding himself alone before the Blessed Sacrament, [Jogues] prostrated himself to the ground, beseeching our Lord to grant him the favor and grace of suffering for His glory." The answer to this prayer, writes Lalement, "was engraved in the depth of his soul" with these words: *"Your prayer has been heard. What you have asked of me will be given you. Be brave and steadfast."* Native American peoples were taken up into these devotional narratives of courage and sacrifice not as models of the civilizing effects of Christianity, as New England's Puritans understood their mission, but as fellow recipients of God's hard love. Father Jogues comforted a recent convert who was being tortured alongside him, saying, "Take courage, my dear brother, and remember that there is another life than this; remember, too, that there is a God who sees everything and who will reward the anguish that we suffer on his account."[23]

Death, sickness, and violence stalked the settlements of the New World, Catholic and Protestant, and both had to come to terms with these realities in the context of their respective religious imaginaries. The Puritans found in violence and sickness evidence of God's approval of them (when God gave them victory over their enemies) or of his displeasure (when the settlements were ravaged by disease and hunger). But for Catholics, pain and death, in all their terrible abundance in the settlements, were not judgments but testing and proof, as well as evidence of God's love. This is what made Catholics transcendently strong; supernatural strength born of faithful suffering was Catholicism's gift to the New World, as well as Catholics' bond to it. The dominant figure of the Catholic settlements was the courageous, willing, and loving victim for Jesus' sake, not the lordly religious ancestors of the New England godly commonwealths. Even Columbus was absorbed into this devotional narrative when Catholic writers emphasized his cruel mistreatment after the third voyage. He too suffered. Another Jesuit martyr, Jean de Brébeuf, expressed this ethos in terms that missionaries across New Spain and New France would have shared: "The joy one feels when he has baptized an Indian who dies soon afterwards, and flies directly to Heaven to become an angel, certainly is a joy that surpasses anything that can be imagined. . . . One would like to have the suffering of ten thousand tempests that he might help save one soul, since Jesus Christ for one soul would have willingly shed all his precious blood."[24]

The same tropes shaped the experience of the founders of the American church in the early Republic too, as well as how they were remembered in the nineteenth and twentieth centuries. Exemplary in this regard is Kentucky missionary, Father Charles Nerinckx, born in the Austrian Netherlands, who was extolled immediately after his death and then later by American Catholic chroniclers for his passionate embrace of "the floating hell" (his words) of the ship passage to America and the subsequent rigors of frontier Kentucky. One of his earliest biographers, Rev. Martin J. Spalding, himself a leading figure of the American church and archbishop of Baltimore (1864–72), offered the following hagiographical account of Nerinckx, casting him in the tropes of the ancient desert and of the sixteenth-century American saints:

> His rest was brief, and his food was generally of the coarsest kind. He usually arose several hours before day, which hours he devoted to prayer and study. . . . He seldom missed offering up the Holy Sacrifice

daily, no matter what had been his previous fatigues or indisposition. Often was he known to ride twenty-five or thirty miles fasting, in order to be able to say Mass. . . . His courage was unequalled: he feared no difficulties and was appalled by no dangers. . . . He crossed wilderness districts, swam rivers, slept in the wood among the wild beasts; while undergoing all this, he was in the habit of fasting, and of voluntarily mortifying himself in many other ways.[25]

Later Catholic historians echoed and elaborated Spalding's portrait, describing in one case how Nerinckx took up residence in a Kentucky graveyard. "This was the spirit of a saint," this biographer writes (in 1915), "and a saint of the severe school of penance and mortification."[26] Exiled from a European environment fiercely hostile to the church (Nerinckx had been hunted by Napoléon's soldiers), the Kentucky missionary seems never to have stopped thinking of the land to which he had escaped by God's grace and plan as a place of suffering, sacrifice, pain, and redemption.

Graphic tales of the deaths of Catholic martyrs on North American soil filled the pages of popular Catholic American history textbooks in the late nineteenth and twentieth centuries. Descriptions of the martyrdom of the Jesuits Lalement and Brébeuf in Sadlier's 1879 *History* recounted the grim details of how Brébeuf's tormentors ripped off his nose and lips and forced a burning branch between his teeth before ripping out his heart and devouring it. Moreau writes that almost all Catholic American history textbooks from the 1870s to the 1960s "include an account of the death [in 1724] of Father Rasles, a Jesuit missionary among the Indians living along the Kennebec River in Maine," at the hands of a party of New Englanders who hacked the priest's body to pieces and then, in the words of one textbook quoted by Moreau, "rifled the altar, profaned the Host and sacred vessels, and burned the church." (Funston in the Philippines falls into this narrative tradition.) Catholic historians called attention to the fact that the first victim of the Salem witchcraft hysteria was an Irish Catholic woman who fell under suspicion because she knew the Lord's Prayer only in Latin.

Such tales were foundational to American Catholic memory and history, to how Catholics in the United States understood themselves as American. Moreau concludes, "Often these death scenes are placed explicitly in the locations of future American states such as Kansas, New Mexico, Michigan and Maine, giving Catholicism a spiritual claim to the land well in advance of Protestant settlers." Look at the place names of a map of the United States, John Gilmary Shea wrote in an essay during the national centennial, and what do you see? St. Augustine, St. Louis, Santa Fe, San Francisco—it was as if the United States were "a medieval painting amid a group of saints." Before there was even an American republic, William H. J. Kennedy and Sister Mary Joseph wrote in their popular 1926 U.S. history textbook for upper grades, Catholic missionaries had "consecrated America" with their blood. Just as "Europe" first existed as a skeleton made of the bits of saints' bones sent to local rulers by the popes in Rome, so "America" in Catholic imagination was initially constituted as a network of places connected by the blood of the saints. Given such different wellsprings of memory, how could Catholic citizenship in the United States possibly be like that of their Protestant compatriots?[27]

∞"I Can't Say Y'ere Not There": From Père Brébeuf to Tony the Dago Mick

What kinds of citizens should Catholics be in the American Century? Addressing the National Catholic Educational Association in 1940, a year before Luce's summons, Brother Philip, FSC, supervisor at the time of the high schools of the Christian Brothers in New York City, urged Catholics in the United States to cultivate a spirit in their homes like that in the "homes of Ireland during the hundred years of persecution." Catholics ought to live, to make Brother Philip's meaning explicit, like a people hunted by Protestants, hiding out in their own country, expecting to suffer and die for their faith at the hands of their fellow citizens. It may be that Brother Philip would not have followed out all the implications of his metaphor, but still, this is hardly a vision of national harmony.[28]

Others did follow through on the metaphor. In a 1933 novella, *Tony*, written by the prolific Jesuit writer Thomas B. Chetwood for Catholic youngsters of the generation that would soon enough assume the burden of American destiny in war and published by the Jesuit father Daniel Lord's press, the Queen's Work, the eponymous hero, a tough "mick" from the "vile and unsightly quarter of a great city," is tortured by a gang of Protestant boys who hang him upside down over the city's greasy, rat-infested river and demand that he declare himself "a dirty yellow-faced Dago [Tony's mother is Italian] an' a Republican an' a Protestant." But Tony cannot speak the lie "I am a Protestant," not simply because he is not a Protestant, but because, as he tells his tormentors, sputtering filthy water out of his mouth, "Protestants say . . . that they ain't no one there."[29]

What Tony means here is that to identify himself as a Protestant would be to deny the real presence of Jesus in the Eucharist and in the reserved sacrament in the parish tabernacle, which is the ground of all other Catholic difference in modernity, and this he cannot do. "I can't say Y'ere not there," he moans over and over, "I can't say Y'ere not there." Tony dies by inches, his death as graphically recounted as Brébeuf's or Rasles's: "First came the terrible desire for air. . . It racked every inch of him up to the feet that were held above him." All through this terrible suffering Tony says, "I can't say Y'ere not there." The repetition of this phrase sustains and comforts him until the moment finally comes when his soul and body are filled with a "strength that was in no way his own." Tony's tortured body, hanging beneath a squalid urban overpass, becomes a tabernacle of the real presence. On the autopsy table this body shines with "a pallid beauty," and like the Roman centurion at the foot of the cross, the police officer present, Lester Bradly, described as an Episcopalian who "belonged to a very exclusive family with influence" and "a graduate of one of the most aristocratic eastern universities," looks on Tony's dead but serenely lovely face and is converted to Catholicism. "There simply must be," Bradly reflects, "without any possibility of question, a life of calm vision and understanding when this life is done." Ten years later Tony's death has reformed the neighborhood's wild girls; the bad boys have become model citizens; and neighborhood ethnic conflict has ceased. Peace and order have come at last to the modern city, all because of Tony's martyrdom at the hands of Protestants. Before there was a republic, as the story went, Catholics had sanctified the land with their blood.[30]

"I should be a better patriot than the next guy," a man who grew up in the 1930s in Cleveland in an eastern European immigrant household told me when we were talking about his childhood in the church, "because I was Catholic." This apprehension was common among American Catholics in the American Century, when most Catholics in the United States had abiding ties to other countries and when other Americans were so highly mistrustful of their Catholic fellow citizens. Catholics had to be better Americans than other Americans because other Americans thought that Catholics did not belong here. But different national origins were not the main reason Catholics were held in suspicion. Catholics were out of place in the nation specifically because what was most fundamental to being Catholic —loyalty to the pope, obedience to authority, love of the Virgin Mary, and devotional practices addressed to the saints—struck Americans as pagan, premodern, and perverse. But above all, Catholics were askew to American civilization because of the antimodern ontology—in Latour's terms, again, the mixing of categories otherwise kept separate—of the real presence. "I can't say Y'ere not there," as Tony says, refusing to be purified as a modern as his fellow Americans want him to be.

Catholics were as patriotic as the next guy, in fact—more patriotic, even, although the irony of U.S. Catholic patriotism throughout the twentieth century is that it derived from stories and memories, real and imagined, of exclusion, persecution, torture, and martyrdom. It was Tony's suffering that made him a good citizen—a citizen possessed of supernatural strength—and a good American. The pain inflicted on his body by Protestants made him effective in the civic life of this Protestant nation. From Isaac Jogues and Kateri Tekakwitha through the frontier missionaries to Tony the working-class Dago Mick, this sensibility gave a distinctive shape to Catholic memory and patriotism. As American national identity came increasingly to be premised on the imperative to extend the country's presumed values and virtue to the rest of the globe, Catholic patriotism remained grounded in stories of spiritual courage and physical fortitude, in the memory of persecution, and, especially, in the passionate willingness to embrace martyrdom, to suffer horrible pain, and to die for the country and for their radically different ontology.

From the 1880s into the 1930s, Catholic stories of martyrdom and persecution were inflected by a new set of memories, moreover, those of southern and eastern European immigrants and their children and grandchildren who remembered industrial and farmland distress, loss of homes, and then working-class sacrifice. Protestant Americans standing securely in the dominant national myth maintained that southern Italians and eastern European immigrants chose to come to the United States in search of freedom and opportunity, which they took as further indication of the global beacon that was America. But this is not what Catholic parents born elsewhere were telling their children. Coming to U.S. shores or northward from the South, from the Caribbean, and from Mexico to its cities and fields was an act of domestic sacrifice and personal mortification undertaken on behalf of loved ones and in the company of the Blessed Mother and the saints. These narratives drew on the common stock of the lives of the saints and martyrs, on devotion to Jesus on the cross and to his Sacred Heart, on the historical suffering of Catholics, and especially on the image of the Virgin Mary as the woman who suffers. To this already-rich inheritance the immigrants and migrants and their descendants added an edge of working-class anger and grief, together with a stoic and accepting attitude toward pain in the body. They translated their toil as workers, miners, and farmers and their struggles as labor-union and migrant farmworker organizers into offerings, first for their families and friends and then, during World War II, Korea, and Vietnam, for the country itself. Physical courage, stamina, and suffering were how they connected themselves to and at the same time challenged the national ethos.

Catholic immigrants and migrants and their children were the nation's victims and its heroes. Italian American novelist Pierto DiDonato's *Christ in Concrete* and the powerful images of crucified workers by the artist and labor-union activist Ralph Fasanella made these associations explicit.[31]

෨Catholics and the American Century: Citizens on the Cross

At the height of the Cold War, the heroically suffering and persecuted Catholic body became the surest evidence of Catholic loyalty to the country. Protestant Americans were weak, Catholic popular periodicals warned, dangerously so, given the grave challenges confronting the times. Modern American Protestants practiced birth control because they lacked the moral and physical stamina to bear the burdens and sacrifices of raising large families; they sought a life of leisure, consumption, and self-indulgence; and they used cosmetics to hide the toll of their dissipation. No Americans have been as fiercely and self-consciously critical of consumerism in the United States as Catholics. Fort Wayne's Bishop Noll, whose imprimatur accompanied the celebratory history of Catholics in the United States cited earlier, was an extraordinarily sharp critic of the nascent American consumer culture. Noll was American Catholicism's Tertullian. The competitive impulse in American Catholic civic traditions moved fully into the sacred narrative during the Cold War. While Protestants spoke of patriotism, Catholics made it real in their bodies. Catholic bodies were keeping the United States safe from the Soviet Union, just as suffering Catholic bodies had sanctified the American wilderness, built the cities and subways, worked the factories and farms of the nation, and forged the labor unions.[32]

The centrality of suffering and sacrifice to how Catholics understood themselves as Americans was most dramatically and powerfully evident in the lives—and above all in the dying—of the two great American Catholic heroes of the Cold War, Maryknoll bishop Francis X. Ford and lay saint Thomas A. Dooley. The handsome, glamorous, and photogenic Dooley, an alumnus of Notre Dame, was a physician and missionary whose published accounts of working amid suffering refugees in Southeast Asia (written with the sponsorship of American intelligence), *Deliver Us from Evil* (1956), *The Edge of Tomorrow* (1958), and *The Night They Burned the Mountain* (1960), became Cold War best sellers. Dooley recounted the persecution of Vietnamese Catholics at the hands of Communists, but it was his immersion in suffering, his physical sacrifices, and his self-denying service to the sick, disfigured, and dying that made him an exemplary American Catholic citizen of his time and after his death a candidate for sainthood. Awful physical suffering is as graphically and disturbingly described in these volumes as in the accounts of the martyrdoms of the North American Jesuits. The church's struggle with communism, exemplified and personalized in the suffering of figures like Dooley, was protecting and preserving the freedom of the West. This was the secret history of the modern world. "I received a note from a priest who had just been released from a Communist torture cell in Red China," Dooley writes in the foreword to *The Edge of Tomorrow*, "where his hands had been crushed between two stones. He was offering a daily *Memorare* [a popular Marian prayer] for the blessings of Jesus on us." Dooley's own excruciating cancer was lovingly recounted in Catholic popular periodicals, which took particularly careful note of his heroic refusal to use pain medication.[33]

Maryknoll priest John M. Donovan's 1967 biography of Bishop Ford describes the bishop's courageous death at the hands of Chinese Communists explicitly in the language of the Passion. "The Bishop fell three times to the rough dirt road," Donovan writes. "Each time he picked himself up with great effort and calmly continued his *via dolorosa* through the mad mob." When they see how this holy man courageously endured torture, Father Donovan reflects at the end of the book, Communists throughout the world will know that the United States means business. They will see that the country is more than a "grasping, colonial" power. A Catholic's heroic death proves America's mettle to China and the Soviet Union and makes it clear that this is not a nation of self-indulgent consumers (or not only this). Donovan includes a barbed comment about the difference between Ford's missionary aims and those of other unnamed but presumably American Protestant missioners "who were intent on the civilizing effects of Christianity." Ford, instead, "preferred to raise their spirit of self-sacrifice and brotherhood than their standard of living."[34]

This was the moral of the story of another Catholic best seller in the era, *4 Years in a Red Hell* by Father Harold W. Rigney, SVD. A holy card available with this book has an image of an Asian Madonna and Child on the front, Father Rigney on the back, and the following text: "Rev. Harold W. Rigney, S.V.D. Divine Word Missionary. Rector, Fu Jen Catholic University Peking (Peiping), China. Imprisoned by the Communists July 25, 1951 to Sept[ember] 16, 1955. I preach the Gospel, and in its service I suffer hardship like a criminal, yes, even imprisonment . . . [ellipsis in original] What persecutions I underwent! And yet the Lord brought me through them all safely (2 Timothy 2:8–9, 3:11)."[35]

What captured Catholic imagination about the discovery of America was the erection of the cross on these shores, with all the accompanying rituals, and the elevation of the cross was central to their vision of citizenship. In 1958, at the height of the Cold War, Fred and Phyllis Schlafly, Fred's sister Eleanor, and Father Stephen Dunker, a former missionary to China who had been imprisoned by the Communists, founded the Cardinal Mindszenty Foundation, named after the imprisoned Hungarian prelate. (There was already a Protestant organization, founded by Fred Schwartz, called Christian Anti-Communism Crusade, but Schwartz rejected the Schlaflys' initial appeals for a joint Catholic-Protestant organization because he knew that his constituency did not trust Catholics and would not work with them.) The aim of the foundation, which had an advisory board made up of priests who had likewise been imprisoned by Communists (Father Rigney among them) was to educate ordinary Americans about the evils of communism and to ready American citizens for spiritual and moral combat to the death. Catholics had something to teach other Americans.[36]

When I was doing research in southern Indiana on Catholic childhoods there, I was told a story about an event at a Catholic school in a small Hoosier town. During the heyday of civil defense drills, around 1960, the principal of this school had all the children brought by grade into the parish church. Then she made them come up toward the altar as if they were receiving Holy Communion, an orderly procedure they knew well, having done it many times before. The children knelt down in rows at the Communion rail, and the principal pointed her hand in the shape of a gun to each child's temple one after the other, pretending to be a Communist, and demanded, "Do you renounce Jesus?" This seems like a horror story today, especially in light of the abuse of Catholic children by religious figures, but for children at the time, raised on tales of Cold War martyrs, it was an easy exercise, one for which they had been thoroughly prepared in mind and body. I do not know this for sure, but I suspect that these children may have found all this exciting and interesting (it got them out of class, after all), and that they enjoyed the satisfaction of knowing exactly what to do—and they knew exactly what to do because they were American Catholics.

∽The Ambiguity of U.S. Catholic Citizenship

The distinctive shape of Catholic citizenship in the second half of the twentieth century was not the product of the sacred narrative alone, nor even of the interplay between the civic and sacred traditions of Catholic public memory, but of the convergence of these traditions of civic culture with the social and political realities of Catholic life in this country over a century. The quality of Catholic citizenship was marked by stories of the North American martyrs and also by the realities of violence in working-class Catholic neighborhoods, by memories of the persecution of priests in Ireland and by the humiliations of class in the United States, by ethnic and racial rivalries, and by the long inheritance of religious prejudice, labor struggles, and unemployment from the turn of the century through the 1950s and 1960s. A vein of violence and anger runs though the language of U.S. Catholic citizenship and public life. This has erupted at different times in U.S. Catholic history and has taken various forms, including domestic violence, neighborhood battles among Catholic ethnic groups (among the children of the immigrants and migrants) and against Jews and African Americans, including African American Catholics, anti-Protestantism, violence in the workplace (and sometimes against labor organizers and union members), and alcoholism.

By the mid-twentieth century Catholic citizenship often took on a swaggering and hostile tone edged with rage and superiority. Catholic conservative commentator Pat Buchanan recalls that at Gonzaga High School in Washington, D.C., he and his fellow students were trained by their Jesuit teachers to be "Gods' marines." The sacrament of confirmation among U.S. Catholic children was intended in the twentieth century to ready youngsters for holy warfare and martyrdom against unnamed (but presumably close-at-hand) political and religious enemies. The red armband children wore when being confirmed signified their enlistment in the Catholic army. "Small wonder we [Catholic kids] were always slugging it out on the streets," New York labor activist Fred Garel writes about his childhood. At another Gonzaga High School, in Omaha, Nebraska, singer Bing Crosby was being formed (in the Catholic word for childhood training) by a disciplinarian, Jesuit father James "Big Jim" Kennelley, who beat his charges with a chain and "had no use for those who cringed at the swing of the chain and the keys or who cried when sent to him for punishment." Historians have noted this vein of violence and aggression in the careers of Father Charles Coughlin and Senator Joseph McCarthy, but Coughlin and McCarthy inherited and manipulated Catholic anger that was already there; they did not create it. From the Civil War draft riots to late twentieth-century attacks on abortion clinics, there have been distinctly violent elements in U.S. Catholic civic culture.[37]

The impress of this inheritance shaping the ideal of Catholic citizenship can be seen in the mid-twentieth-century stories about hard-boiled street priests, a popular Catholic genre that might be called clerical noir. Model citizens of church and country, involved in daunting and physically danger-ous activities on behalf of otherwise-forgotten and abused populations, these clerical heroes are canny about the nasty ways of the world, impatient with the niggling scruples of democracy, and comfortable with booze and the company of thugs and cops, but they are also deeply pious, self-abnegating, and self-punishing. The hard-boiled priest combined the qualities of the martyr and the ward boss, the shamus and the desert father. This was the kind of priest who would "walk up to any hoodlum or gun killer," one such story begins, "and shove his gun down his throat." Clerical noir thrillers of-fered a model for midcentury clergy and beyond that of Catholic civic virtue.

The sentence about the gun-down-the-throat priest is from a 1951 biog-raphy of Bishop Bernard Sheil of Chicago, founder of the Catholic Youth Organization and, in his starstruck biographer's words, "the most manly man." Sheil is said to have the face of "a philosopher [or] a buccaneer." Tens-ing his taut muscles, the priest jumps out of the shower in the morning, we are told, and rubs his body down with a rough towel that feels like sandpa-per before beginning his daily calisthenics, a "routine of violence" that would send ordinary men (non-Catholic men, certainly) "limping back to bed." The homoerotic undercurrent of clerical noir rises to the surface here. On his "powerful legs" the priest accompanies more than twenty boys on their way to the scaffold in Cook County Jail. In one case, as a hand-cuffed boy falls through the opened trap, he grabs hold of Sheil's hand, nearly pulling the priest down into the hole with him. The rope snaps. "Blood dripped from Father's fingers where the chain of the handcuffs had ripped through his flesh [it is not clear whose flesh is being referred to here— Sheil's or the dying boy's], but his eyes were closed as he continued to pray."[38]

Pain, rage, sacrifice, and violence swirled around the hard-boiled priest in the city imagined as desert and in the American public square remade as the site of hagiographic myth. The hard-boiled priest exemplifies the mid-twentieth-century model Catholic citizen and patriot in a genealogy that descends from the martyrs of the North American frontier to the heroes of the early American church, Charles Nerinckx and others, to Bishop Ford and fellow victims of the Reds, Dr. Tom Dooley (not a priest but devoutly— and incorrectly—believed to have been celibate by his faithful), and to Bishop Bernard Sheil.

It was with this ambiguous civic inheritance that Catholics in the United States entered the period of American history that began with John Kennedy's assassination and the presidency of Lyndon Johnson and continued through the Reagan years. The confidence in this era among Catholics that they were becoming ordinary Americans, with which I began this chapter, is now a commonplace among sociologists and historians of U.S. Catholicism. But the numbers mask the full story. To understand U.S. Catholic life in this period and its impact on U.S. public life, it is necessary to remember that the Catholics who "came of age" in the 1960s had been raised on tales of holy heroism, of the tough priests of clerical noir, and of courageous Cold War martyrs and in working-class neighborhoods or on struggling farms, where the hatred of Catholicism by other Americans was not forgotten, and where the sense of Catholic specialness was sharpened by resentment and betrayal. They were the heirs of both traditions of Catholic national consciousness, the civic and the sacred. These men and women found themselves on the front lines of the era's most contentious changes, where social transformations mattered the most and hit the hardest, in the places where they lived, in their workplaces, and at worship. The combination of the distinctive U.S. Catholic political imagination with the violent fracturing of the broader political landscape and the rapid transformations of Catholic devotional culture proved to be a potent, at times toxic, mix.

The ambiguity and ambivalence of this civic inheritance were evident in the streets of U.S. cities, outside abortion clinics, in the parking lots of Selective Service offices, on the lawns in front of the homes of African Americans who dared to move into ethnic Catholic neighborhoods, and in parishes where street priests in the mold of clerical noir, among them Boston's Paul Shanley and New York's Bruce Ritter, used their aura of fierce and angry heroism and self-sacrifice to hide their abuse of children, who were themselves raised in the virtues of suffering, endurance, sacrifice, and surrender. Arrogance, intolerance, self-righteousness, and cruelty grew in the soil of U.S. Catholics' sense of their transcendent superiority as citizens and citizen-victims. The ethos of U.S. political conservatism from the 1980s to the present owes much to this Catholic inheritance, brought fully into the public sphere by, among others, Pat Buchanan (who left Gonzaga eventually to become adviser and speechwriter to presidents Nixon and Reagan); Supreme Court justices Antonin Scalia and Clarence Thomas; L. Brent Bozell (William Buckley's brother-in-law, author of Goldwater's "autobiography" *The Conscience of a Conservative*, and an innovator in violent and ritualized antiabortion protest); and the Schlaflys. The public tone of such Catholic conservatives as citizens has the feel about it of the old clerical noir.[39]

The point is not that Catholics are either better than other U.S. citizens (which is the old temptation of Catholic history) or worse than other U.S. citizens (an even older temptation in U.S. history and memory). Rather, it is that Catholics in the United States have understood their citizenship in ways that cannot be absorbed or assimilated into the broader U.S. story or into other enactments of U.S. citizenship. It is not identical with the spirit of the American Century, although it contributed to it. The men and women who thrust rosaries in the faces of young women and their families going into abortion clinics are U.S. Catholic citizens, as was Sargent Shriver, founder of the Peace Corps, and Michael Harrington, whose 1962 book *The Other America* helped inspire the antipoverty programs of the 1960s and 1970s that Catholic conservatives of the 1980s so excoriated. But it is not a question of either/or, good Catholics/bad Catholics. Catholics have been as good and as bad citizens as anyone else; their behavior in the public square has been as tolerant and as intolerant as that of other U.S. citizens. But the grounds of their citizenship and of their public presence have been different. This difference, which has been profoundly influential in U.S. political and social history throughout the twentieth century, is due to that angle at which Catholics have lived in the modern world and in the United States.

⬅The Ironies of American Catholic History

There are a number of ironies in the history I have been exploring here. One is that by making their patriotism about the suffering, mortified, disciplined, and sacrificial body, Catholics in the United States were at the same time instantiating and validating the American Protestant identification of Catholics with the body. American Catholic patriotism and citizenship embodied the American Protestant fantasy of Catholics. Another irony is that modernizers within the American Catholic church, the Americanists of the late nineteenth century and the progressive reformers of the 1960s and 1970s, failed to understand that the devotional practices and orientations they were most eager to prohibit—because in their view such idioms, rooted in the dolorous piety of pain, seemed out of step with American society—were the very practices and images by which ordinary Catholics were aligning their destinies with modern America. But perhaps the greatest irony is that because this ethos of ontological citizenship was a matter of the body, formed in Catholic flesh by practices and sensations of devotional life and by the most rigorous religious training of children seen in modern American culture, Catholics across the political spectrum in the late twentieth century had difficulty forgetting in an age when forgetting was the expectation and the mark of modern belonging. This was so despite prodigious efforts within the church itself in the latter part of the century to encourage historical amnesia. As it turns out, Catholics really cannot be purified for modernity.

Again and again adult Catholics who grew up in this way of being in the world told me when we were talking about their childhoods in the church that in times of personal and social crisis in the challenging 1960s and 1970s they found their bodies acting in old devotional ways many years after they thought that they had rejected them for more modern ways of being Christian and citizens. They began murmuring Hail Marys when street protests for social justice took a violent turn (as one former vowed woman religious told me about a riot in Gary, Indiana, in the 1970s) or making the sign of the cross. Catholics make bad moderns, in short, because they have trouble forgetting, no matter how hard they try, and this is so because even if they manage to forget with their minds, their bodies betray them. Catholic memory has proved to be a potent ground for Catholic citizenship in the United States and for the particular ways in which Catholics have been American, especially in the American Century, precisely because American Catholic memory is so deeply at odds with the story that is otherwise told about the American past. Catholics are just destined to be impure citizens.

⌘ Postscript

This effort to describe the angle at which Catholics have lived American life, including American political culture and national memory, began as a conference paper. I was vigorously challenged by members of the audience at the meeting where it was first presented for what they saw as my effort to revive the old and now presumably discredited notion of Catholic exceptionalism in American history. This charge took me aback because as an American historian who studies Catholicism, I have long and resolutely set myself against this idea, broadly speaking. I have not wanted to see Catholicism written out of mainstream American history (granted that the mainstream is itself an unstable and changing construction) or subtly nudged to the margins, like unfamiliar relatives standing around out of place at a wedding or a funeral. But my understanding of the traditions that have gone into the making of Catholic citizenship and then the implications of this for Catholic public life evidently looks like exceptionalism by another name.

The idea of historical "revivals" has always struck me as misbegotten, however, because the river of time flows on, circumstances change, and something that looks very much like something from an earlier time cannot be that earlier thing because the world around it is so fundamentally different. So it is with the notion of Catholic exceptionalism, which I prefer to call Catholic askewness to the modern. Catholics lived in the United States with values, religious practices and imaginings, political views, experiences of family life and of the social world, and historical memories and stories that were all deeply incongruous with mainstream American values, religious imaginings, and memories. This was true for many reasons, among the most important of them being the distinctive ontology of Catholic religious life, which understood supernatural figures to be really present in the things of this world and available to humans in a direct way, which led Catholics to reimagine American history as a Catholic narrative peopled by bloody holy figures. It was true as well because so many Catholics in the United States had come so recently from somewhere else and because they belonged to a global religious community that was larger than their American citizenship. And it was true because mainstream American values, religious imaginings, and memories, although never stable or simply given, had their deepest roots in the inheritance of Protestant/Catholic hostility (from which Catholics in the United States were likewise not free or innocent). But none of this takes Catholics out of American history.

Several generations of American Catholic historians, to whom I am deeply indebted, have argued that American history cannot be studied or taught without reference to Catholic experience on these shores, from the colonial period to the present. We have a way to go in this regard. Books are still being published with the aim of "making sense of the twentieth century," to take one relevant recent example, with nary a reference to Catholics or Catholicism (other than, predictably, Father Coughlin or Senator McCarthy).[10] But some things have clearly changed in the past few decades. Catholics have both benefited from and contributed to the wider critical revision of American historiography under way since the 1960s and the new social and cultural historiographies. To see that Catholics have always been in the mix of American history, however, does not mean that they have been the same as other Americans, even when they used identical words, such as "freedom," "justice," or "fairness." Nor does it mean that the ways used to tell the story of Americans who do not think that the Host is really God and who do not bring the saints into their everyday lives will work as well for those who do think and do these things. Catholics have always been in the mix and have always been different, and carefully exploring this difference is key to understanding U.S. Catholic history.

But it is also key to understanding U.S. history: we have come to the point now where we can turn around and see that looking at the history of the United States through the lens of the study of U.S. Catholics and Catholicism and from the perspective of the Catholic imaginary challenges many of the old, taken-for-granted narratives of American civilization, raises new questions, and demands some theoretical and historiographical creativity and innovation. We need to figure out, for instance, how figures like Saint Jude, Saint Martin de Porres, or the Blessed Mother as our Lady of Lourdes, for example, or as Nuestra Señora de Guadalupe have been agents in this history, as they have been for Catholics in the United States, and when we have figured this out, we can go on to think about other such supernatural figures who are acting in other American social and religious environments; or how the history of American women is refashioned by including in it the work and lives of the many thousands of vowed women religious, immigrant and American born, who were responsible for building, governing, and sustaining much of the vast institutional landscape of American Catholicism while living religiously passionate and dedicated lives of obedience, self-sacrifice, submission, and mortification; or how Catholic political orientations and constructions of subjectivity not only have constituted an alternative to established American notions but have fundamentally contributed to the shape of American moral, political, and psychological history.

Some years ago Yale historian Jon Butler referred to this way of approaching the past of the United States through a Catholic lens as a "historiographical heresy." Although Butler was thinking primarily of religious history, historians since have demonstrated the power of this heresy to open new ways of thinking about U.S. history itself.[41] But to do this effectively, those of us who approach U.S. history though the lens of U.S. Catholicism must also be robustly historically heretical about history and historiography. Yes, Catholics are distinctive and different, but this does not mean that they are out of the picture. They are different and distinctive and fully in the picture. To understand U.S.—not U.S. Catholic—society and politics, urban history, the politics of race and class in this country, popular culture, and the history of the arts, among other things, it is necessary to hold together in creative tension the fact that Catholics have and have not been like their fellow citizens before the American Century, amid its challenges and possibilities, and since.

⎯⎯ CHAPTER 2

Re-viewing the Twentieth Century through an American Catholic Lens

LIZABETH COHEN

I have two interrelated goals for this chapter: first, to appraise the state of the field of the history of the United States in the twentieth century with an eye to how historians might advance the field; second, to consider how these goals for future work might at least partly be addressed by studies of U.S. Catholicism. I will also issue two caveats. What follows is no gospel on "the state of the field" of twentieth-century U.S. history but rather a personal meditation on what I see as the challenges and opportunities facing historians in the United States in the twentieth century. Someone else undertaking the same task would likely have a different assessment. And while I will propose future directions for histories of American Catholicism, I should make clear that I am far from expert in the subject, although my research over the years has led me to investigate aspects of the social history of Catholic experience in America. I value the opportunity presented by this

I am grateful to D. Clinton Williams for helping me while I was resident in Oxford by providing me with materials on the Catholic Church in Boston and the church's role in the Boston busing crisis, including the fine seminar paper he wrote during fall semester, 2006, cited in note 24. I would also like to thank him, Herrick Chapman, Nico Slate, Gareth Davies, John McGreevy, Scott Appleby, and Kathleen Cummings for their feedback on earlier drafts of this chapter. In addition, coteaching the recent historiography of U.S. history with Stephen Tuck to master's students at Oxford University while serving as the Harmsworth Professor during 2007–8 prepared me well to write this chapter.

chapter to share my personal observations about past historical work and my ideas about where the field might move from here.

In the course of considering this vast field of twentieth-century U.S. history, I inevitably draw on my own work as a historian of this era and this place. Through four major projects—*Making a New Deal: Industrial Workers in Chicago, 1919–1939* (1990; 2008); *A Consumers' Republic: The Politics of Mass Consumption in Postwar America* (2003); a popular Advanced Placement and college-level textbook, *The American Pageant* (1998; 2002; 2006; 2010; 2013); and my current book project, an investigation of the rebuilding of American cities in the post–World War II era—I have participated in two decades of U.S. history writing and have analyzed multiple dimensions of the twentieth-century American experience.[1]

Twentieth-century U.S. history is not static. It is as much a product of moments of authorship as of moments in history. Had I been taking stock of the history of the United States during the first half of the twentieth century some fifty years ago, I might very well have recited a version not unlike the one historians Samuel Eliot Morison and Henry Steele Commager—giants in the field at the time—presented in their widely used textbook *The Growth of the American Republic*, published by Oxford University Press in 1950 in its fourth edition.[2] On the surface the narrative would be familiar, as captured in these chapter titles: "The American Colonial Empire"; "The Progressive Movement," followed by separate chapters on Presidents Roosevelt and Wilson; then "War and Peace"; "Normalcy and Reaction"; "The New Deal"; "The Second World War"; "The Truman Administration"; and "The Responsibilities of World Power." Additions in the 1962 fifth edition included chapters titled "Society and Culture in the Postwar Years" and "Politics and Policies of the Eisenhower Administration." If I had followed Morison and Commager's lead, who, we might reasonably ask, would have been my major historical protagonists? Not surprisingly, we would have found a cast of characters dominated by white men in leadership positions, particularly presidents—Theodore Roosevelt, Robert La Follette, William Howard Taft, Woodrow Wilson, A. Mitchell Palmer, Warren Harding, Calvin Coolidge, Herbert Hoover, Franklin Roosevelt, Winston Churchill, General Dwight Eisenhower, Harry Truman—you get the picture. Very occasionally, a woman or two would have shown up. Jane Addams and Lillian Wald were described in the chapter on Progressivism as "once regarded as misguided zealots," now "recognized as the most effective reformers of their generation."[3] But no suffragists like Carrie Chapman Catt or Alice Paul and no Eleanor Roosevelt or Frances Perkins appeared.

Nonwhites were also few and far between. The 1950 edition of the text still contained a passage on slavery dating back to the book's first edition in 1930 that by the late 1950s African American parents and leaders were angrily pressuring Morison and Commager to remove: "As for 'Sambo,' whose wrongs moved the abolitionists to wrath and tears, there is some reason to believe that he suffered less than any other class in the South for its 'Peculiar Institution.' . . . Although brought to America by force, the incurably optimistic Negro soon became attached to the country, and devoted to his white folks."[4] By the 1962 edition the most offensive passages in the slavery section had been removed, and discussion of what the text called the "civil rights controversy" had appeared, described as "the first time that Southern Negroes began to take matters in their own hands" and overcome their long-standing "passive rather than active role." Here Morison and Commager were referring specifically to "Negro students, inspired by the example of Gandhi's passive resistance movement," who "began to 'sit in' at lunch counters in drug stores and shopping centers." But other than the student protesters of 1960, the makers of the civil rights movement, according to Morison and Commager, were President Truman when he desegregated the armed forces, Gunnar Myrdal when he published *An American Dilemma* (1954), Chief Justice Earl Warren and his unanimous Supreme Court when they ruled for integrated schools in *Brown v. Board of Education*, President Eisenhower when "he dispatched federal troops to Little Rock to preserve order and protect Negro children," and Attorney General Robert Kennedy when he "outlawed discrimination in interstate travel."[5] The Montgomery bus boycott and its now-familiar instigators—Rosa Parks, Martin Luther King Jr., and Alabama State College English professor Jo Ann Robinson and her Women's Political Council, which provided many of the boycott's foot soldiers—are nowhere to be seen. Nor are the Little Rock Nine, the National Association for the Advancement of Colored People except in a note on its founding in 1909, the Congress of Racial Equality, the Freedom Riders, and many others.

Most striking in Morison and Commager's midcentury version of twentieth-century U.S. history is their handling of human agency. When powerful white men were not the ones making history, the "United States" or "America" or "the Americans" were frequently the subject of sentences, revealing Morison and Commager's assumption of unity of identity and action. More unexpectedly, I found many statements that had no clear subject, indeed, no one actually making history, and thus conveyed an undisputable inevitability in history's unfolding. Here are a few examples from just one chapter chosen at random, "The Truman Administration": "The most impressive fact about the domestic scene was the continuation and extension of wartime prosperity"; "Poll taxes, however, resisted both political and constitutional attack"; "Loyalty investigations and purges, and the requirement of loyalty oaths were extended into many other fields, notably those of labor and education."[6]

These observations about consensus-era U.S. history surely are not new, but it is worth recalling just what that history looked like before the tidal wave of revisionism hit in the late 1960s and 1970s. What we now take for granted and might at times even cynically dismiss as the tired old triad of "race, class, and gender" was truly a revolution in historical research and writing. Whatever we choose to call it—the new social history or "history from the bottom up," with its major subfields of the new labor and working-class history, black history, women's history, and immigration history—had a formative impact on American history. Consider the seventh edition of *The Growth of the American Republic*, which appeared in 1980 under the authorship of Morison, Commager, and their new team member William E. Leuchtenburg and was by no means the most social history–oriented of the era's textbooks.[7] Now we find statements like the following: "Woman suffrage was written into the constitution in 1920; millions of women crowded into jobs in factory and office; and increasing numbers of them took part in public life. A generation that observed Jane Addams and Eleanor Roosevelt could not seriously believe women less competent than men in public affairs." Or, "The real spark for the civil rights revolution came not from the President or Congress, not even from the Supreme Court, but from the Negroes themselves." Need I say more?

As I explained in the new introduction I wrote for the second edition of *Making a New Deal*, I was under the magical spell of the new social history when I conceived that project first as my University of California at Berkeley dissertation in 1986 and then as a book published four years later. I was particularly excited by this new approach that made ordinary Americans important actors in making history and the "local" a revealing stage on which to capture their activity, whether "local" referred to a huge city like Chicago, a smaller-scale ethnic community or neighborhood, or a membership organization such as a labor union or a women's association. I aimed in my book to make three additional contributions to social history as it was then evolving: first, to bring the kind of social-historical investigation that had reshaped eighteenth- and nineteenth-century American history to twentieth-century American history, still at the time a chronicle of presidential administrations or decades; second, to overcome the fragmentation into historiographical subfields that had emerged in social history by the early 1980s, making it increasingly difficult to view historical actors as having multiple racial, ethnic, class, and gender identities; and third, to bring a more political orientation to social history. By this last objective I meant both probing people's political thoughts and behavior and linking their social lives to larger questions of politics and power in the United States. Here I had been influenced by historian critics of social history like Tony Judt who lamented some social historians' tendency to write "history with the politics left out" and by social scientists like Theda Skocpol who called for "bringing the state back in" and paying greater attention to politics and political structure. I took from these debates a challenge to bring the rich, multivocal research of social history to bear on the political history of the twentieth century. I did not agree with some critics of social history who argued that the daily content of people's social and cultural lives did not matter. My view was that we had to do a better job of figuring out how that content mattered in shaping major developments in politics and power. I aimed to write a politically inflected social history or a socially inflected political history or, better yet, to abandon those distinctions altogether.

Making a New Deal appeared in 1990 and became part of a generation of social history writing about the twentieth-century United States, authored from the late 1970s through the 1990s, that included the work of many participants in this volume and the conference that preceded it: Leslie Tentler's *Wage-Earning Women: Industrial Work and Family Life in the United States, 1900–1930* (1979); Robert Orsi's *Madonna of 115th Street: Faith and Community in Italian Harlem, 1880–1950* (1985); David Gutiérrez's *Walls and Mirrors: Mexican Americans, Mexican Immigrants, and the Politics of Ethnicity* (1995); John McGreevy's *Parish Boundaries: The Catholic Encounter with Race in the Twentieth-Century Urban North* (1996); Thomas Sugrue's *The Origins of the Urban Crisis: Race and Inequality in Postwar Detroit* (1996); and R. Marie Griffith's *God's Daughters: Evangelical Women and the Power of Submission* (1997). A very long list of other works could be included in this era of twentieth-century U.S. social history; I will single out only a few here to capture the full range of subject matter: Jacqueline Dowd Hall and her collaborators' *Like a Family:The Making of a Southern Cotton Mill World* (1987); Gary Gerstle's *Working-Class Americanism: The Politics of Labor in a Textile City, 1914–1960* (1989); and George Chauncey's *Gay New York: Gender, Urban Culture, and the Making of the Gay Male World, 1890–1940* (1994).[8]

As the 1990s wore on and turned into the early twenty-first century, new cutting edges inevitably emerged within the field of twentieth-century U.S. history. First, whereas once it had seemed that everyone identified as a social historian, suddenly now everyone was proclaiming himself or herself a cultural historian. In practice, this meant that scholars were paying more attention to literary and cultural texts—many of them nonelite—and to the use of language in those texts, sensitive to how historical subjects' experiences were inevitably refracted through discourse. That language, it was argued, provided the historian—himself or herself a product of a different historical moment—with whatever evidence was available about the past. In the new era of cultural history, teasing out contradictions increasingly replaced arguing for causality in the teleology of many historical arguments. In the twentieth-century U.S. field, this "cultural turn," as it was called, focused attention on many new kinds of texts, from Christina Klein's analysis of Rodgers and Hammerstein's musical *South Pacific* and James Michener's novel *Hawaii* in her book *Cold War Orientalism: Asia in the Middlebrow Imagination, 1945–1961* (2003) to Sarah Igo's investigation of the emergence of what she calls a "statistically normal American" through the Middletown studies, the Gallup poll, and Alfred Kinsey's reports on human sexual behavior in her book *The Averaged American: Surveys, Citizens, and the Making of a Mass Public* (2007).[9]

In a second new historiographical development in the 1990s, U.S. historians expanded their treatment of the "subaltern" beyond racial minority groups and first- and second-generation immigrants to encompass the vast mainstream of Americans who had not previously been viewed as having racial or ethnic identity. What became known as "whiteness studies" argued that from the arrival of the Irish in the mid-nineteenth century through the many population influxes of the late nineteenth and twentieth centuries, European immigrants to the United States—and in some cases native-born poor whites—transcended their narrowly defined ethnicity by learning to see themselves as white as opposed to black or brown, thereby building common cultural bonds and gaining political privileges that set them apart from their darker neighbors (or, more frequently, nonneighbors). Not only did they absorb this self-defining racial bifurcation from popular culture such as vaudeville theater, Hollywood movies, and popular advertising, but they also reinforced it when they excluded those they considered nonwhite from their neighborhoods, labor unions, and voting booths. Although this field first congealed as an interpretation of the Irish working class in the nineteenth century by David Roediger and Noel Ignatiev, before long historians such as Matthew Jacobson, George Lipsitz, Bruce Nelson, and Roediger himself in a second volume extended the analysis into the twentieth century.[10]

Third, just as historians expanded their interest in race beyond narrowly defined racial populations to a more universal process of constructing racial identity or "racialization," so historians of men, women, and gender began seeing "gendering" as a complex, ubiquitous process. No longer was gender only about excavating the lives of women and, to a lesser extent, men. Inspired by a paradigm-shifting article in the *American Historical Review* by French historian and gender theorist Joan Scott in 1986, "Gender: A Useful Category of Historical Analysis," scholars brought gender analysis to historical dynamics that on the surface did not seem to be animated by gender. Scott argued that "gender is a primary way of signifying relationships of power" and that by decoding the gendered language of governments and nation-states we can gain deep insight into the nature of politics, power, and ideology in any given society. "Political history," she claimed, "has, in a sense, been enacted on the field of gender."[11] What followed were wide-ranging and influential studies of masculinity and femininity as they played out in the American polity from imperial adventures to the creation of the welfare state. Linda Gordon's *Pitied but Not Entitled: Single Mothers and the History of Welfare, 1890–1935* (1994), Gail Bederman's *Manliness and Civilization* (1995), and Alice Kessler-Harris's *In Pursuit of Equity: Women, Men, and the Quest for Economic Citizenship in 20th-Century America* (2001) are only a few of the many studies that explored what Kessler-Harris calls the "gendered imagination"—the way gender sensibilities and biases were deeply embedded in the nation's foreign and domestic policies.[12]

A fourth shift in recent American historiography has been the emergence of new topics of inquiry, in some cases the flip side of subjects explored by social historians in the 1970s and 1980s. Two fields in particular have attracted—and continue to attract—the attention of historians. Whereas the founding generation of social historians early on fixed their attention on producers, drawn particularly to workers' struggles to organize unions, during the last decade historians—myself included—have shifted their attention to consumers. My book *A Consumers' Republic: The Politics of Mass Consumption in Postwar America* (2003) is part of a cohort of work that includes Grace Hale's *Making Whiteness: The Culture of Segregation in the South, 1890–1940* (1998); Lawrence Glickman's edited volume *Consumer Society in American History: A Reader* (1999); Jennifer Scanlon's edited volume *The Gender and the Consumer Reader* (2000); and Meg Jacobs's *Pocketbook Politics: Economic Citizenship in Twentieth-Century America* (2005).[13] In a similar fashion, after years of probing the historical dynamics of liberalism in twentieth-century America through topics ranging from Progressivism, the New Deal, and the Great Society to the Congress of Industrial Organizations and civil rights, historians affected by the political "right turn" of the last quarter of the twentieth century began to investigate conservatism. Nancy Maclean's *Behind the Mask of Chivalry: The Making of the Second Ku Klux Klan* (1994), Lisa McGirr's *Suburban Warriors: The Origins of the New American Right* (2001), and Matthew Lassiter's *The Silent Majority: Politics in the Sunbelt South* (2006) are only a few examples.[14]

Other topics driving significant new work include the new western and borderlands history, legal history, and, building on its significance in contemporary U.S. culture, religious history.[15] Given the focus of this volume, I point out that alongside a healthy crop of historical books on twentieth-century Protestantism and Judaism there has been a notable flowering of work on American Catholics from a rich variety of perspectives, including David O'Brien's *Public Catholicism* (1989), Mary Lethert Wingerd's *Claiming the City: Politics, Faith, and the Power of Place in St. Paul* (2001), Evelyn Savidge Sterne's *Ballots and Bibles: Ethnic Politics and the Catholic Church in Providence* (2003), Leslie Tentler's *Catholics and Contraception: An American History* (2004), and James T. Fisher's *On the Irish Waterfront: The Crusader, the Movie, and the Soul of the Port of New York* (2009).[16] Although these and other historians have paid increasing attention to religion as a crucial factor in shaping American politics and social relations, some critics lament the functionalism of that approach to religion and urge more attention to religious faith and practice in defining the cultural experiences of Americans. Historians of Catholicism have pioneered investigation into the spiritual meaning many Americans have found in religion through interpreting the devotional rituals and artifacts of believers, such as their prayers and practices, religious objects, and church buildings, and the multitude of other ways in which religion has suffused daily life. Robert Orsi's studies of Italian immigrant religious observances in New York City and the cult of women's devotions to St. Jude, the patron of hopeless causes, stand out as models of how investigation of religion can both penetrate Americans' interior lives and shed light on the larger social and cultural history of twentieth-century America.[17]

The latest trend in the historiography of the United States is what we have come to call the "internationalizing" of American history. This approach aims to escape the assumption of American exceptionalism that has been embedded in so much of our history writing—that the United States followed its own unique path, distinct from Europe and the other colonies the Old World spun off. Some proponents of American exceptionalism over the years even made further normative claims, that this exceptional America escaped many of the dangers of Europe's past—undemocratic political regimes, entrenched social classes, and limited economic mobility. The new international approach investigates whether and how the United States followed a distinctive path rather than assuming that it did. It decenters the United States in a variety of ways: by explicitly comparing the U.S. historical experience with that of other nations; by recognizing that professional history writing was part of the nation-state project, and therefore transnational movements of people and ideas—across national borders and spanning nodes of extrastate interaction such as the worlds of the Atlantic, Pacific, and Indian oceans—deserve more attention; and by asserting that long before the era of global capitalism, states and people operated within a global framework. American history is thus undeniably a part of such worldwide dynamics as exploration, settlement, enslavement, industrialization, immigration, nationalism, imperialism, and environmental degradation. Thomas Bender articulated the two major arguments at the heart of his treatise *A Nation among Nations: America's Place in World History* (2006) as follows:

> The first is that global history commenced when American history began, in the decades before and after 1500. The second follows directly from the first: American history cannot be adequately understood unless it is incorporated into the global context. It then becomes a different kind of history with more explanatory power. It reconnects history with geography. It incorporates causal influences that work across space as well as those that unfold over time. It enriches our understanding of the historical making and remaking of the United States. It is, moreover, the only way to map and appraise the changing position and interdependencies that connect the United States today to the other provinces of the planet.[18]

There are few among us who would challenge the importance of what we might call "the international turn." It has undoubtedly made most U.S. historians more alert to critically important comparative and transnational dimensions of U.S. history, whatever their particular subject. But like all panaceas, it is not perfect. I would like to raise a concern that struck me after reviewing three of the most prominent new international histories of the United States: Bender's *A Nation among Nations* (2006); Eric Rauchway's *Blessed among Nations: How the World Made America* (2006); and Daniel T. Rodgers's *Atlantic Crossings: Social Politics in a Progressive Age* (1998). Bender's and Rauchway's books are synthetic works that encompass only the early decades of the twentieth century. Bender aims to put five important events in American history in global context: the colonial experience in the context of the larger era of discovery, the American Revolution in the context of the crisis of empires, the Civil War in the context of nineteenth-century liberal nationalism, the Spanish-American War of 1898 in the context of broader imperialism, and the Progressive Era in the context of the expansion of industrial capitalism and social liberal strategies to cope with it. Rauchway also zeroes in on large themes like capital, labor, welfare, and warfare in the period 1865–1918. But in their admirable effort to replace the American historian's usual close-up lens with a wide-angle one that better locates the United States in the larger world, both authors end up focusing more on elites and their ideas than on ordinary people's experiences. The American protagonists of Bender and Rauchway's treatments of the late nineteenth and twentieth centuries are presidents like Theodore Roosevelt and Woodrow Wilson; reformers like Jane Addams, Richard Ely, and D. Carroll Wright; and capitalists like J. Pierpont Morgan. Rodgers's *Atlantic Crossings*, less of a survey and based more on primary research, is a book I admire very much, but it, too, in its attention to those Rodgers labels as "cosmopolitan progressives" who were "brokers" of reform ideas from Berlin to San Francisco, focuses our attention on many of Bender and Rauchway's protagonists, as well as other influential writers and doers like Frederic C. Howe, Florence Kelley, Paul Kellogg, Catherine Bauer, and Lewis Mumford.

Although there are certainly more women making history in these new internationalized versions of the American past than Morison and Commager ever acknowledged in *The Growth of the American Republic*, it is hard not to notice that the cast of thousands who crowded the stage in the social history of the 1970s and 1980s and continued to play important roles in cultural history, whiteness studies, gendered political history, and historical investigations of new topics like consumption and conservatives are suddenly less visible. Powerful white men—and a few women—seem to dominate center stage. My purpose here is not to accuse these three fine historians of negligence. I know from my own recent effort to internationalize the presentation of U.S. history in the *American Pageant* textbook that elites who cross national boundaries are particularly helpful guides to the transnational flow of ideas and social policies. And for whatever reason, these three pioneers in internationalizing American history—Bender, Rauchway, and Rodgers—are by inclination, as evidenced in their earlier work, historians of political and intellectual elites. My larger point here is that in our enthusiasm for decentering the United States in history, we need to be watchful not to slip back into the days of Morison and Commager and forget some of the important lessons of the new social history—that ordinary people shape history and that "the local" is an important stage for watching them act. Although not all historical work will—or should—be transnational, for that work that is, the question then becomes: Is it possible to have "history from the bottom up" and the world, the local and the global, at the same time?

I propose that historical analysis is not a zero sum game, and that historians can—and should—move back and forth across registers of local, national, and international history. I will label this "broadband" transnational history, making use of a term in telecommunications for a signaling method that handles a wide range of frequencies at the same time.[19] This approach, moreover, can broaden the cast of influential actors beyond what the first generation of internationalizing historians has considered. It also is not without some compelling models. The twentieth-century fields that have most effectively probed the possibilities for broadband transnational American history by moving nimbly among local, national, and international arenas are the histories of immigration and of the civil rights movement, particularly during the Cold War era. As early as when I was in graduate school in the late 1970s, long before the "discovery" of international history, the new immigration history pioneered following American immigrants back to their country of origin and exploring how Old World patterns—of family, work, religion, authority structures, and community interactions—affected their New World experiences. I remember the publication of John Briggs's *An Italian Passage: Immigrants to Three American Cities, 1890–1930* in 1978 as heralding an exciting, cosmic shift, a recognition that immigration history had to be written from both shores. More work in the same vein quickly followed, particularly as historians who moved back and forth across oceans and national borders discovered that more often than we had previously realized, immigrants did the same.[20]

More recently, enormously rich work by Brenda Plummer, Penny Von Eschen, Robin Kelley, Mary Dudziak, Thomas Borstelmann, Carol Anderson, Nikhil Singh, Jonathan Rosenberg, Ruth Feldstein, and James Campbell, among others, has laid out a powerful analysis of how African Americans had long linked their struggle for freedom to a diasporic consciousness of pan-Africanism and anticolonialism. By the Cold War era, not only had black internationalism intensified in the aftermath of World War II and the crumbling of European empires, but the white American establishment struggled to resolve the blatant contradiction between promoting itself as the paragon of liberty and equality in contrast to communism, on the one hand, and, the reality of deeply embedded racial discrimination in the United States, on the other hand. As many of these historians argue, the international pressures of the Cold War exerted crucial leverage in advancing the civil rights agenda.

Concern over America's image abroad and civil rights activism at home were inextricably linked in a causal chain reaching from Birmingham to Washington to New Delhi. By introducing race into transnational history, this literature on civil rights has also propelled the field of internationalized American history beyond the Euro-American encounter to include Africa, Asia, and Latin America.[21]

∞ Transnational American Catholicism

If writing a broadband transnational history that moves agilely among the local, the national, and the global is the great challenge awaiting twentieth-century U.S. historians, I propose that American Catholic history offers an opportunity for innovation similar to immigration and Cold War civil rights history. After all, the Roman Catholic Church is a global institution operating on multiple levels from the Vatican in Rome to the Catholic Church of America to local archdioceses and dioceses to neighborhood parishes. What happens on any one of those frequencies has connections to, and implications for, most of the others.

In making this case, I will draw on the book I am currently writing on the rebuilding of American cities after World War II, revealed through the life and career of a pivotal figure in urban renewal during the second half of the twentieth century, Edward J. Logue. Logue was the chief—some said the czar—of redevelopment in the urban-renewal laboratory of New Haven in the 1950s, in the building of the "New Boston" in the 1960s, and as head of the New York State Urban Development Corporation, a unique and powerful statewide redevelopment agency, from the late 1960s to the mid-1970s. His last big job, as president of the South Bronx Development Organization from 1978 to 1985, involved him in efforts to revitalize devastated neighborhoods in the South Bronx. He died in 2000. Logue provides a vehicle for me to examine half a century of strategies to revitalize U.S. cities in the era of mass suburbanization.

What, you might be wondering, does Ed Logue have to do with developing a transnational American Catholic history? In my effort to understand how Logue's urban-renewal schemes were received by the power structure and ordinary residents of the cities in which he worked, I have been drawn to investigating influential mediating institutions, churches among them. In Boston the Catholic Church played a critical role in the city's efforts to revitalize itself in the 1960s after decades of economic stagnation. During the 1950s alone, Boston had lost 13 percent of its population to the suburbs, which grew 50 percent over the decade, and more than 48,000 manufacturing jobs, contributing to an 8 percent drop in city employment while suburban jobs increased 22 percent. Only two new office buildings had gone up in thirty years, the city's tax base was declining precipitously while the tax rate was the highest in the nation, and the city was near bankruptcy. It surprised no one when a *Fortune* magazine headline asked rhetorically, "What Can a Sick City Do?" When Logue and Mayor John Collins managed to push through a renewal plan in the early 1960s that involved a quarter of the city's acreage and half of its population in ten target areas, including several white working-class neighborhoods dominated by Irish Catholics, the church's support proved decisive.[22]

What I have learned, however, is that a full analysis of the Catholic response to urban renewal in Boston requires consideration of a wide spectrum of actors from the pope in Rome and the reforms emerging from the Second Vatican Council of 1962–65 to Richard Cardinal Cushing's actions as head of the Archdiocese of Boston and to local parishioners and pastors in embattled neighborhoods such as Charlestown. Let us start at the global and work back to the local.[23]

As historians of Catholicism have chronicled, from 1962 to 1965 the Roman Catholic Church thoroughly reinvented itself through the deliberations and decrees of the Second Vatican Council. Launched by Pope John XXIII and continued after his death by Pope Paul VI, the ecumenical Council called for "updating" in multiple dimensions: in the nature of liturgy, ritual, education, and relations within the hierarchy and between the clergy and the laity; in attitudes and policies toward pluralism and religious freedom; in relations between Catholics and other Christians and Jews; and in the realm most relevant to my inquiry, the church's involvement in the world, including the complex social problems confronting the urban communities located within most dioceses.

During the time of Vatican II, the Archdiocese of Boston was headed by Richard Cardinal Cushing, who had held that position since the death of his predecessor, William Cardinal O'Connell, in 1944. To the secular mass-media magazine *Time*, which devoted a special issue to Catholicism in August 1964, Cushing, more than any other American bishop, epitomized "the surge of church renewal." Even before the assembling of the Council, Cushing had anticipated much of its openness to change by radically improving relations between Boston's Catholic Church and other denominations. Of most interest to me, he led the church actively in efforts to mobilize previously antagonistic groups to join together to improve the city. Whereas Cardinal O'Connor had shared the separatist orientation of James Michael

Curley's corrupt political machine, Cushing allied himself with the new wave of Irish reform politicians—Mayor John Hynes and his successor, Mayor John Collins—who were reaching out to the Yankee downtown interests that Curley had antagonized for years.

The most important vehicle for broaching these paralyzing divides between downtown business interests and the ethnic, often Irish, neighborhoods and their political representatives was a new institution founded in 1954 called the Boston College Citizen Seminars, where business and labor leaders, public officials, and members of the civic elite—including religious leaders of all faiths—came together to begin to discuss the city's deep problems. The seminar was started by Boston-born Jesuit priest W. Seavey Joyce soon after he was named dean of the School of Business Administration at Boston College, and it continued meeting throughout the 1950s and 1960s, providing a neutral, Catholic-sponsored base for building trust and then rebuilding much of the city's infrastructure. Under Cushing the church recognized that its own future was as entwined with the city's fate as that of local manufacturers and downtown banks and department stores. If Boston continued to bleed population and jobs to the suburbs, the church as an enormous and powerful urban institution would suffer along with other city-based organizations and institutions.

The other major commitment that Cushing's Boston Catholic Church made that was crucial to launching the city's urban renewal was delegating his close adviser Monsignor Francis J. Lally to serve first as one of the original members and then, in 1960, as chairman of the Boston Redevelopment Authority (BRA), a new administrative entity created in 1957 as an independent public authority to deal exclusively with redevelopment, particularly federal urban-renewal funding. Lally had been Cushing's right-hand man in matters of civil rights and interfaith relations, and it was a progressive act to name him editor of the archdiocesan weekly newspaper, the *Pilot*, in 1952 and to promote him for the BRA post in 1957. When Logue arrived in Boston from New Haven in the spring of 1960 at the invitation of recently elected Mayor Collins with big plans to revitalize the city, Lally's enthusiastic support made his appointment and his proposals possible. Without it, Logue would never have been approved by a divided BRA Board because the old-guard Irish pols were dead set against Logue, an outsider, coming in to remake their city. Lally's—and through him the cardinal's—endorsement, communicated through leadership on the BRA, editorials in the *Pilot*, archdiocesan instructions to parish priests, and many other kinds of support, remained critical throughout Logue's tenure in Boston.

By the time the official decrees of the Second Vatican Council were pro-mulgated in the mid-1960s, Boston's church was already implementing many of Rome's new reforms. Cushing, in fact, brought many of his home-grown, open-minded commitments to the Council's deliberations in Rome and helped push them in progressive directions. He boldly supported the proposed declaration of religious liberty, successfully introduced a statement absolving the Jews of any culpability for Christ's death, and, less successfully, tried to take the call to substitute the vernacular for Latin one step further by proposing—and offering to pay for—the installation of a simultaneous translation system so that those like him who were not proficient in ecclesi-astical Latin could nonetheless participate fully in the council's delibera-tions. Given these predilections for reform, what Vatican II gave to Cushing and his Boston Church was legitimation for partnering with other influen-tial forces, including the Protestant business elite, to renew the city. Without that, the church would have been much more vulnerable to internal and external pressures to keep to church business narrowly defined.

One of the pressures from within that Vatican II helped Cushing's arch-diocese withstand was resistance from parishioners who lived in some of the neighborhoods targeted for urban renewal and who adamantly resisted the proposed changes. A prime example was the insular, Irish Catholic, working-class—one could even say poor—community of Charlestown. The Charles-town story is too complicated to explore fully here. Suffice it to say that both the urban renewers and their opponents had a case: the neighborhood was in a deteriorating condition that desperately needed attention, and de-spite the BRA's claims to the contrary, "Townies," as they were known, were right to fear that redevelopment would fundamentally change their com-munity. The Charlestown struggle became a crucial contest between Logue's BRA, which prided itself on promoting a new-style urban renewal based on "planning with people" and rehabilitation rather than demolition, and the anti-urban-renewal forces, who understandably feared either another West End disaster or a different kind of death by gentrification.

As the battle lines were drawn from 1961 to 1965, the Catholic Church became an important ally of the BRA's vision for a renewed Charlestown. Monsignor Lally moved into the rectory of St. Catherine's Church in Charlestown, and parish priests at that and the other two area parishes, St. Mary's and St. Francis de Sales, were instructed to sermonize about the positive aspects of urban renewal. After two years of acrimony the BRA triumphed at a key public hearing in March 1965 when three hours of de-bate (in which local priests supported the BRA's plans as the only way to save their dwindling parishes) were brought to an abrupt halt by a local priest suddenly calling the question. In what was considered a very close—if not questionable—counting of hands, the BRA's plans passed. Redevelopment went forward in Charlestown, albeit with some accommodations to residents' demands.

But a decade later, in the midst of the busing crisis of the mid-1970s, anger that had festered since the battles over urban renewal flared up again and contributed to Charlestown becoming an important base for the resistance to school integration through mandatory busing.[24] In particular, Catholic women active in Charlestown's antibusing organization, Powder Keg, and Louise Day Hicks's ROAR (Restore our Alienated Rights)—some of them veterans of the earlier urban-renewal struggles—challenged the pro-busing cardinal who now headed the archdiocese and their parish pastors, many of whom were personally sympathetic but felt constrained in their ability to offer public support because of the church's official endorsement of Judge W. Arthur Garrity's busing order.

The Boston Catholic Church was now led by someone these antibusing activists considered an outsider—Portuguese Humberto Cardinal Medeiros, originally from Fall River, Massachusetts, more recently from Brownsville, Texas—who had become an outspoken advocate for the state's Racial Imbalance Act and busing as an imperfect but necessary remedy for deep racial bias in the operation of the Boston School Committee. In the reform-minded wake of Vatican II, Rome had promoted the scholarly, pious, and socially committed Medeiros to head one of the most important sees of the Catholic Church in America. But Medeiros faced a rocky road. Succeeding the beloved Cushing, enjoying little of the base in Boston that South Boston native Cushing had had when he took over, and suspected for his racial and ethnic otherness as the first non-Irish Boston cardinal in almost a century and a half, Medeiros began his tenure politically weak and grew only weaker when he took such actions as prohibiting transfers from public to parochial schools to dodge busing. By 1976, in the depths of the busing battle, he dared not even enter Charlestown or South Boston for fear of being stoned.

Significantly, the dictates of Vatican II remained relevant to this local struggle because both sides invoked them to justify their positions: Catholic antibusing proponents argued that one of the council's major documents, *Gaudium et Spes*, granted parents the responsibility to educate their children in their school of choice, while the cardinal claimed that Vatican II required Catholics to act morally in service to the common good. Moreover, the Catholic women who spearheaded the attack on forced busing with prayerful protests built their strategy around the authorization they felt

Vatican II had given the laity to act independently of the church hierarchy. Ironically, Vatican II had aimed to reconnect ordinary Catholics with their church, and in many ways it succeeded in reenergizing the faith. But in a city like Boston its legacy, as played out in struggles over urban renewal and busing, also contributed to weakening the church's hold over its parishioners, who would be further aggravated in succeeding decades by a devastating series of parish closings and the notorious clergy sexual-abuse crisis of 2002.

∞ Opportunities for Catholic Historians

This case study of the centrality of the international Roman Catholic Church to the local urban renewal of the City of Boston highlights a unique opportunity awaiting Catholic historians. They are ideally situated to take on one of the most important challenges facing the field today: how to internationalize our understanding of U.S. events, institutions, and ideas without abandoning the commitment historians have made over the past four decades to broaden the range of people whose experience matters in analyzing U.S. history. I cannot think of a better historical subject that requires consideration from the top down as well as from the bottom up, one that shows as powerfully the interconnectedness between the international and the local, than Catholic history as it stretches from the global reach of the Roman Catholic Church to the daily lives of ordinary parishioners. Historians of U.S. Catholicism are thus poised to lead the way in enriching and renewing the writing of general twentieth-century U.S. history by writing a broadband, transnational kind of U.S. Catholic history.

Much is possible. I look forward, for example, to what Catholic history can contribute to a more fully realized transnational history of American immigration. Take the predominantly Catholic Mexican American population. Following Robert Orsi's lead in chapter 1 of this volume, historians could explore what alterations in the practice of Catholicism by Mexican Americans moving between Mexico and the United States revealed about their transition to American life. (See the chapter by David Gutiérrez in this volume.) What better way to understand the very private side of the immigrant experience? And when Mexican Americans helped make a city like San Antonio at least 41 percent Catholic, more than twice the next-largest religious group, the Protestants, a powerful, internationally oriented Catholic Church became critical for defining the distinctive urban society and politics of the late twentieth-century U.S. Southwest.

Or, to take a very different kind of historical problem, the history of global birth-control efforts cannot be fully understood without investigating the ideology and actions of the Roman Catholic Church as well as contraceptive practices not just in developing countries but also in the United States, with the third-largest and probably the wealthiest and most influential Catholic population in the world. (See R. Marie Griffith's chapter in this volume.) In other words, there is an unbroken chain for historians to follow from the intimate decisions American Catholic couples made about sexuality to the United Nations' global policies to control fertility.[25]

The possibilities for expanding U.S. historical narratives awaiting historians of twentieth-century Catholicism are limitless. I, along with many other twentieth-century U.S. historians, await their discoveries with great anticipation.

∞CHAPTER 3

The Catholic Encounter with the 1960s

THOMAS J. SUGRUE

"What in the name of God is going on in the Catholic Church?" asked the *National Review* in 1964. Scholars, whether or not they share the conservative periodical's alarm about the politics and theology of postconciliar Catholicism, agree that something profound changed in the American Catholic Church in the mid-1960s. Studies of the liturgy and devotional practices, the priesthood, Catholic education, family life, belief, and public opinion view the 1960s as the critical turning point in the history of the church in the United States. Historian Philip Gleason points to "the disintegrative impulses of changes in the post-conciliar years."[1] Chicago archbishop Joseph Bernardin writes of "a fundamental shift in historical consciousness" in the period. Others highlight "revolutionary change," a "spiritual earthquake," and a fundamental "crisis" or a process of "decomposition, decay, apostasy."[2] The 1960s marked, in best-selling author Charles R. Morris's words, "the end of the Catholic culture."[3]

The notion of the 1960s as a moment of disruption and cultural shift is not peculiar to Catholic historiography. In one of the earliest and most perceptive articles about the "cultural revolution" of the late 1960s, critic

For comments and criticism, I wish to thank Scott Appleby, Kathleen Sprows Cummings, James T. Fisher, and the participants at the 2008 Catholicism and the American Century conference.

Benjamin DeMott wrote: "We've come to relish plurality of self. We behave as though impatient or bitter at every structure, form, convention and practice that edges us toward singleness of view or 'option,' or that forces us to accept this or that single role as the whole truth of our being." Although DeMott was not concerned with Catholicism, he identified the fundamental challenges that the "cultural revolution" posed to Catholic America. How could a church defined by its ostensibly timeless rituals, repeated habitually each Sunday, survive what he called the sixties-era "detestation of the habitual"? How could an institution posited on an understanding of a divine order mediated through the papacy, the priesthood, and the Magisterium survive the 1960s "belief in the power of unmediated experience"? How could the individualism and experimentation of the 1960s not erode traditional understandings of authority and community that defined the Catholic experience?[4]

DeMott's understanding of the 1960s as a cultural revolution continues to shape our understanding of the period as a moment of rupture. Most Catholic histories of the 1960s offer a version of what I call "sixties exceptionalism," in this case an interpretation of the period as the end of tradition. Histories of the Catholic 1960s focus overwhelmingly on two shocks to the system, one endogenous, the other exogenous. The first was the Second Vatican Council, which launched a period of intense theological debate, a rethinking of the role of the church in the world, a reconceptualization of clerical authority, and a reconfiguration of rite, ritual, and devotion. The second was the impact of the political, social, and cultural changes in U.S. society writ large during the 1960s, which reinforced and compounded the tectonic shifts in everyday life, belief, and religious practice among Catholics.[5]

This interpretation of the 1960s is compelling but incomplete. It downplays the long process of social, cultural, and political change that remade the United States—and the Catholic Church—over the course of the twentieth century. It foregrounds short-term changes and ignores continuities. It rests on an ahistorical, static understanding of what came before the 1960s. It emphasizes Catholics as the objects of change, not the agents of change. It ignores the profound role that Catholics played in the reconfiguration of American politics and society in the mid-twentieth century. And it downplays or overlooks the ways in which Catholics set the terms for debates about public policy that would remake the United States over the last third of the twentieth century.[6]

The non-Catholic historiography of the 1960s unfortunately does not provide much material for those who want to challenge the tired clichés of sixties exceptionalism. Scholarship on the sixties is full of gaps, largely because its formative questions were shaped by a generation of scholars who focused on one side of the period: the rise of the New Left and the collapse of an alleged "liberal consensus." The first draft of history was written by participants in the student revolts of the 1960s and by liberal and neoconservative observers who chafed at what they saw as the "excesses" of the antiwar and black power movements, the Great Society, and the war in Vietnam. Like mainstream Catholic historians, these scholars and pundits emphasize rupture and discontinuity, albeit of a secular variety. Many former New Leftists celebrate the liberatory impulses of the 1960s when radical social movements struck a blow against the conformity and homogeneity of the postwar years by fostering a culture of participatory democracy and personal liberation. Disillusioned liberals and conservatives offer a darker view of these changes, directing their attention to the "unraveling" of liberalism, the result of the destructive forces unleashed by Dionysian counterculturalists, chiliastic racial separatists, and nihilistic, violent student revolutionaries. The very titles of the most influential syntheses of the 1960s capture the prevailing arguments about the sixties as apocalypse: *The Unraveling of America*, *Fire in the Streets*, *Years of Discord*, and *Coming Apart*.[7]

By the early 1990s a new generation of scholars, most of whom came of age in the more conservative 1970s and 1980s, began to decenter the New Left. They reacted against the first wave of sixties historiography in which conservatism appeared as a reactive force, politically impotent until it was confronted with hippies, AmeriKKKa-bashing leftists, and lawless blacks. In conventional narratives of the 1960s the rightward turn in American politics was the by-product of a populist "backlash" against liberalism's failures. But revisionist historians of liberalism and conservatism demolished the underpinnings of the backlash thesis through social histories of grassroots politics and sophisticated analyses of the state and political development. Particularly influential were scholars who engaged in painstaking reconstructions of the New Right as an intellectual, political, and social movement. Challenging the notion that right-wing politics emerged de novo in the late 1960s, they uncovered a deep-seated antiliberalism that remade American politics well before the campus uprisings, the urban riots, and the love-ins and happenings of the late 1960s. Already by the late 1940s right-wing business leaders were marketing the concept of "free enterprise" as fundamentally American. Republicans began trolling for converts among southern whites in the late 1950s by denouncing the black freedom struggle. And cells of newly empowered conservative activists built a political base through countless coffee klatches, reading groups, and evening meetings where they plotted the takeover of local school districts from liberals, atheists, and suspected Communists and began mounting campaigns for higher office.[8]

At the same time, the notion that the 1960s were the apotheosis of statist liberalism came under siege by a variety of political scientists and historians, many of whom argued that programs like the War on Poverty, long described as the zenith of American state building, were actually rather conservative in their origins and limited in their effects. In his field-defining essay "Was the Great Society a Lost Opportunity?" Ira Katznelson argued that the social programs of the 1960s were constrained in their scope and scale, fundamentally nonredistributive, and cautious as a consequence of the collapse of a economic-based liberalism during the domestic cold war of the 1940s. Other scholars emphasized the long-standing racial and gender exclusions of liberal social programs, their emphasis on citizenship and uplift rather than on economic redistribution, and their fundamental pro-business orientation.[9]

Conventional frameworks for thinking about liberalism and backlash in the 1960s also came under siege by urban historians who uncovered a ubiquitous "crabgrass-roots" antiliberalism that defined local politics in places like Detroit, Baltimore, Oakland, Chicago, and New York well before the tumult of the 1960s. Other scholars challenged the prevailing notion that the post–World War II United States was a nation of consensus, homogeneity, and cultural conservatism. Women's historians chipped away at the conventional stereotype that the 1950s were marked by the hegemony of the nuclear family and that the 1960s destroyed it; social movement historians found deep currents of radical activism in the seemingly complacent postwar years; and cultural historians found expressions of popular rebellion in everything from films to comic books to car detailing. Gay and lesbian historians pried open the closet and found thriving, if persecuted, homosexual communities in big cities—and even in small towns and rural communities—well before Stonewall. And scholars of sexuality found that the sexual revolution of the 1960s was a public expression of long-term changes in sexual norms that began early in the twentieth century.[10]

Even historians of student radicalism, the narrowest and most hidebound subfield of 1960s historiography, began to break open the long-hermetic history of the New Left, challenging the heroic self-fashioning of memoirists and finding common ground among student radicals and such unlikely allies as Social Gospel Protestants, postwar psychologists, and even big business. Building on the important insights of sociologist Daniel Bell, a cadre of revisionists reinterpreted the counterculture as an expression of post–World War II consumer culture, the product of an increasingly fragmented marketplace that was shaped and reshaped by Madison Avenue advertising executives and corporate marketing departments. The performance of countercultural styles was, in the words of historian and critic Thomas Frank, part of an effort to "commodify dissent."[11]

Historians of the most influential social movement of the 1960s—the African American freedom struggle—uprooted the prevailing assumptions of civil rights historiography. One body of scholars uncovered the history of "the long civil rights movement," arguing against chronologies that put too much emphasis on the "classic phase" of the movement from 1954 to 1968. Others challenged the binaristic framework for thinking about racial integration and black power, finding that the emphasis on the nonviolent freedom struggle effaced a history of black self-defense, anti-imperialism, and separatism that long predated the moment in 1966 when Stokely Carmichael famously uttered the two words "black power."[12]

The new scholarship, putting the 1960s in the broader trajectory of postwar American history, has resulted in a historiographical shift. New histories of the 1960s view conservatism as ultimately more important and influential than the New Left, offer a new, more nuanced view of mid-twentieth-century liberalism and its travails, and see the period's "cultural revolution" as one part of a *longue durée* of social, political, sexual, and cultural transformations that dated to the early twentieth century. But this historiographical revision remains unfinished. It has yet to topple the textbook orthodoxies about the 1960s that still shape how we teach, write, and opine on modern U.S. history. Many topics, especially those that do not conform to images of the "tumultuous" 1960s, have yet to be explored in detail. Business and economic history remains on the margins of our accounts of this period. The history of the mass media—despite its obvious importance—has attracted only a handful of talented historians, who have largely left the field to cultural theorists and communications scholars. And even well-developed subfields go cold when they move into the 1960s. The 1960s witnessed an acceleration of the process of white suburbanization, a phenomenon generally consigned to the 1950s and ignored thereafter. The remapping of metropolitan America in the 1960s and beyond, especially the rapid movement of commerce, industry, and the white population out of central cities, shaped economic, social, cultural, and political life in ways that were ultimately as far-reaching as the transgressive politics of the youthful radicals who still dominate our narratives.[13]

For several years, in my course on the history of the United States in the 1960s, I have asked my students to conduct oral histories of people who lived through the era. They have tracked down ex-hippies (among them one of Jimi Hendrix's many fleeting lovers), would-be prophets (including a depressed activist who renamed himself Job and took a gloomy pilgrimage of self-abasement across America), and campus leaders (mainly former members of Students for a Democratic Society). But most of my students come to me with the perplexed observation that their informants were "not doing anything in the sixties." Their discovery, although frustrating, is a teachable moment. Most Americans in the 1960s were not swept up directly by the counterculture, the New Left, or the civil rights and black power movements. They were managing their households, raising their families, driving long distances from home to work, and spending long hours in front of their television sets. They were also dealing with the tensions and contradictions between normative depictions of the nuclear family and a reality that increasingly confounded it. A well-rounded history of America in the 1960s must include those whom Catholic historian James Fisher calls the "many whose own striving 'sixties' bore no resemblance to the decade of myth."[14]

One of the deafening silences in the scholarship on the 1960s—and the one most pertinent here—is the history of religion. The subfield of religious history has taken off in recent years, but cutting-edge work on lived religion, religious activism, and theology, public policy, and the state has scarcely affected histories of America in the 1960s beyond accounts of black churches and the African American freedom struggle. Where religious groups do appear, they play bit roles, usually typecast. Mainstream Protestantism flits across the stage only for the announcement that it is in decline before it shuffles off, never to be heard from again. Judaism appears as the foil to black power before it bows out with a lamentation for the lost golden age of black-Jewish relations. And evangelicals, despite their growing numbers, wait silently in the wings for their appearance as a deus ex machina in the 1970s. Novelty trumps continuity, resulting in more ink spilled on the spread of New Age religious practices and the popularization of Buddhism and Hinduism (both interesting and important, if small-scale, phenomena, to be sure) than on the denominations that accounted for a majority of America's churchgoers.[15]

An observant student reading any good textbook or synthetic account of U.S. history in the mid-twentieth century will discover a mysterious paradox: somehow the churchgoing Americans of the God-fearing 1950s dropped their religious enthusiasms in the ostensibly secular 1960s, just a few years after the words "under God" were added to the Pledge of Allegiance. Most historians seem to have stopped reading the moment they came across the hyperbolic and decidedly premature obituaries, widespread in journalistic and scholarly accounts of the time, reporting the "death of God."[16]

Still, there are openings. The best younger historian of the 1960s left, Doug Rossinow, makes a persuasive case for exploring the political history of Christianity as a constitutive part of youthful radicals' search for "meaning" and "authenticity." Political scientist Hugh Heclo provocatively describes the 1960s as an "awakening," analogizes movement leaders to "New Lights," and views the period as a "search for a higher public moral order in a policy culture denying that there could be any such thing." And cultural historian of religion Amanda Porterfield also compares the 1960s to previous great awakenings in American history. But they are prophets howling in the historiographical void, at least for the moment.[17]

Despite the fact that Catholics constituted more than one-fifth of the nation's population in the 1960s, they seldom make anything more than fleeting appearances in any major accounts of the period. The absence of Catholics from the broad narratives of the 1960s is primarily the result of the blindness that most nonreligious historians have to lived religion, spirituality, theology, and institutional history. Mainstream intellectual historians from midcentury on began their search for the "American intellectual tradition" in Puritan thought and ended it with the struggle between theology and secularism in late nineteenth- and early twentieth-century philosophy. The foundational notion of "American exceptionalism" that shaped the discipline of American studies rested on the assumption that Protestant individualism defined American identity. Social historians were even more allergic to religious beliefs and practices, except insofar as they served the material interests of elites. Drawing from a Marxian tradition, they understood religion as instrumental, as a vehicle for elites to exert social control over the masses, discipline blue-collar workers, and reform the poor.

But the absence of Catholics in modern American historiography is also the consequence of the largely internalist orientation of twentieth-century Catholic historiography, which, despite the path breaking, crossover work of scholars like Philip Gleason, John McGreevy, Leslie Woodcock Tentler, and Robert Orsi, remains largely trapped in the Catholic ghetto at the very historical moment when the most decisive transformations in Catholic life dissolved the ghetto, brought Catholics into the very heart of the public sphere, and, in ways that merit further exploration, made the modern United States more Catholic just as Catholics themselves became more American. Like specialists in other subdisciplines in the increasingly fragmented discipline of American history, Catholic historians mostly write for each other.

Reading Catholic history from the perspective of a social and political historian trained at secular universities, I suggest that it is high time for twentieth-century American historians to integrate Catholics into their work and grapple with the fundamental problems that Catholic history poses to their paradigms—and vice versa. That requires greater attention to the ironies, interconnections, and the unexpected syncretism of mid- and late twentieth-century Catholic and non-Catholic life.

There is a road map for this newly integrated scholarly agenda in the words of many important religious historians themselves. Nearly forty years ago Philip Gleason argued that "the Catholic revolution both influenced the general American cultural crisis and was influenced by it."[18] More recently, Amanda Porterfield has provocatively argued that the 1960s witnessed the "infusion of Catholic sensibilities into mainstream American culture," even if she boils it down to a colorful, if rather dubious, connection between various forms of New Age spiritual seeking and "radical sacramentalism that burst out of its Catholic shell."[19]

Bringing Catholic history into the center of American history in the 1960s offers a radically new way of thinking about the period. In unexpected ways, historians of Catholicism (despite the still deeply entrenched focus on the Second Vatican Council as disruptive) actually reinforce arguments against sixties exceptionalism. A rich body of scholarship, mostly by historians of Catholic theology and liturgy, speaks directly to one of the major currents in the revisionist historiography of the 1960s. "If there had never been a Second Vatican Council," argued David J. O'Brien, the erosion of Catholic communities, particularly in the rapidly expanding suburbs, "would have created enormous pressure for change." Many new Catholic parishes became venues of weekly worship, less entwined with other communal institutions and everyday life than they had been in the tight-knit ethnic communities of the immigrant church.

Likewise, Catholic understandings of marriage and the family evolved in relationship to postwar popular culture in ways that reinforce the conclusions of historians who find significant changes in gender, family, and sexual practices predating the 1960s. In the postwar years North American families turned inward. The nuclear family—not the norm for most of U.S. history—supplanted other household arrangements, including boarding and extended families that were common in the nineteenth and early twentieth centuries, especially among Catholics. Larger currents in popular culture, especially the sexualization of music, film, and advertising, transformed everyday sexual practices. By the 1960s Catholics were just as likely as non-Catholics to engage in premarital sex and just as likely as Americans of other religious backgrounds to conceive children outside marriage. And married Catholic couples, like their mainstream Protestant and Jewish counterparts, increasingly separated marital sexuality from procreation.[20]

But such changes were not wholly the result of Catholic immersion in American popular culture. Catholic teaching that celebrated sexual pleasure as an essential part of companionate marriage was popularized by groups like the Christian Family Movement and played a role in legitimating the practice of nonprocreative sex. By the time of the Second Vatican Council, Catholics were primed to be suspicious of long-standing church teachings that seemed to contradict new popular and theological understandings of sex. Popular interpretations of Vatican II—most important, the notion of the church as the "people of God" on pilgrimage rather than as a static, hierarchical institution—made it easier for lay Catholics to discount unpopular church teachings on contraception and, to a lesser extent, homosexuality and abortion. Many ordinary Catholics believed that the reforms of Vatican II gave them permission to practice ethical autonomy. The decline in the sacrament of confession led them to feel less obliged to take responsibility for theological deviation. Such changes within Catholic practice were validated by the growing suspicion of authority in American life generally. Theological change and societal change were mutually reinforcing.[21]

The American Catholic turn from authority to democracy, from institutional obedience to theological autonomy, was also the product of shifts in everyday Catholic practice in the mid-twentieth century. Post–World War II Catholic prayer, devotion, and catechism were shaped by what Joseph P. Chinnici calls a "pedagogy of participation" that fostered dialogue between clergy and laity in place of a unidirectional flow of authority from the top down. All these changes together laid the groundwork for the Second Vatican Council and, at the same time, made it possible for Catholics to join—and contribute to—larger cultural transformations in the mid-twentieth-century United States, including a growing emphasis on individual fulfillment and a new politics of participatory democracy.[22]

From within the walls of the church, Catholicism was changing profoundly in the years before the Second Vatican Council. But Catholic lives were also ineluctably transformed by the major social transformations that affected millions of postwar Americans regardless of their religion: the processes of suburbanization and embourgeoisement. In Catholic historiography the move to the suburbs marks the end of the "ghetto church" as Catholics joined the ranks of the middle class and abandoned the tight-knit neighborhoods that surrounded their urban parishes. But the history of Catholic suburbanization, its impact on Catholic understandings of family and community, and its implications for Catholic politics remain mostly unexamined. A remarkable body of scholarship has highlighted the role of Catholics in the transformation of racial politics and urban life in the mid-twentieth century. But suburban Catholics are mostly missing from histories of the Catholic encounter with race, liberalism, and conservatism.

In 1970, for the first time, Catholic median incomes exceeded those of white Protestants.[23] The stereotypical urban working-class Catholic, living in a close-knit urban parish in the shadow of factories or on the waterfront, had become an endangered species. The fundamental question shaping much of the recent work on Catholics and race—why Catholics stayed in their urban neighborhoods longer than white Protestants and Jews—tells only one part of the story of metropolitan change. A majority of white Catholics did not stay in their urban enclaves, even if a vocal minority did. After World War II Catholics moved—often with astonishing speed—to outlying municipalities. The glue of parish and school was not enough to preserve most urban Catholic neighborhoods, which grew less white, grayer, poorer, and more Protestant throughout the postwar years. The emphasis on urban life has led scholars to downplay the role of Catholic suburbanites in law-and-order politics and in struggles over civil rights and education (which highlight urban resistance to desegregation at the expense of a more nuanced metropolitan understanding of the issue). Urban Catholics were the most visible participants in the northern grassroots movement opposing school desegregation and busing, but suburban Catholics—those who fled rather than fought neighborhood change—were equally important players in the emergence of a new suburban politics.[24]

To understand Catholic suburbanization, we need to reread the work of Catholic sociologists in the postwar years, who were acutely aware of the process of suburbanization and worried mightily about its impact on parish life, on family structure, and on Catholic values. Postwar suburbia, with its single-family detached homes, its car culture, and its unbridled consumerism, threatened Catholic identity on several levels at once. In the late 1940s, reacting to the fast pace of suburbanization, sociologist and Jesuit priest Joseph Fichter found that Catholics had come to view the parish as a "service station where the people had their religious and spiritual needs satisfied" while they forged more enduring ties on the basis of their shared educational, social, and racial identities. In 1959 Andrew Greeley, then a young parish priest in Chicago, combined his pastoral and social scientific observations in a prescient study of suburbanization and its consequences. "The suburbanite with his income over $7,500, his large family, and his own home," wrote Greeley, "represents a profound social revolution." Greeley's book hinged on a question that preoccupied nearly every religious author writing about suburbanization: "Is there any room for God in an age of plenty?" Ultimately, Greeley's answer was yes, for "the Holy Spirit might work in the suburbs, too," even if "His work in the suburbs might take on, initially at least, a distinctly suburban tinge."[25]

However mysterious the workings of the Spirit might be, Catholic and non-Catholic suburbanites made new communities that differed fundamentally from the urban neighborhoods that they viewed, with a mix of romance and disdain, through their rearview mirrors. Catholic attachment to place, despite the power of parish boundaries, was increasingly fickle. Catholic understandings of territoriality and the sacralization of space were profoundly altered by the process of suburbanization. In postwar Philadelphia, for example, the Catholic archdiocese engaged in a massive program of suburban school building while it closed many inner-city schools and dramatically reduced expenditures to renovate old and deteriorating inner-city schools. The thinness of parish boundaries and the hardness of political boundaries were clearest when Catholic school attendance zones crossed city lines. In one West Philadelphia parish white parents petitioned to send their children to a newly built suburban high school rather than the one that had traditionally served their parish on the "grounds of safety and the better quality of suburban schools." The suburbanization of Catholics also proved to be corrosive to Catholic education (in ways that might be suggestive for a larger study of the relationship of suburbanization, institutional change, and the formation of social capital). Although dioceses engaged in a massive building program to construct schools in booming suburbs, Catholic school enrollments dropped in many nonurban communities, in part because of the attenuation of parish affiliations, in part because many suburbs offered excellent and free public schools. Why should a Catholic parent pay, in effect, a dual tax: tuition for parochial schools and local levies on property to fund public schools?[26]

The relationship of Catholics and taxation is yet another area that is potentially rich for historical inquiry. Catholic suburbanization coincided with a growing grassroots rebellion against taxation, fueled in part by rising discontent over costly federal social programs that seemed to benefit minorities and urban residents at the expense of suburban whites. Compounding grievances about taxation were rising assessments in communities with expensive schools and public services. Suburban municipalities in most of the United States created and reinforced the inequitable distribution of power and resources by place. Where you lived, to a great extent, determined your access to public goods and services and how much you paid for them in the form of taxes. Catholics, especially those who continued to pay for parish schools, had their own reasons for joining the tax rebellion. One sign of the shifting politics of Catholic suburbanites was growing discontent among those asked to provide subsidies for surviving inner-city Catholic schools. In a debate in Philadelphia about the gap in resources between city and suburban parish schools, one suburban parent fretted about calls to equalize school funding. "Why should their children suffer just because the people in the cities aren't doing their share? If the parents are contributing more in the suburbs, the children in the suburbs should get the benefits." But for Catholics, the battleground was not just city versus suburb. For Catholic parishioners who, in effect, paid a double tax for parochial and public schools, local taxation was especially burdensome. The intense national debates in the 1960s, 1970s, and beyond about public funding for Catholic education touched on more than church-state issues. They were, for Catholics, part and parcel of the growing antitax movement. Ultimately, they contributed to one of the most profound political changes of the late twentieth century: the erosion of support for the state, a decline in a sense of broad social responsibility, and the legitimation of free-market understandings of social relations themselves.[27]

Greeley suggested another important connection between suburbanization and the transformation of Catholicism. "In the suburb," he wrote, "the Catholic is regarded, at last, as a full-fledged American."[28] Catholic grassroots politics and religious practices were made anew by the reorientation of political interests and identities in the suburbs. The relationship of Catholicism and Americanism, one of the major currents of American Catholic historiography, played out with special intensity on suburban terrain, where Catholics found themselves in places that were no longer insular, and where a de facto ecumenism (Sunday mornings excepted) prevailed. In the postwar years, especially in the long 1960s, Catholics made their peace, both intellectually and socially, in their political theory and in their lived experience, with Americanism.

R. Scott Appleby argues that one of the most dramatic legacies of twentieth-century American Catholic history is that conservative and liberal Catholics now "share a basic orientation and set of assumptions about the United States and its worthiness as a model for the Roman Catholic Church." Or, to borrow a phrase, by the 1960s Catholics were all Americanists now. "In the early decades of this century," writes Appleby, most Catholics assumed that "Roman Catholic and American visions of human nature and society are not easily reconciled, and may in some important regard be irreconcilable." A synthetic approach to mid-twentieth-century U.S. history will help explain the social, cultural, and political changes that allowed

Catholics to come to peace with Americanism and, just as importantly, how mainstream Protestants and Jews made a tentative peace with members of a church that they had recently denounced as authoritarian and un-American.[29]

Part of the explanation for that reconciliation can be found in the growing interaction of Catholics and non-Catholics in the era beginning with World War II. In most metropolitan areas Catholics and non-Catholics lived in proximity to each other to an extent unimaginable a few decades earlier, and they found their increasing familiarity and propinquity reinforced by their churches' growing openness to non-Catholic ideas, indeed, to the very legitimacy of views of U.S. society once considered heretical. The story of Catholics, Americanism, ecumenism, and Americanization is at once a Catholic history and an American history.

The simultaneous and interacting shifts in Catholicism and in everyday life help explain what might otherwise be a wholly inexplicable phenomenon of the mid-twentieth-century United States—the strange political marriage between Roman Catholics and conservative Protestants. The courtship began in the de facto ecumenism of the heterogeneous postwar suburbs. It got serious as Catholics and conservative Protestants, despite their deep-rooted theological differences and cultural antipathies, found themselves united by the Cold War. The engagement was blessed by the Second Vatican Council, which encouraged interfaith dialogue and respect. And even though the marriage was often unhappy, it was held together by the conservative reaction to the cultural transformations of the 1960s, particularly public displays of sexuality and the culmination of second-wave feminism.[30]

No sensible historian or cultural observer could have predicted in 1920 or 1940 or even 1960 that conservative Catholics and Protestants would make common political cause, whether in the pages of the *National Review*, in the corridors of the American Enterprise Institute, or in the plethora of lobbying groups dedicated to restoring the patriarchal family, thwarting sexual liberation, and restoring a now-common system of "Judeo-Christian values." Anti-Catholicism had long been taken for granted in both liberal and conservative Protestant circles, from the alarmist writings of liberal Paul Blanshard to the "whore of Babylon" ravings of religious rightist John Hagee. From the nineteenth century onward, Catholics had fretted about Protestant indoctrination in the public schools. Even ordinary Catholics, immune from the larger theological debates about the relationship of Catholicism and Protestantism, had a visceral distaste for Protestant perfectionism that is perhaps best captured by Michael Novak's description of Catholic Chicagoans' angry reaction to civil rights activists who marched in their neighborhoods. The "tactic of demonstration is inherently WASP and inherently offensive to ethnic peoples," he argued. "A protest march is a moralizing finger jabbing into a neighborhood sick to death of being moralized."[31]

But Catholics grew more open to lived ecumenism as steadily increasing numbers of Catholics attended public schools and secular universities, as rates of interreligious marriages skyrocketed, and as Catholics found themselves living outside the ghetto. The walls between Protestants and Catholics began to crumble. Intellectuals like L. Brent Bozell could adhere to the triumphalism of Catholics United for the Faith and, at the same time, align with non-Catholic candidates on the religious right.[32] Michael Novak jettisoned his populist disdain of the WASP and, under the aegis of the American Enterprise Institute, worked to stitch together the Protestant ethic and Catholic social teaching into a seamless garment.[33] Catholic neoconservatives, wrote a sympathetic George Weigel, "scouted the terrain of a new American ecumenism" and joined "an intense, engaged conversation with evangelical, fundamentalist, and Pentecostal Protestants" over a "shared concern for the politicization of Christian social witness."[34]

The new form that Catholic Americanism took at midcentury shaped Catholic participation in national politics—one of the most important and understudied themes in the history of postwar America. The key moment was 1960, when John F. Kennedy, aspiring to be America's first Catholic president, appeared at the meeting of the Greater Houston Ministerial Association and assuaged Protestant fears that he would be a tool of the papacy in the White House. There was, ultimately, little distinctively Catholic in John F. Kennedy's politics other than his ease in mingling with audiences at Knights of Columbus halls. His accommodation to the political mainstream meant jettisoning most explicit manifestations of his Catholic faith other than Sunday churchgoing. Kennedy's politics put him on one end of the ecumenical spectrum: in his campaign and in office he reconciled his thin Catholicism with liberal principles of individual rights, free speech, and the separation of church and state.[35]

Even if at midcentury the Catholic Church viewed itself as a total way of life, offering its members a lens to view things both intimate (like family, sexuality, and child rearing) and public (foreign policy, economics, and human rights), in practice Catholic politics in the 1960s was heterodox. Catholic political figures synthesized Catholicism and Americanism differently, in the process offering different valuations of Catholic social teaching and its relationship to national and international politics. On the right, William F. Buckley Jr. and his brother-in-law and Barry Goldwater's speechwriter, L. Brent Bozell, brought a distinctly ultramontane form of Catholicism to bear on the intellectual trajectory of the New Right. St. Louis maverick

Phyllis Schlafly inflected conservative politics with a Catholic vision of the Cold War and of the family. In the center, former Harvard professor and Johnson administration official Daniel Patrick Moynihan authored the most influential and controversial study of the African American family to date. *The Moynihan Report* synthesized a generation of work on black family pathology with a Catholic understanding of normative family life. But like that of many Catholics at midcentury, Moynihan's politics of family was not orthodox in its adherence to Catholic moral teaching. Like many of his coreligionists who came of age in an era of an empowered laity, Moynihan supported birth control and reproductive rights, a position that enraged many other coreligionists.[36] To his left, Thomas P. O'Neill, a product of the Irish Catholic machine of Massachusetts, defended a localistic politics that was at once a reflection of the Catholic notion of subsidiarity and, at the same time, an expression of the pragmatic liberalism that brought home the bacon to his constituents. Even further to the left, Michael Harrington, a former Catholic Worker, helped the United States discover the poor and fashioned a Democratic socialism that owed much to his training in Catholic social teaching and his encounter with Dorothy Day's personalist theology. Cesar Chavez, who led what was arguably the most important movement for social justice in the 1960s after the African American civil rights struggle, organized mostly Catholic Hispanic workers, built alliances with the church, and shaped a labor politics that had deep resonances with a long tradition of Catholic labor politics.[37]

The history of national electoral politics in the 1960s is a reminder of the dangers of leaving out the Catholic perspective. After southern whites, Catholics constituted the most influential segment of the New Deal coalition. But the role of Catholic voters, politicians, and policymakers in defining liberalism remains mostly unstudied. Thirty years ago practitioners of the "new political history" explored Catholicism and anti-Catholicism as ethnocultural variables in shaping partisan affiliations in the nineteenth-century United States but sacrificed an analysis of the content of politics to a narrower quantitative study of voting behavior.[38]

Twentieth-century historians have paid even less attention to Catholics as political actors. In some of the most influential histories of working-class politics in places where Catholics made up sizable majorities of the electorate, among them Chicago, Lynn, and Detroit, religion appears irrelevant. (When I was writing *Origins of the Urban Crisis*, I too overlooked Catholicism until timely dissertations by John McGreevy and Gerald Gamm led me to return to my sources and confront the abundant evidence that urban Catholics had a territorial consciousness that profoundly shaped their understanding of home ownership, racial change, and neighborhood politics.) At best, scholars briefly evoke the role of Catholics in the New Deal coalition, usually making the important if rather obvious point that Catholics tended to be urban and working-class. But documenting Catholic affiliation to the Democratic Party is not the same as explaining the Catholic impact on liberalism and its troubled course through the mid- and late twentieth century.[39]

John McGreevy's study of Catholics and liberty offers an important lens for rethinking the relationship of Catholicism to the New Deal and its discontents. "Since the beginning of the nineteenth century Catholic revival," writes McGreevy, "Catholics had emphasized the common good more than individual right, and the dependency of any one person on family, neighborhood, workplace, and church." Those principles shaped twentieth-century Catholic thought on the economy and led Catholic thinkers like Father John A. Ryan to reject economic libertarianism. At a moment of intense debate about the proper role of the state in society, the American Catholic bishops argued in their 1919 Program of Social Reconstruction for robust government intervention to improve the living conditions and wages of American workers. It is exactly that sense of dependency, institution, and place that played such a central role in shaping Catholic political identities. The New Deal certainly attracted Catholic voters for the same reasons that it appealed to blue-collar workers across racial, regional, and ethnic divides. But it also provided an opening for Catholic activists and policymakers to bring Catholic ideas about labor and capital, social responsibility, and the family wage to the fore of national politics. It is likely that the gendered nature of New Deal programs like Social Security, Aid to Dependent Children, and Unemployment Insurance owe at least something to the assumptions about women and work that Catholic lawmakers and their constituents brought to the table.[40]

The New Deal was a compromise that preserved the delicate balance between local control and federal power and balanced many competing interests, among them the southern states rights' wing of the Democratic Party, northern blacks who clamored for recognition, urban laborers, and local elected officials in both the North and the South who lobbied for social programs with maximum federal support but minimum federal regulation, whether in housing policy, employment programs, or welfare assistance. The New Deal's combination of localism and federalism also embodied for many of its Catholic defenders a model of the notion of subsidiarity, and it reflected Catholic social teaching, most notably regarding the redemptive value of labor and the necessity for a family wage to provide workers' security and to preserve the role of the father as breadwinner for his household.[41]

By the 1940s and 1950s, as national politics turned rightward, political debate turned to the scope and scale of government and the relationship of the state to the economy. Critics of the New Deal denounced federal programs as the essence of socialism or communism. In the mid-1940s advocates of "free enterprise" began a lengthy national campaign of advertising, popular education, and broadcasting to celebrate unbridled capitalism as fundamentally American. The successful attempt to enhance the image of business, combined with deep-seated Catholic fears of atheistic communism, gave rise to a growing suspicion of federal bureaucracy that led many Catholic voters to eschew their Democratic identities and pull the lever for Republican candidates like Dwight Eisenhower while supporting the anti-Communist crusade of Wisconsin Senator Joseph McCarthy. How Catholics made their peace with "free enterprise," especially given the long history of Catholic social teaching that criticized unregulated capitalism and supported labor, remains to be fully explored.[42]

Catholic voters also gave post–New Deal Democratic politics a valence that remains almost wholly unexamined. When public opinion researchers in the 1950s examined Catholic voters, they found a distinctive bundle of political characteristics that defied easy categorization as conservative or liberal. Catholics tended to be staunchly anti-Communist. In comparison with Protestants and Jews, they harbored stronger negative views of African Americans. But they were also strongly pro-union, supported generous welfare provisions, and were internationalist in their orientation. By the end of the 1960s, despite the cultural and political tumult of the era, those attitudes had changed relatively little. A 1970 study reported that Catholic Democrats were "more anti-Negro and more religiously conservative than Republicans" and that overall, Catholics were liberal on foreign aid, the United Nations, and labor. If anything, the Catholic encounter with the 1960s led many Catholics, at least in practice, to cling to an unfashionable mix of political views that defied easy categorization at a moment when pundits and scholars described American politics as polarized.[43]

This was even more the case outside the realm of electoral politics, but Catholics also brought a distinctive style to protest movements, especially on the left. The antiwar movement brought Catholics into an ecumenical orbit of protest politics dominated by liberal and left-leaning Protestants, but it provided one vehicle for the integration of internal and external forces. Catholics, especially students, were drawn to the antiwar movement for many of the same reasons as their non-Catholic counterparts.[44] But when Catholics moved into the center of the antiwar movement—which had been dominated by Protestant activists for most of American history—they transformed it. Before Vietnam members of traditional peace churches and Social Gospel–influenced mainline denominations spearheaded antiwar activism. Social Gospelers vocally opposed World War I and allied themselves with the Depression-era Oxford movement against war. And a vocal minority of pacifists, most of them Protestant, resisted military service in World War II. A smattering of Catholics, most of them associated with the Catholic Worker movement, joined the ranks of conscientious objectors in twentieth-century wars, but they were a barely visible minority.[45]

The 1960s antiwar protests, by contrast, included a sizable contingent of Catholic activists. A small but growing movement of left-wing Catholics in the United States drew inspiration from their Protestant counterparts, in particular the individualism and perfectionism that manifested itself in notions of the primacy of conscience. But they also drew inspiration from personalist philosophy and the Catholic Worker movement's emphasis on solidarity with the poor and oppressed. The democratic energies unleashed by the Second Vatican Council—and in particular Rome's call for engagement in the world—further inspired young Catholic activists to oppose the war. When American Catholic activists joined in ecumenical antiwar efforts like Clergy and Laity Concerned about Vietnam, they adopted the language of conscientious objection and personal responsibility, but they did not simply jettison their Catholicism. Their collective protests, shaped by a distinctively Catholic understanding of the body of Christ, took a quasi-sacramental form. Fathers Daniel and Philip Berrigan, the most visible peace protesters, evoked a long Catholic history of martyrdom and redemptive suffering in their writing and action. Catholic antiwar gatherings combined established styles of protest (picketing, chanting, and civil disobedience) with Catholic-inflected, richly symbolic acts, such as the pouring of blood (sometimes real, sometimes simulated) onto draft cards. Revivifying biblical practices of burnt sacrifices, they immolated draft cards (although, in a distinctively sixties-era twist, they doused them in napalm, a gelatinous form of gasoline used in aerial attacks on Vietnam). Priests and laypeople sprinkled holy water at protests, chanted prayers, read the litany of the saints, and even, on occasion, performed exorcisms at draft induction centers and military installations.[46]

Catholic students, sharing in a widespread youthful alienation with "mass society," searched within their own religious tradition for styles of worship and prayer, models of action, and structures of community in what they saw as an increasingly impersonal, atomized society. Young Catholics were best described by Daniel Berrigan as uninterested in "the internal questions of the Catholic community," but instead concerned with the role of faith in a troubled world. Many radical Catholics combined their political engagement with the search for an authentic Catholicism that countered the "malaise" and rootlessness of modern society and the rule-bound practices of the traditional church. "More people than we readily imagine," wrote Berrigan, "have reached a stalemate of such proportions as chill the joy and assail the integrity of marriage, work, religion, education of children, the direction and meaning of life itself." Witness against war and solidarity with the poor and oppressed were vehicles both for individual redemption and for restoring an "authentic" participatory community that would remake the modern United States and the Catholic Church alike.[47]

Whether in the suburbs or on campus, whether radical, liberal, or conservative, Roman Catholics played a central role in the reconfiguration of U.S. politics and society, particularly the challenge to liberalism from both the Right and the Left and the rise of a distinctive postliberal political order. My examples from social and political history are but a starting point for what is a necessarily intertwined history of Catholics and modern U.S. social and political life. Ultimately, our understanding of the history of the 1960s and, more broadly, of the post–World War II United States will remain incomplete if Catholics are not incorporated. The experience of a group that constituted somewhere between one-fifth and one-quarter of all Americans cannot remain on the margins of our historiography. It should be impossible to write modern U.S. history with Catholics left out. That most twentieth-century U.S. historians, myself among them, have downplayed or ignored religion and its impact is telling evidence of the limitations of our scholarship to date. It is time for the Catholic encounter with the modern United States to be followed by a more comprehensive and nuanced history of the modern United States' encounter with Catholicism.

CHAPTER 4

Crossing the Catholic Divide

Gender, Sexuality, and Historiography

R. MARIE GRIFFITH

In the historiography of American gender and sexuality, Catholics remain an uneasy fit. A breach continues to exist between scholarly work that takes Catholics as its primary subjects and an ostensibly broader mainstream narrative that, more often than not, tends to neglect them. This gap or divide persists whether the authors in the latter camp see their work as being about "secular" history or about religious history, perhaps because Protestantism has so often functioned as an unmarked category in secular studies of sex and gender. Notwithstanding the durability in U.S. history of Protestant anti-Catholicism, Catholics have long participated in all arenas of U.S. life, including those seen as especially pertinent to gender and women's studies: movements both for and against women's rights, gay rights, contraceptive access, and legal abortion, for example. The sources of the enduring scholarly divide are therefore not self-evident. So why does it prevail? Certainly, those who work on gender and sexuality in U.S. culture, whether from a Protestant or purely secular point of view, should find much of interest in Catholic history and much to learn from the ways in which Catholics have wrestled in diverse, sometimes conflictual ways with these matters. More practically, then, how might Catholics be incorporated more adequately into

I wish to thank the many colleagues who read and responded to this chapter during its lengthy germination. I am especially grateful to Eva Payne for her invaluable assistance in the final stages.

the wider historical narratives of sex and gender in the United States? And how could the presence of Catholics, in turn, transform the broader picture in significant, illuminating ways?

This chapter sets out to address these questions by exploring particular instances of the Protestant/Catholic divide in U.S. historical scholarship about gender and sexuality.[1] It does not aim or pretend to be comprehensive; rather, I focus particular attention on some sources of the gap, as well as some possibilities for remedying it in new scholarly work. The mutual enmity between U.S. Catholic leaders and liberal sex reformers during the first half of the twentieth century—Margaret Sanger and Alfred Kinsey, in particular— provides one lens for thinking about some (though by no means all) historical contexts that established the divide, while a prospect for bridging it becomes visible in the life of the sex reformer Mary Steichen Calderone, a liberal Protestant who sought energetically in the later part of the century to work across the religious rupture with Catholics. Understanding Calderone's work and commitments may help historians consider the importance of crossing the Protestant/Catholic divide. Her story can also enable us to recast the stories we tell about the past.

"Understandings of gender and sexuality," as John McGreevy puts it, "would eventually become the central dividing line between Catholics and U.S. liberals, and divisive within Catholicism as well."[2] It is no surprise, then, that the subject of gender, above virtually all others, continues to be a source of historiographical disruption as well. Women were always engaged in these battles on the ground: McGreevy gives clear documentation of various suffragist writers arguing sharply against the "idolatrous perversions of the Romish faith" and seeing the Catholic Church as having been ever "the deadly opponent of progress and freedom."[3] Moreover, women continue to be major players in Catholic-liberal debates today—debates over equal rights, same-sex marriage, and abortion, for instance, to name only a few hot-button issues. Catholic-liberal tensions over gender and sexuality have been divisive not only for people in the pews or the political arena, however, but also for those in the academy, including Catholic and non-Catholic historians. In the midst of my own project on religion and sexuality in the twentieth century, I wonder at the fact that scholarly accounts often subtly play into popular caricatures of divisive figures—whether sex reformers or conservative bishops—rather than working to undermine them. More important, I wonder what we may gain in the historical study of twentieth-century religion, gender, and sexuality if we scrutinize our own historical narratives for remnants of political exaggerations and subject them to rigorous critical inquiry and rethinking.

∞Catholicism in the Historiography of Gender and Sexuality

When Catholics are not altogether invisible, they tend to play a univocal role in most mainstream scholarly studies of gender and sexuality.[4] In the classic text by John D'Emilio and Estelle Freedman, *Intimate Matters: A History of Sexuality in America*, the chief Catholic actors are ones whom the authors denigrate as "purity crusaders": opponents of legal birth control, the Legion of Decency, the National Organization for Decent Literature, and an activist Roman Catholic hierarchy intimidating pro-choice Catholic politicians are the Catholic protagonists here.[5] The same crusading Catholics appear in Beth Bailey's more recent account, *Sex in the Heartland*, where again the only sign of Catholic diversity is the prevalent lay rejection of the birth-control ban in the wake of *Humanae Vitae*.[6] In an even more extraordinary example, the term "Catholic" appears only once in Jane Gerhard's widely read and ostensibly comprehensive history, *Desiring Revolution: Second-Wave Feminism and the Rewriting of American Sexual Thought, 1920 to 1982*; it refers to the Indiana Provincial Council of Catholic Women's campaign against the sex researcher Alfred Kinsey.[7] In much of this literature, even when historical actors are plainly Catholic, they are not identified as such.[8] Despite years of scholarship establishing a broad range of Catholic views and participation across the full political spectrum, historians of sex and gender are wont to see Catholics in monolithic terms as livid militants, inflexible church authorities and their lay minions obediently toeing the line, or, more ominously, as victims of and accessories to sexual hypocrisy.

Like many taken-for-granted assumptions, this one rests on some empirical evidence and a lot of speculation, extrapolation, and inherited prejudice. On the empirical side, historians and sociologists have certainly established that Catholics tend to adopt more traditionalist views of sexual morality than all but the most conservative Protestants; moreover, that U.S. Catholic leaders at various times have been active political opponents of birth control, avant-garde film and literature, and gay marriage is true, however diverse the opinions of less influential parishioners. Simply by remaining in the church, moreover, Catholics appear to non-Catholics to have consented, however reluctantly, to a male-over-female system of governance that the Magisterium teaches as God's ordained plan. Meanwhile, every time new revelations about clergy sexual abuse and its systematic cover-ups emerge, outsiders critical of the church's secrecy—perhaps more broadly, of its enduring devotion to a male, purportedly celibate clergy—may feel a sort of sickened vindication that is easily translated into anti-Catholic sentiments (even if they are suppressed politely when Catholics are within earshot). Many historians of women and sexuality, vocally supportive of a feminism they see as necessarily rejecting all social gender hierarchies along with many traditional prohibitions on sexual relations between consenting adults, understandably see Catholics, even liberal or progressive ones, to be old-fashioned by definition on the issue of gender. As Kathleen Sprows Cummings rightly notes in explaining the disinclination among most women's historians to view Catholic women as historical subjects, "Many Catholic women of the past—celibate, seemingly subservient, often antisuffrage—are decidedly unappealing to modern women."[9]

Here, then, is an identifiable gap, although it may go unacknowledged in the larger historical profession beyond Catholic circles.[10] If there is such a thing as mainstream gender studies in the contemporary academy outside confessional arenas—as seen in nonsectarian university programs and departments that focus on women, gender, and sexuality—then its focal goal is one of wholly deconstructing gender and sex as social constructs and axes of power relations rather than self-evident biological verities.[11] Gender is in no way natural but rather performative, we learn from the gender theorists most often cited; and even sex itself is not what the male-female binary society and culture have instilled in us but, rather, a spectrum or multiplicity of possibilities.[12] Homosexuality, transgenderism and transexualism, and all things queer emerge to prove wrong the assumption of a clear and essential difference between biological male and female, not to mention the cultural assumptions of masculine and feminine. Sexual relations between consenting adults typically appear, in this context, unproblematic as such; moral questions arise on the grounds of truth telling and deception, of how persons treat one another, rather than from precepts based on the Bible or Roman Catholic canon law (which, many note, presume that women are the property of men). A field that in its earlier "women's studies" incarnation drew its inspiration from the project of recovering female actors—women—once invisible to history has developed into a discipline whose principal academic work is to liberate subjects from imposed gender identifications altogether, including forms of sexual repression and closeting that are perceived to cause shame and self-loathing. In short, the study of gender and sexuality is conjoined with a specific set of presuppositions and moral analyses, most or all of which are linked to current legal debates about civil rights and to political activism in the contemporary public sphere.[13]

It may be little wonder, then, that those who self-identify as Catholic stand in imperfect accord with that world. Whatever else Catholics are, unless they have exited or been excommunicated, they remain part of a church that prohibits sexual activity outside heterosexual marriage, and of a religious culture that insists on the reality—indeed, as the Catholic ethicist Aline Kalbian has argued, the fundamental primacy—of the biological binary male-female.[14] Dissent, of course, is widespread and broadly tolerated—indeed, one often hears liberal U.S. Catholics expressing delight in their disagreement with the Magisterium—and it is not always clear to those on the outside where the limits of such dissent may lie. But it is certainly clear that Catholic feminists exist across a diverse spectrum, and that they hold views on gender rather different from those promulgated in high Vatican circles.[15] To be a Catholic feminist means, at minimum, that one takes a serious interest in the social constructedness of "gender," including its religious sources, and that one cares about remedying the injustices that have accrued to women (both inside and outside the church) because of false assumptions about their nature. To that extent, Catholic and non-Catholic gender scholars are aligned. At some point beyond this ground of general agreement, however, the paths appear to diverge, a divide visible in subject matter as well as conceptual or theoretical frameworks.

With regard to subject matter, it is apparent that many Catholic scholars of women and gender have had a particular interest in women religious, Catholic sisters whose vocation and gender identification have been at odds with the social roles of wife and mother that have been enthusiastically promoted in U.S. culture.[16] This fact makes sense for a number of good reasons, notably that women religious, as Mary Henold has argued, have played a crucial role in the history of Catholic feminism, as well as the history of U.S. Catholicism more generally.[17] Scholars who have focused attention on women other than sisters have often continued to look at bounded female religious cultures—for instance, the Italian Catholics of East Harlem, the Women-Church movement, or Catholic women's colleges (including the Mighty Macs of Immaculata College; note that the cover of Julie Byrne's book sports a garbed nun determinedly holding a basketball).[18] Analyses that focus on ordinary Catholics and tell a broader U.S. story, such as Leslie Tentler's *Catholics and Contraception*, remain relatively uncommon, while gender analysis remains rudimentary if not neglected in many of the larger histories of U.S. Catholicism.[19]

Outside Catholic circles, meanwhile, scholarly interest in nuns has been sparse at best, and although a few books that focus on Catholic women have been widely influential in the field—above all, Robert Orsi's *Madonna of 115th Street*, one of the most significant books in U.S. religious history of the past quarter century—they have not successfully prompted a scholarly wave of Catholic inclusion to match the growing efforts to include, say, women and African Americans in comprehensive accounts of U.S. religious history.

As for the conceptual divide, the assumption that "gender" is constructed even while "sex" is more or less fixed pervades the scholarship of Catholic feminists (among others) in a way that marks them off from the work that is most celebrated today in mainstream gender studies. Paula Kane, for instance, makes clear her presumption of the fixity of sex in the opening introductory paragraph of her excellent coedited volume, *Gender Identities in American Catholicism*. Speaking for her coeditors, James Kenneally and Karen Kennelly, Kane writes, "By gender, in contrast to the biological referent of 'sex,' we refer to the social construction of masculinity and femininity and the social relations between men and women." Shortly thereafter Kane notes that "each sex" has oppressed its own kind throughout history. That there are two distinct sexes is a point so obvious that it does not require explication. Rather, illuminating "how religion structures, maintains, and debates notions of gender" is the aim. Kane clarifies her own view of gender studies and its disjuncture from Catholic history in a revealing passage: "The expansion of women's studies since the 1970s and the appearance of men's studies and gay/lesbian studies in the 1980s are now often merged under the rubric of 'gender studies.' In many ways, the academic landscape mirrors similar shifts within Catholicism: the splintering of liberals and conservatives, the increasing fragmentation of believers in general, combined with an ultimate utopian desire to overcome these tensions to reach a better understanding of difference."[20]

Kane's basic account of the overriding aim in gender studies today—to reach a better understanding of difference—sounds about right as far as it goes. What is intriguing, however, is her frank appraisal of this project as utopian, a pointed criticism that describes the alleged desire to overcome these tensions—evidently, the tensions among different generations of scholars who have disparate allegiances (to women's studies, men's studies, queer studies, and so forth). If it is utopian to imagine harmonizing the variations extant today in gender studies, then these differences (some of them, anyway) must be irreconcilable. Although Kane resists saying so directly, her meaning is plain: disputing the natural category "women" diverts energy from the more urgent project of analyzing the social constructions that make up "gender." Her "Suggested Readings in Gender Studies" list makes this point all the more evident: the works are almost uniformly social historical in nature, one notable exception being Gayle Rubin's "Thinking Sex" (an essay that seems, in fact, palpably out of place here).[21]

My point in lingering on Kane's explication of gender studies is not to argue against it in favor of queering Catholicism; indeed, my own scholarly projects and methodological approaches are far closer to Kane's than to those of the gender theorists she sets aside. Rather, I want simply to emphasize that Catholic studies' usual occupation of a more traditional wing of gender scholarship makes fairly good sense for historians, if not necessarily for activists.[22] Again, Kathleen Sprows Cummings's work illuminates this point because she focuses on Progressive Era Catholic women such as Katherine Conway who "challenged gender prescriptions" on Catholic grounds, decidedly not because they wished to become "New Women."[23] Such women are of scholarly and perhaps also personal interest to female historians who happen also to be Catholic. They also interest many non-Catholic historians of religion who are interested in a broad range of ways in which religious women have been historical subjects and have lived out their religion in creative ways. Citation indexes and course syllabi would doubtless show that such women remain less interesting (or certainly less visible) in many other arenas of gender studies. This fact may be due, in part, to gender studies' general suspicion of religion and to the field's ongoing interrelation with current legal and political debates about sexuality, marriage, and abortion.

Successfully crossing the Catholic divide, then, requires both realism about the stakes embedded in gender studies in the contemporary academy and, just as importantly, scrupulous clarity about the possible gains of making this journey in the first place. It is not enough to try to induce guilt in Protestant and secular historians by foisting on them some sort of special obligation to incorporate Catholics just to be inclusive. Historians who mostly study secular or Protestant women in twentieth-century North America, for instance, must have a clear rationale for going beyond their own meticulous archival research into unfamiliar territory. Is the point merely to learn about previously unknown historical figures? To show that we have overcome the anti-Catholic prejudices of our past? Or is it to subvert and supplant the imperialist trappings of Protestant scholarship that claims to be more broadly "American"? In other words, is the aim to add to our knowledge of the diverse actors in American culture (add Catholics and stir) or to do something more original and genuinely transformative?

To address this intriguing question, I turn to some of my current research as a way to explore some of the gains to be found when historians of gender and sexuality attempt to cross the Catholic divide. The story I wish to tell eventually focuses on the U.S. sex reformer Mary Steichen Calderone, a pioneer in the promotion of sex education in the public schools and also, it turns out, something of an advocate for Protestant-Catholic collaboration, or at least mutual understanding and respect. I recount Calderone's story not to paint an unrealistically rosy picture of Christian rivals suddenly getting cozy after centuries of distrust and animosity; rather, I hope to suggest new insights that may emerge from a careful exploration of stories like Calderone's and may even lead to the reformulation of our broader historical narratives. Before getting to Calderone, however, I want to illustrate the context of Protestant/Catholic divisions through the public reception of two U.S. sex reformers, Margaret Sanger and Alfred Kinsey.

∞ Liberal Reformers Lambaste Catholics, and Vice Versa: Margaret Sanger and Alfred Kinsey

If we wish to understand twentieth-century tensions between Catholic and non-Catholic Americans over questions of gender and sexuality, there is no better figure with whom to begin than Margaret Sanger. Sanger was arguably the first nationally significant twentieth-century figure in the long engagement of religion with sexuality, and Leslie Tentler has noted "the widening gulf between Catholic and Protestant perspectives on marriage" that occurred in the wake of Sanger's fight for legal contraception.[24] The acrimonious events and political realignments of the 1920s secured Sanger's reputation as the most divisive figure in the religious history of American sexuality.

Catholics, along with some conservative Protestants, denounced Sanger as "diabolical" in her own day, and many have continued to view her judgmentally into our own time.[25] (The fundamentalist-modernist controversies that pervaded this period make it difficult to put boundaries around particular groups as representative "evangelicals," so the term is unhelpful here.) Feminists during her own lifetime had an often contentious relationship with Sanger, who basked in her own limelight and disdained mainstream feminists for the compromises they willingly made with the legal system and for their sympathies with alternative points of view. Later generations of women activists hailed Sanger for her courageous stand against patriarchal tyranny and the relentlessness of her crusade for women's right to control their own bodies and to experience sexual intimacy not bound to procreation. Anti-Catholics saw religiously affiliated Protestants as practical allies of freethinkers and secularists on the question of birth control; indeed, Sanger worked tirelessly behind the scenes to secure the partnership of liberal Protestant leaders, a meeting of minds that resulted in broad church support for contraception (within marriage) by the early 1930s. More than any other figure before or since, Sanger drew the battle lines that have defined the United States' great political and religious battle over sex. And the opponent she battled most fiercely was the hierarchy of the American Catholic Church, in the person of New York archbishop Patrick (later Cardinal) Hayes.

Was Sanger the courageous heroine lauded by feminists, the little woman who took on the inordinate sexism of a patriarchal institution and scored an extraordinary victory against its repressive policies? Was she instead an immoral, sex-obsessed racist, a horrific eugenicist whose name ought instead to be inextricably linked with Hitler, Stalin, and Mussolini?[26] Astute and fair-minded historians attempt to avoid both extremes, writing of Sanger as a complicated and savvy figure who spoke in distinct ways to different audiences in her quest to foster a range of strategic alliances for the cause of birth control. McGreevy and Tentler write of Sanger with significantly more restraint than David Kennedy did in his highly critical Bancroft Prize–winning study of 1970, *Birth Control in America: The Career of Margaret Sanger*, although they are far less impressed with her than Ellen Chesler in her laudatory and meticulously researched biography, *Woman of Valor* (1992, 2007).[27] This charitable effort by Catholic historians to present Sanger fairly is significant, particularly since (as all these studies rightly point out) Sanger built her campaign by stoking U.S. anti-Catholic prejudice.

But an understanding of Sanger on her own terms is beyond the scope of both McGreevy's *Catholicism and American Freedom* and Tentler's *Catholics and Contraception*, and both show signs of some distaste as well as avoidance. Sanger was "flamboyant," writes Tentler—surely true, though on its own a limiting if not trivializing characterization that sidesteps the convictions and extraordinary effort that Sanger put into securing new rights for American women. Both McGreevy and Tentler rely for their portraits of Sanger on the doctoral dissertation by the Catholic historian Kathleen Tobin-Schlesinger, "Population and Power: The Religious Debate over Contraception, 1916–1936" (University of Chicago, 1994), which was later published by Tobin as *The American Religious Debate over Birth Control, 1907–1937* (2001).[28] But in writing about how the birth-control debate became "Catholicized," Tobin here and elsewhere (in her contribution to Sally Barr Ebest and Ron Ebest's *Reconciling Catholicism and Feminism? Personal Reflections on Tradition and Change*) narrowly (mis)reads Sanger and Protestants of the period almost solely as racist eugenicists driven by class prejudice and rabid anti-Catholicism.

"Sanger took every opportunity" to condemn Catholic organizations while also claiming a broad following among poor Catholic women, writes

Tobin with critical skepticism. "From the early years of her crusade, Sanger condemned the Catholic Church for holding onto antiquated superstitions that she considered more medieval than modern and for mixing in politics, infringing on her right to free speech, and attempting to impose its beliefs on all Americans. These kinds of comments helped to shape the debate over birth control into one divided between Catholics and non-Catholics."[29] Investing Sanger with vast and deeply malicious power, Tobin writes of Sanger's deftness in pretending that the issue of birth control was "a simple platform of the women's rights movement," "cloaked in radicalism." With her allies, Sanger maneuvered so that the Catholic Church was "forced into a position of self-examination" but heroically "increased efforts to preserve human life" and "maintained its original stand."[30] Tobin's larger point is that once feminists properly understand how racist and classist Sanger was and how deeply those feelings persist in international development programs, they can come (anew?) to "actively and openly embrace children, as well as women who choose to have children," rather than sticking with what Tobin calls the "antimother and antichild" emphasis of second-wave feminism. ("It is important to recognize the racist and classist discrimination inherent in the early-twentieth-century movement to distribute contraceptives and to realize that those feelings persist" [212].)

One can sympathize with Tobin's broader aims (aims that, of course, many non-Catholic feminists have always shared) while wondering about her depiction of Sanger, which seems quite obviously to distort the woman misleadingly. Tentler's thorough reading of contraception debates is sophisticated and far more nuanced than Tobin's, and the citations to Tobin's portrayal of Sanger are insignificant insofar as they relate to Tentler's own concern. The larger point, though, is that the demonization of Sanger thereby continues uncontested—another brick in the wall separating Catholic and Protestant historiography.

Sanger's conflict with Hayes and other Catholic leaders points to other anxieties of the period, ones not limited to race, religion, and the Catholic hierarchy. We could, for instance, read it through the lens of a much larger debate in this period about gender that persisted and perhaps even intensified after the ratification of the Nineteenth Amendment in 1920. That debate was about female autonomy, the expansion of spheres, choice, and freedom of speech, among other things. As voters, women had now secured rights of citizenship unknown to their foremothers; and many questions remained unanswered. For what purpose would women use their newfound freedom? What would be the impact on the home and on conventions of domesticity and family life that had restricted female autonomy? In this period of uncertainty and turmoil, as Tentler aptly notes, Sanger seemed to represent the worst sort of threat. This debate about gender was deeply interwoven with an equally significant debate about religion amid modernity and about the status of science in relation to religion in the modern world. Was religion an essentially conservative force, as Sanger thought? Was it an institution that sought unrestricted propagation for itself in service to its rich, powerful male leaders? Or was it a potentially progressive and vital institution, caring for the poor in a heartless world and agitating for a living wage over and against the capitalistic exploitations of the period? Surely the story about Sanger and the Catholic-Protestant debates she so deftly exploited would shift in important ways if we expanded our analysis beyond eugenics and anti-Catholicism to focus more on the coalescence of these forces—gender, science, free speech, and modernity—that played out so explosively in the sex wars of the twentieth century.

This is but a mere snippet of reflection on how the characterizations of Sanger may map onto historiographical divisions between the narrative worlds of Catholic scholars (however diverse such scholars may be in their religious and political views of gender, sexuality, birth control, and feminism) and the narrative worlds of those outside those circles. Sanger's liberal defenders continue to cast her as a courageous opponent of religious authoritarianism, while Catholic historians, even liberal ones, seem still to read her through the lens of vicious class prejudice, eugenic disregard for the sanctity of life, or promotion of a frivolous hedonism. These are not reconcilable narratives, and both of them seem ultimately to trivialize the profound humanitarian concerns that ground the positions on the other side (Sanger or Catholics). Sanger's is a story that warrants greater fairness on all sides.

What, then, about Alfred C. Kinsey? Kinsey (1894–1956), the entomologist-turned-sexologist whose taxonomic reports on U.S. sexual behavior electrified the nation, remains today one of the most divisive U.S. figures of the twentieth century. To admirers like the sexologist Robert Latou Dickinson and the publisher Donald Porter Geddes, Kinsey was a pioneering scientific researcher in an age of moral hypocrisy, a tireless investigator of human desire and intimate behavior whose contributions to human history ranked with those of Marx, Darwin, and Adam Smith. To critics like Monsignor Maurice Sheehy, head of Catholic University's Department of Religious Education, he was a dissolute pseudointellectual bent on shredding the moral fabric of the nation by wrecking the family, and his work was unmistakably "the most antireligious" of the time. Towering scientist and liberating revolutionary to some, lascivious fraud, religious threat, and likely Communist to others, Kinsey stood with Senator Joseph McCarthy as one of the most divisive personages of the 1950s.[31]

Like Sanger, Kinsey's forays into sex drew fierce opposition from religious leaders, mostly Catholics and conservative Protestants (the latter chiefly fundamentalist). Also like Sanger, Kinsey remains extraordinarily controversial, as is illustrated by the hullabaloo that greeted Bill Condon's 2004 biopic.[32] Kinsey also worked tirelessly, often behind the scenes, with a number of prominent mainline Protestant leaders who, directly citing Kinsey and his famous studies, called for significant changes in Christian sexual ethics. Through these allies, Kinsey's influence eventually bore fruit in the many cooperative efforts that enthusiastic supporters saw positively as "re-evaluat[ing] attitudes toward marriage and sex, in light of biblical theology and scientific findings" and "develop[ing] a positive Christian ethic on sexual behavior which will be relevant to our culture."[33] Although Kinsey did not publicly advocate feminism or the expansion of women's public roles, shifts in Protestant models of gender would accompany, if not reinforce, his rethinking of sexual morality.

Catholic and conservative Protestant commentators expressed outrage at Kinsey's studies from the very start. The Jesuit publication *America* published an editorial lambasting *Sexual Behavior in the Human Male* (1948), even before its publication, as "pandering to prurience." "The sound conclusions of genuine science are part of God's truth and as such are never to be disowned, flinched from, hushed up. But there is a vast difference between the recognition and use of scientific truth by those who have a legitimate interest in it and its helter-skelter popularization among those who have no ground for interest save curiosity. As well might one popularize for the masses a strictly scientific treatise on the compounding of poisons."[34] A sharpened Catholic reaction made national news in mid-September when the National Council of Catholic Women passed a resolution deploring Kinsey's volume as "an insult to the American people" and "a disservice to the nation which can only lead to immorality."[35]

Other Catholic commentators soon followed suit, condemning Kinsey's Darwinian biologism (which they perceived to reduce human affections and behavior to amoral instincts) and ostensible ethical relativism while raising further questions about the study's sample and statistical conclusions.[36] Such critiques did not initially appear to influence parishioners, however, at least according to Protestant pollsters: George Gallup's mid-February poll of Americans across the country found that "both Protestants and Catholics in the population express approval of the Kinsey study, although Protestants are more in favor than Catholics are." According to Gallup, Protestants approved of the study as a "good thing" at a rate of 57 percent, compared with 10 percent who thought it a "bad thing" (the rest had no opinion or mixed responses), while Catholics who expressed an opinion approved of it at a rate of 49 percent to 19 percent.[37]

Even as liberal Protestants praised Kinsey's frank look for bringing to light problems that needed pastoral attention, public denunciations grew among conservatives, many of them Catholic priests who took offense at Kinsey's declaration of the abnormality of celibacy. As Sheehy complained to one journalist, "Dr. Kinsey's report gives the impression that if one has not some hidden or overt means of sexual expression he is beyond the pale of normalcy."[38] But however personally the celibate clergy took Kinsey's low appraisal of their lifestyle, they mostly elevated their critiques to higher levels of broad concern. The mere fact of broaching such previously unthinkable topics as homosexuality, pedophilia, bestiality, and all manner of extramarital sex was not "scientific" but plainly lascivious, critics argued, and hence indefensible by any civilized standard.

The publication of Kinsey's next major study, *Sexual Behavior in the Human Female* (1953), reaped astonishing fanfare as well as unprecedented excoriation. Once again, Catholics were among the most acrimonious critics. For example, the Catholic editor of the Ashland, Wisconsin, *Daily Press* described Kinsey's book as a "direct and devastating attack upon Christian civilization" and "a dirty, beastly attack upon American womanhood"; Kinsey himself he called "one of the most loathsome wretches ever produced in human form, or else an individual utterly bewitched by the forces of evil and darkness."[39] The Indiana Provincial Council of Catholic Women's denunciation (already mentioned as an oft-noted event in the history of sexuality in the United States) compared the distribution of Kinsey's ideas to the culture of Nazi Germany.

Hovering over these sermons was the specter of bawdy, degenerate women, treacherous in their refusal to submit obediently to the morality of church and home. Their flouting of authority and seeming eagerness for sexual emancipation aligned them in the conservative mind not only with free lovers of earlier generations but also with feminism, long an enemy to conservatives who insisted on a divinely ordained male clergy and patriarchal family structure. Echoing older arguments against women's legal and political rights, conservative ministers stoked in their hearers the fear that if women's sexual behavior was allowed to run wild, American civilization itself would crumble to dust. Meanwhile, in this scenario, communism and the devil would rise victoriously, the evil children spawned illegitimately by female promiscuity. The perversion of women was conjoined with liberalism in the conservative religious worldview, and many of Kinsey's critics associated the report's female interviewees with the promotion of liberal morals and liberal religion. A liberal religious and sexual revolution seemed already under way, and those infidels who preached such a vile gospel of tolerance were surely to blame. It was only a matter of time before conservative Protestants and Catholics realized their compatibility and came to understand the expediency of forgiving the sins of the past—anti-Catholicism and anti-Protestantism—to achieve a virtuous future.

Popular appraisals of Kinsey have been no less divided than those of Sanger. But the historiography, contentious though it is, does not follow simple Catholic versus non-Catholic patterns; instead, there is a strong bias against religion generally in much of this scholarly work, as is seen, for instance, in the familiar story of his stringently religious father, an account habitually embellished well beyond documentary evidence.[40] The elder Kinsey, the story goes, was "the sternest, the strictest, the most unforgiving" of Victorian-era Methodists, a man who permitted his family few indulgences and dispensed regular punishments. The family's social life, "such as it was," according to Kinsey biographer Jonathan Gathorne-Hardy, "was restricted to a few of the Hoboken Methodists—gloomy gatherings, exchanging platitudinous pieties, the children enjoined to respectful silence." Kinsey's God, another biographer, James H. Jones, surmises, was "the God of the Old Testament," a harsh patriarch built on all the "mean-spirited, hate-filled, and fearful" things Kinsey presumably heard in church. "Given his harsh religion and overbearing father," Jones concludes, "young Kinsey must have suffered in full measure the pain and agony to which seriously religious children can fall victim." In due course young Alfred rebelled bravely against his father's dreary religion and thereafter stood firm against all other forms of superstition and hypocrisy.[41]

This affecting parable has usefully served interpreters, both sympathetic and critical, who wish to psychoanalyze the adult sexologist, making him the childhood victim of sexual repression who would rise heroically to conquer his cruel upbringing. Regina Morantz, in her 1977 *American Quarterly* article on Kinsey, took for granted the legend as developed by Kinsey's irreligious colleagues when she explained Kinsey's crusading zeal by the fact that "his parents were strict and puritanical" and that he was "the product of a deeply religious home." "When Kinsey rebelled," she continued, "science offered him a set of values which emotionally rivaled his juvenile commitment to religion."[42] This mythic trajectory drove the plot of the 2004

Hollywood biopic *Kinsey*, which featured John Lithgow's memorable if deliberately exaggerated depiction of the sex-obsessed Christian father, now inflated from the staid engineering teacher he was in real life to a towering fire-and-brimstone preacher perfectly calibrated to the big screen. Like Gathorne-Hardy's engaging biography that helped shape it, the film further elaborates the legend that Kinsey's loathing of religion was thoroughgoing and relentless because of his patriarchal, puritanical rearing. The boyhood injuries of phobic piety seemingly explain a man goaded by outrage, a scientist ever at war against forces of religious suppression in American society.[43]

Here the narrative that begs for reappraisal is the secular account that reviles all things religious or Christian and equates serious religious conviction with fanaticism. Perhaps this is why Catholics have been such convenient villains for those who tell this story, for their most dramatic pronouncements certainly fit this pattern. The stories of both Sanger and Kinsey, where liberal Catholic sympathizers are virtually invisible, play directly into the scholarly divide that separates Catholics from the "main" history of gender and sexuality in the United States. Fortunately, theirs are not the only stories to be told. We turn next to a figure whose life and work begin to exemplify what we may learn from incorporating the Catholic story.

∞ Mary Steichen Calderone's Interreligious Work: Catholic Contacts

Mary Steichen Calderone, who had carried on a warm and lengthy correspondence with Kinsey during his lifetime, became one of the most influential sex educators of the twentieth century, first as medical director of Planned Parenthood and later as the founder and director of the Sexuality Information and Education Council of the United States (SIECUS). During her years at Planned Parenthood (1953–64) and, indeed, throughout the remainder of her life, Calderone did her utmost to reach out to Catholics. By all visible measures, she did so in a spirit of deep interest and generosity, believing that if she exposed her own humanity to Catholic women and men, they would reciprocate. In one of the earliest surviving accounts, on June 26, 1956, she wrote to Sister Mary Nora at St. Joseph Hospital in Memphis, Tennessee, in response to a letter (which has not survived). She included copies of three pamphlets, "The Nurse and Planned Parenthood," "To Those Denied a Child," and "Education for Marriage." Then she continued:

> I would like to add this personal note. I very much appreciate the spirit in which you wrote and would like you to know in return that being a Quaker I am deeply concerned with protecting the right of every human being to believe and worship in his own way. I deeply respect the belief of the Catholic church and understand the principles on which it is based. I would never do anything to try and influence a Catholic in any way.

Calderone went on to defend her commitment to making contraception available to those who wanted it, but she made sure that Sister Mary Nora understood that this was not about imposing her own norms on others.

> You ask me about the spacing of babies. Along with number of babies this is more and more a question on which we all realize there can and must be no didactic answer. What is too close together for one mother is just right for another. What is too many babies to handle for one mother is fine for another. I am thinking of the article "How America Lives" in this month's *Ladies Home Journal*, describing a wonderful young Catholic family in California. We are often suspected of being critical of such families, but this is far from the case. We believe in the kind of families that couples want. We also believe in the medical science that makes it possible for married couples to achieve these wants and please do not believe that when we say want we mean selfish wants. We know that human nature is not like this. The truly religious and warm mother will actually want the number of babies that come to her. It might be better for her health both physical and emotional, however, if she could perhaps have a breathing space between pairs of babies say.

Noting that as a mother of three widely spaced children she spoke "from experience," Calderone continued to point out the emotional and health benefits for both mother and child of planned spacing.[44]

Words of outreach and an earnest effort to understand and empathize with Catholics characterized other correspondence as well. In 1958 Calderone wrote a letter to Jack Heber of the *St. Joseph Register* in Kansas City, Missouri, about his recent article on birth control. The letter, opening with assurance of "how much I admire" the article for its "well documented and thoughtful statement of the Catholic position," was as candid as it was charitable in seeking to discuss the issue of birth control (no response from Heber exists in the archives).

> Actually you know the Catholic and the non-Catholic position is not so far apart. Our basic desire is the same: stable, happy monogamous

families. The understanding shown by the Vatican in several statements of the need of parents in some instances and conditions of stress to space their children simply echoes our own feelings of concern for mothers and fathers all over the world.

Calderone wrote of herself, as she often did, as a deeply religious and highly moral woman. She could, she noted, respect the Catholic position against contraception; why could Catholics not accept her own view as equally moral?

> When I take my children to the Friends meetings and sit in silence among those plain, sober, and thoughtful people, I often send my thoughts to my Catholic friends, praying that they will offer to us the same kind of understanding that we offer to them. In other words, we are as deeply devout as they, and I often wonder if they really think that we have horns just because our group has approved birth control as highly moral, as have the other great denominations quite officially, such as the two Lutheran groups, the Anglican Episcopal Church, the Methodist Church General Conference, the General Council of Congregational Christian Churches, etc. In other words, who is to determine the immorality or the morality of non-Catholics? I am sure that you will agree that Catholics may determine this only for themselves and not for members of the other religious groups.

That last point was precisely what many Catholics and Protestants could not agree on, which Calderone certainly knew; but she remained optimistic that her outlook could be heard and that agreement could be reached. Insisting on Planned Parenthood's profound commitment to happy, monogamous marriages and to solving the problems of infertility (and not simply birth control), Calderone presented herself here and elsewhere as a "highly moral" person who deserved a hearing from Catholics. "I have written to you at such length," she pleaded, "hoping that these sober thoughts could be passed on by you to other thoughtful Catholics."[45]

Calderone was equally charitable toward Catholics in her first major book, *Release from Sexual Tensions*, which adopted the same high-minded tone as her correspondence and plainly sought to draw Catholic readers no less than others. The text gave frank counsel to couples about the ordinary difficulties, sexual and otherwise, to be faced in marriage, and its list of suggested readings included *The Catholic Marriage Manual*, by George A. Kelly. Calderone also commended the church's Pre-Cana and Cana conferences (for engaged and married couples) as well as the rhythm method (although she urged that this be "practiced with extreme care under the guidance of a knowledgeable physician" and extolled safer contraceptive methods for those whose religion allowed them). Sounding like the liberal Quaker she was, she wrote hopefully that those who followed the "fundamental part" of their religion could see that "the love and worship of God" were more important than "the details and dogma" of particular systems.

Perhaps the most telling sign of Calderone's distance from orthodox (Catholic and Protestant) precepts of the time was her insistence that within marriage "anything is proper so long as it pleases both husband and wife and allows both to achieve emotional peace." Or, as she put it later in the same book, "Indeed, there is one great truism that I wish everyone, particularly wives, could learn. It is that sex in itself, with a person whom you love and who loves you, is good, and nothing you do in this relationship could possibly be wrong." Catholic and conservative Protestant writers would later write volumes of marriage manuals in this same vein, but it was not the style of that time. However fair Calderone aimed to be toward religious views more conservative than her own, she was not about to mask or soft-pedal her own beliefs, which here and elsewhere she presented as medically and therapeutically sound.[46]

What *Release from Sexual Tensions* revealed about Calderone, above all, was her sheer optimism that religious people were reasonable enough to understand the compatibility of faith and sexual openness. She devoted an entire chapter to religion and the tensions it could cause in marriage, but her point was to argue that these could straightforwardly be remedied once religion had been confronted with open eyes. The chapter's opening line cut to the chase: "If there is any area in which sex has no business being a problem, that one area is religion." Recognizing the fundamental truth taught by all religions—the obligation to express thoroughgoing love to others, "preferably beginning with the one nearest and dearest to you"—couples ought to be able to handle anything that came their way. More broadly, charitably recognizing the "common thread" in all religions would, she believed, thwart any priggish desire to legislate one's own peculiar dogma for those who held a different conception of the moral life.[47]

However magnanimous her approach, Calderone was not above being nettlesome to Catholics when she needed to be. In February 1962 she wrote the first of several letters to Father John C. Knott of the Family Life Bureau of the National Catholic Welfare Conference (NCWC). Stating her "great concern for the need of Roman Catholics for a sound presentation of the Rhythm Method," she assured Knott that her concern "stems from my belief as a Quaker that sound methods of family planning acceptable to their religious beliefs should be broadly available to everyone in this difficult world." Since Catholic writers had provided no clear guidelines for this method, Calderone continued, Planned Parenthood had done so in a newly published pamphlet called "The Safe Period," aimed explicitly at Catholics for whom no other method was permitted.[48] She hoped that this publication would be of real use to Catholic couples wishing to space (or limit the number of) their children, couples who had heretofore received no clear information—or, worse, erroneous information—from church leaders. She enclosed several pamphlets in this mailing. Some months later, having not heard back from Knott, she sent him six more, adding, "I think you will be interested to know that we sent a copy of this pamphlet to Roman Catholic Schools of Nursing and are beginning to receive requests for it. If we can have taken a small step towards better understanding in our mutual concern for the stability of the family under the stresses of modern life, I shall be most thankful."[49]

Calderone wrote to the unresponsive Knott again in June, stressing again "my sincerity in working towards mutual understanding between Catholics and non-Catholics" on issues pertaining to marriage, sexuality, and the family. Mentioning the upcoming National Catholic Family Life Convention that Knott would be hosting, she offered to provide him with mimeographed copies of her recent talk to Planned Parenthood affiliates, along with "as many copies of our little pamphlet the 'Safe Period' as you would care to use." Making the point clear, she added, "At our recent exhibit at the American Nurses Association, many Catholic nursing Sisters stopped by and picked 'The Safe Period' up with gratitude. In addition, I have had some letters of deep appreciation from directors of Roman Catholic Schools of Nursing, asking for many more copies for their teaching program." She wanted, above all, for Knott to understand the religious convictions that drove her to do this work, the compassion and care with which she approached Roman Catholics; and the plain reality that she, not he, was on the side of the future:

> There is no question but that the day is rapidly arriving when Public Health and tax-supported hospital services will very definitely include family planning as a part of their maternal health services. My concern as a Quaker is that this shall be accomplished with the least damaging controversy possible—with as deep a concern for the welfare and feelings of Roman Catholics as for that of the non-Catholics,

whose religion places upon them the obligation to use medical methods of contraception. If I can help in any way to move us all along the
road to this goal, I shall feel that this is my way of serving God.

Calderone chose her words carefully, signing off, "Yours in fellowship."[50]

Hearing nothing back from Knott, Calderone reached out to his associate, the Reverend Henry V. Sattler, assistant director of the NCWC's Family Life Bureau. Her letter (of March 7) was much like those to Knott, and
eventually, on June 29, Sattler penned a reply. Writing with like-minded
candor and civility, Sattler summarized the Catholic opposition to birth
control, adding that "I do agree that we must mutually respect the good will
of all those who are thinking in this field." He took strong umbrage at the
implication in Calderone's letter that Catholics were causing "divisiveness"
with their public stand against birth control, pointing out that disagreements must be aired honestly and that, in the United States, "The freedom
to be different is a Constitutional right." Just as Methodists were not accused of being "divisive" when they made public arguments against alcohol
consumption and mass advertising, so too should Catholics be free of this
charge when they attempted to persuade others of their positions.[51]

Most personally offensive to Calderone was the imputation of immorality that she felt Catholics directed toward her and all other non-Catholics
who favored birth control. She complained to Dr. John Battenfield of Long
Island's Mercy Hospital:

> Often even the most highly placed Roman Catholic clergy speak of
> people like myself as if we were pagan or immoral. Far from it, if they
> would but get to know us better, as is fortunately happening. Indeed,
> my own book, "Release from Sexual Tensions," which was a choice of
> the Pastoral Psychology Book Club, is all the way through a litany in
> support of monogamy and stable family life. That my belief is that
> family planning should be the servant of marriage should not separate
> me from my Catholic colleagues, for the simple reason that Pope Pius
> XII himself indicated the same belief—differing, of course, only in the
> method.

Indeed, Calderone's views would be considered rather conservative today in
Planned Parenthood circles. Far more than Sanger or Kinsey, she was in this
period, first and foremost, a promoter of love and empathic connection
within monogamous, heterosexual marriage. She simply could not understand how Catholic leaders could continue to construe her and other persons like her as debased and immoral.

Other correspondence shows that Calderone encouraged impatient physicians to help their Catholic patients understand the rhythm method rather than attempting to persuade them to use medical means instead. To one New York doctor whom she saw as overbearing in this regard, she wrote admonishingly, "I have always been convinced that a physician should not be involved in any way in the struggle of a woman between her religion and her conscience. . . . The burden of a decision as to what method is acceptable must lie on the individual Catholic woman for her own discussion with her Priest." Calderone's care in this regard irritated the doctor, H. H. Neumann, who responded:

> I believe that the individual physician is entitled to speak up freely. The requests of the Catholic Church are at times so incongruous and absurd and spoken of with so much insincerity and hypocrisy mixed with fear, even by devout Catholics, that a reassuring word by their physician may do a great deal to comfort his patients in their conflict of conscience. The irritating, somewhat arrogant virulence of the Catholic clergy towards other viewpoints is such that I wonder whether infinite patience and retreat is the correct attitude. I find it disturbing that in our local Planned Parenthood meetings physicians repeatedly ask not to have their names mentioned as participants in order not to jeopardize their position in the local hospital. If there is that much intolerance on one side, I am not sure whether constant concessions are the best attitude to take.[52]

Plainly, Calderone was able to develop a reputation within Catholic circles for a spirit of openness and generosity. In subsequent years she developed collegial relationships with two priests in particular, the Jesuit John L. Thomas and the Paulist George Hagmaier. Both served on the board of directors of a new organization she founded in 1964, the Sexuality Information and Education Council of the United States (SIECUS). Calderone was inspired to resign from Planned Parenthood to start SIECUS largely through her contacts with liberal religious leaders, mostly Protestants, but she made sure to include Catholics—one of whom was John Rock, the doctor who helped develop the birth-control pill. Ten years later she told an interviewer:

> Father John Thomas was one of the first people on our board—a Jesuit. A beautiful man. He wrote in the second or third issue of the Newsletter (begun in February 1965) a lead article called "Sexuality and the Total Personality." That is a very beautiful little piece in which he speaks of

sexuality as a major aspect of personality. That really was new think-ing. Because people really were in the habit of looking upon sexuality as a series of acts, isolated acts, that you did or didn't do or did with some persons and not with others and always in bed and usually under rather restricted circumstances.[53]

Thomas, a sociologist at Georgetown University whose work focused on marriage and the family, could and did speak differently on the subject, al-though in ways that Calderone later claimed to have supported.

But could the relationship have been as cozy as Calderone recalled? The differences between their points of view were extreme. In a 1959 article, "The Catholic Position on Population Control," Thomas set out those dif-ferences quite clearly (without directly referencing Calderone, although she was medical director of Planned Parenthood at this time and so may have been known to him). "The Christian who believes that the human person is a unity of body and soul, endowed with faculties of intellect and will, and possessing an essential relationship of origin, dependence, and destiny to his Creator, will judge the morality of birth control differently from one who maintains that man has no essential qualitative difference from other higher forms of animal life," he averred. "This point appears to be all too frequently forgotten in current controversy." Indeed, Thomas's point could be extended well beyond birth control to matters pertaining to sexuality more generally, because he wrote that disagreements about the "licitness" of particular acts "must logically be based on differences concerning basic moral principles, and since these are based on our concept of the nature, origin, and destiny of man, any worth-while discussion of disagreements must ultimately cen-ter on this point."[54]

Calderone's other Catholic associate, George Hagmaier, held views that appear to have been somewhat closer to her own. In his highly regarded 1959 book *Counselling the Catholic*, Hagmaier highlighted the crucial role that sex education played in one's subsequent life. "A very important aspect of self-acceptance involves the kind of sex education, or lack of it, which the growing child is given," he wrote.

Sex education means not only a progressing familiarity with the pro-cesses of reproduction; it includes the concepts a child has of masculin-ity or femininity, his growing capacity to give and to receive affection, and the kind of relationship he has to his own father and mother. There is perhaps no single area of human development in which adult behavior is more significantly influenced by attitudes developed in early childhood. Pope Pius XII made it very plain that it is a grave duty of parents to instruct their children by revealing gradually, simply, and truthfully each fact and detail which the child has the capacity to assimilate.[55]

Nearly any Catholic could agree with these points. What was more remarkable, and closer to Calderone's own views, was Hagmaier's attention to the communication of "healthy attitudes toward sex," not mere information; and his insistence that parents were often all too "Victorian, Puritan, or Jansenist" in their inhibited prudishness when tenderly broaching the subject. "Children of such parents come to regard sex with uneasiness and misgivings, and are soon afraid to ask further about it" (10). Significantly, Hagmaier supported the teaching of sex education in the schools.

In May 1966, through the intervention of Hagmaier, Calderone was able to attend an important colloquium on women's sexuality convened by Cardinal Suenens at Louvain University in Belgium. According to the report she later wrote (apparently to other SIECUS administrators), some sixty participants attended the event, hailing from France, Italy, West Germany, Austria, Holland, Great Britain, Ireland, and the United States, as well as Belgium. The group assembled was a mix of physicians, nurses, lawyers, clergy (chiefly pastoral counselors), and academics of various sorts. Despite the fact that the meeting focused on women's sexuality, Calderone was the lone woman in the U.S. delegation, which otherwise consisted of Hagmaier, a Paulist priest who was then teaching courses on marriage and the family at Catholic University; Louis Dupré of Georgetown University; Elmer Gelinas of St. Mary's College, California; Thomas Hayes, a biophysicist at the University of California at Berkeley; John Noonan of Notre Dame, whose book on contraception and natural law had been published the previous year; Bernard Pisani, an obstetrician at St. Vincent's Hospital in New York; and Reuben Hill, a sociologist (and Mormon) at the University of Minnesota who worked in the areas of marriage and family life and who also served as a program officer in population studies at the Ford Foundation. At this event Calderone was approached by Canon Charles Moeller, undersecretary to the Congregation for the Doctrine of the Faith, who spoke with her at length.

> [He] finally asked me if I would undertake to send him personally, those books and publications from the U.S. that would seem to have the most relevance to all of the complicated matters under discussion, particularly as they relate to sex and marriage. He noted specifically the new study by Masters and Johnson on Human Sexual Response. I reminded him that although the findings of this important study

would undoubtedly be recognized as having definitive value and importance to our knowledge and understanding, the methods of the study might lead to difficulties not only in his, but in other churches. His reply . . . : "Yes, but it is essential that our theology be based on the most accurate scientific knowledge." I accepted his charge, needless to say, and am now going to be looking for the funds that would allow the SIECUS Board to choose and purchase books and other materials not only for Canon Moeller, but for the new Institute at Louvain University.

With the heady, ecumenical spirit of the Second Vatican Council still filling the air, Catholics reached out to Calderone just as she had for some time been reaching out to them. Calderone recalled that she "found a kind of radiant comradeship with the clerical group" that she described as "most warming." Above all, she appreciated the humble spirit and common purpose that guided the group's discussions. "What seemed to me of the greatest importance was the message of Cardinal Suenens: We are engaged not only in a search for real truth, but in this search we are all groping our way, unable to distinguish at all times between fact, mythology or rules based on outdated or non-valid concepts," she wrote. "The key word he used was 'tatonnement,' what a blind person does as he gropes his way along an unfamiliar street."[56]

Notwithstanding the warmth of these relationships, conflicts could and did emerge. Thomas, for instance, detailed his disagreement with Calderone in his essay in *Sexuality and Human Values*, and eventually he resigned from the SIECUS board. And, in an oral history interview conducted in 1974, she recalled the stinging words directed at her by the Catholic conservative William F. Buckley, Jr.[57]

Still, of her many accomplishments, Calderone was particularly proud of her outreach to Catholics. She singled out a speech she gave at the University of Notre Dame in March 1968 about "how Planned Parenthood can cooperate with Roman Catholics" as one that "gave me great satisfaction." "What I said to the affiliates was, don't sell the rhythm method down the river. Don't run the Catholics down. (As a Quaker I was good and sick of that.) If that's the only method a Catholic woman can use, then teach it to her as well as possible, don't try to subvert her faith to other methods. Instead, make the rhythm method a part of the services offered by Planned Parenthood."[58]

In a 1976 presentation at the International Congress of Sexology in Montréal, Québec, she reminded her listeners that the chief enemies of sex education had long been church leaders, who remained powerful obstacles in this field. "Historically, the prime contender for control of the sexuality of a person by an outside agency is, and continues to be, religion." A deep suspicion of pleasure and privacy was at the root of religion's repressive force, in her view: an "almost paranoid fear that exists, not only of sexual pleasure itself but also of the recognition of one's body as a valid source of that pleasure." Rather than noting, as she often had, that many liberal Protestant and Catholic leaders were working for change in this regard, she cited several studies to demonstrate that laypeople were simply circumventing their leaders on matters ranging from masturbation and birth control to a wide array of sexual practices outside marriage (some of which she acknowledged were "distasteful" and "worrisome," although these could be averted, she insisted, by better programs of sex education). Calling for "a coalition of strengths" to bring professionals together in service to a "universal approach to realistic sexual knowledge for *all* ages and socioeconomic groups," Calderone noted that religion "can be especially helpful in such a coalition," but only if religious leaders were willing to agree with this statement: "That sexuality itself is morally neutral, but that how we learn or are taught to use it throughout life has heavy moral implications." "Such moral implications," she insisted, "should—and indeed must—transcend differences in religious dogma." Working together in this way would turn what were internal sexual battlegrounds into "private peacegrounds."[59]

∞Reframing the Story of Gender, Sexuality, and Catholicism

This chapter has explored three non-Catholic liberals who played a pivotal role in twentieth-century American sexual history, focusing attention on the one who worked hardest to bridge the Protestant/Catholic divide, Mary Steichen Calderone. In the historiography of American sex and gender in the twentieth century, Catholics largely appear as conservative foils to these kind of liberal icons. Liberal Catholics make few appearances in the standard accounts apart from those written by Catholic historians. In their lifetime Sanger, Kinsey, and Calderone were lauded by secular and Protestant (and doubtless some Catholic) liberals while attracting scorn from religious conservatives, Protestant and Catholic alike; and all three remain contentious figures in scholarly works. Indeed, if we take at face value most of the narratives handed down about the history of sex and gender in U.S. history, we see only the "culture wars" spawned by divisive reactions to public figures such as Margaret Sanger and Alfred Kinsey. Protestant liberals and American Catholics have ever been at odds on issues of gender and sexuality, and that, certainly, is also the story taken up by scholars of the debates over sex education, in which Calderone figures importantly. In accounts by Mary Breasted, Janice Irvine, and Jeffrey Moran, Catholics appear only as the enemies of sex education and sex reform.[60]

Catholic obstreperousness in the face of good liberal sex reform has become the overarching historical narrative. Even when conservative evangelicals and fundamentalists joined the opposition, Catholics remained the main villains in the story. When the clergy sex-abuse scandals publicly erupted in 2002–3, signs of liberal schadenfreude pervaded liberal accounts in scholarly no less than journalistic circles. The topic of clergy sexual abuse and its extent and cover-up through the very highest levels of the church reinforces the tendency of many non-Catholic Americans to see the Catholic approach to gender and sexuality as unique—appallingly so. (This is not so much an anti-Catholic position as an expression of enmity against the Catholic hierarchy, but it should surprise no one that liberals outside the Catholic fold do not always see the point of drawing the distinction.) From that angle, the times have never looked worse for incorporating Catholics into a broader narrative of gender and sexuality in U.S. history.

But Calderone knew that U.S. Catholics were an internally plural community, not a monolith, and she made alliances with progressive Catholics throughout her career. Sifting through her writings and correspondence illumines the cooperation and communication between some Protestants and some Catholics on issues of family planning. The cooperation was deeply rooted in religious commitments. We see Calderone engaging in discussions of sex and marriage with international Catholic leaders in an atmosphere of open questioning and mutual respect. We see Catholic nurses using Calderone's teaching materials from Planned Parenthood to help Catholic women make reproductive choices in line with the church's teachings. We see Calderone forging partnerships, however tentative, with Catholic priests such as George Hagmaier and John Thomas to identify a shared moral ground on which to base education about sexuality. These examples begin to suggest the multifaceted nature of the respective Protestant and Catholic approaches to gender and sex and the interactions between them on these issues. Such complexity is eclipsed by narratives that portray liberal Protestants as sexually amoral and anti-Catholic, and Catholics as backward pawns of the church hierarchy. Calderone's story serves as a reminder of men and women who did not fit these stereotypes and who believed that bridging the divide between Catholics and Protestants was the proper Christian way to influence changing ideas about gender and sexuality in American culture. It suggests that the partnerships between Catholics and Protestants may be a fruitful avenue for research on religion, gender, and sexuality in the United States. By attending to figures who bridged the Catholic/Protestant divide in their own lives, scholars may begin to bridge it in their scholarship.

Examining these partnerships and debates also underscores how much is at stake in the public debate about gender, sexuality, and reproduction: both Catholics and Protestants were wrestling with fundamental questions of what it meant to be a human being, and the purpose of human life. Calderone strove to understand and to dignify persons whose religious ideas she did not share (indeed, whose religious ideas she may have deplored). She did so in the hope of coming to fruitful collaboration on matters of great significance about which they could agree. In the urgency of our time, with vast questions facing us about human rights, human life and flourishing, and with the possibility and potential of civil and religious partnerships for the common good, this broad-minded, incorporative vision remains strikingly relevant.

∞ CHAPTER 5

The New Turn in Chicano/ Mexicano History

Integrating Religious Belief and Practice

DAVID G. GUTIÉRREZ

Scholars who specialize in the study of religion and religiosity in the ethnic Mexican and pan-Latino populations of the United States have long lamented the fact that their work—and the theme of religion more generally—has not drawn more central attention from humanists and social scientists working in interdisciplinary Chicano and Latino studies.[1] They have a valid point. Although one could argue that a small number of notable religious studies titles have recently "crossed over" into the consciousness of Latino studies scholars whose own work generally does not focus on religious questions, it is equally clear that religion and religiosity have not been central themes of inquiry since the study of the nation's Latino populations became academically legitimated and (more or less) institutionalized in U.S. colleges and universities in the late 1960s and 1970s. Fortunately, however, since the 1980s and early 1990s there have been signs that the divide between secularist scholars and religious studies specialists is beginning to be bridged.

Of course, since the vast majority of ethnic Mexicans and other Latinos historically have been Catholic, the earliest scholarship on Latino religious history tended to focus on the Catholic tradition. The work of Moises Sandoval in the early 1980s is an influential example of this foundational work.[2] Later, with the publication of social-historical monographic works such as Ramón A. Gutiérrez's award-winning book, *When Jesus Came, the Corn*

Mothers Went Away (1991), Jeanette Rodríguez's *Our Lady of Guadalupe* (1994), Timothy Matovina's *Tejano Religion and Ethnicity* (1995), Alberto Pulido's *Sacred World of the Penitentes* (2000), Frederick Dalton's *Moral Vision of César Chávez* (2003), and three important anthologies published by the Cushwa Center and the University of Notre Dame Press in 1994, analysis of Catholicism has begun to inform the broader currents of the history of Mexicans and Mexican Americans in the United States.[3] In addition, the publication of a number of important anthologies and conference proceedings comparing Latino Catholicism with other religious traditions has also contributed to what has become an unprecedented period of dialogue and intellectual cross-fertilization between comparative religious studies scholarship and the field of interdisciplinary Latino studies.[4]

This chapter represents a modest and far-from-comprehensive effort by a secular, religiously skeptical Chicano historian whose work has not centered on religious themes to explore some of the issues and analytical possibilities raised by the expanding nexus between recent scholarship on Latino Catholicism and other religious traditions and the main currents of one crucial element of interdisciplinary Latino Studies—that of the evolution of Chicano/Mexicano history and historiography of the late twentieth century.[5] To explore this increasingly influential intersection, I begin with a brief discussion and critical speculation on the role Catholic and comparative religious studies scholarship has played (or not played) in the main currents of Chicano/Mexicano historiography. I then offer an argument about the major conceptual and categorical conundrums contemporary scholars of Mexican American and Mexican immigrant history currently face in their collective agenda of research and interpretation. Finally, I consider some of the ways recent Catholic and comparative religious studies scholarship provides a bridge between conceptual and historiographical paradigms that first emerged nearly forty years ago, on the one hand, and contemporary analytical frameworks that may be better suited to understanding the changing demographic, cultural, and political realities characterizing the lived experiences of ethnic Mexicans and other Latinos, on the other.

Religion and the Evolution of Chicano/Mexicano Social History

In the introduction to his history of Mexican American Catholicism in Houston, Texas, the social historian Roberto Treviño muses about the ambiguous role the study of religion has played in Mexican American history and historiography. He astutely notes that although Mexicans and Mexican Americans have always been strongly and even stereotypically associated in public consciousness with their religious traditions, practices, and what some see as their "superstitions," comparatively few Chicano historians have engaged religion or religiosity as central categories of historical analysis. Indeed, Treviño notes that much of what motivated him to pursue his case study in the history of what he calls "ethno-Catholicism" in a Mexican American community was a desire to offer something of a corrective to this trend by using the study of religion to develop a better understanding of the foundations of Mexican American society and culture. In the process Treviño hoped to help move Mexican American religious history beyond its intellectual "infancy." From his standpoint, given the centrality of religious belief and practice in the Mexican and Mexican American tradition, analysis of religion and religiosity is crucial if we are to gain a broad and deep understanding of the central animating dynamics of cultural production, reproduction, and change in ethnic Mexican communities over time.[6] Indeed, this kind of reframing and rethinking has typified seminal work by historians of religion such as Gutiérrez, Rodríguez, Matovina, and Pulido.

A number of theories have been advanced about why the study of religion and religiosity has not been a primary scholarly focus in Chicano and Latino history. On the most basic level, it is clear that many interpreters of U.S. Chicano, Mexicano, and Latino history are reluctant to engage the intricate lacuna any empirically based researcher faces when she or he attempts to delve into the history of consciousness and especially the history of ordinary people's relationship with the spiritual, the supernatural, and the ineffable.[7] But this reluctance to engage religion more systematically is somewhat surprising since it seems to run counter to other powerful trends in Chicano and Latino cultural and historical scholarship. In recent years Chicano and Latino scholars have shown little hesitation in venturing beyond the study of Latino theology and institutional relationships to examine any number of pan-Latino cultural artifacts and modes of cultural expression, including close analysis of the political and cultural meanings of the zoot suit, the deeply gendered, quasi-religious coming-of-age ritual known as the *quinceañera*, the significance of machismo and "insider" joking among Chicano and Mexicano men, and virtually all forms of popular film, music, art, and dance. But comparatively few intrepid scholars have been willing to grapple explicitly with fundamental questions concerning the significance in Latino communities of religious faith, cosmology, religious practice, and the general relationship of the mystical and the spiritual to everyday behavior and social practice.

This apparent reluctance to engage such themes and, in some cases, the tendency to avoid philosophical and metaphysical research altogether can be attributed in part to the uneasy place the study of religion occupies in the contemporary secular university, apart from formally constituted religious studies or philosophy programs. Given the political and cultural tensions among evangelical Christians, Muslims, and Jews on the global stage, perhaps it is not surprising that the study of religion in university settings is widely considered to be fraught with controversy.[8] And this is to say nothing of the influence on academe of the blistering indictments of organized religion and religiosity by the so-called New Atheists, ranging from the comedian-pundit Bill Maher to influential critics of religion and best-selling authors such as Richard Dawkins, Sam Harris, the late Christopher Hitchens, and others.[9]

One of the most important reasons, if not *the* major reason, Latino studies scholars have been reluctant to engage systematically with religious belief and practice is the generally unsettled nature of the fields of Chicano and Latino studies. Although it is probably an exaggeration to suggest that the fields of interdisciplinary Chicano and Latino studies are in the midst of a conceptual and historiographical crisis, the explosive growth of the nation's ethnic Mexican and pan-Latino populations over the past half century has raised serious questions and heated debate about the continuing viability of conceptual frameworks of analysis that were first developed at the height of the Chicano and Latino civil rights movements of the 1960s and 1970s.

At that time of political turmoil and intellectual ferment, the field of Chicano history emerged as both an intellectual project of archaeology and recovery and an active political project. This sweeping historical project was intended both to critique institutions and structures of the dominant society and to insist that Mexican-origin people were historical actors who deserved to be heard. Drawing inspiration from germinal statements of cultural awakening and ethnic pride—such as Rodolfo "Corky" Gonzales's epic poem *Yo Soy Joaquín* (1967); the First Chicano Youth Liberation Conference's ringing manifesto of self-determination, *El Plan Espiritual de Aztlán* (1969); the call to intellectual arms issued by Chicano higher-education activists in their own manifesto, *El Plan de Santa Bárbara* (1969); the establishment of the critical academic journals *El Grito* (1967) and *Aztlán* (1970); and the landmark 1972 publication of Rodolfo Acuña's historical shot across the bow, *Occupied America: The Chicano's Struggle toward Liberation*—Chicano scholar-activists forged a collective project that directly challenged the domination of what one cultural critic termed "epistemic imperialisms" and another described as the "categorical violence wrought by colonialism on subaltern social groups."[10]

In some respects reflecting developments that were unfolding in the conflictual African American and third world cultural politics of the time, the emergence of modern Chicano historiography in the late 1970s was part of a larger trend by which individuals of Mexican descent sought new ways to challenge existing asymmetries of power while simultaneously attempting to foster self-esteem, solidarity, and political mobilization among the constituents they collectively defined as the "Chicano community." A critique of institutional Catholicism and other forms of constituted religious authority marked some of the Chicano ideologies espoused at the time. Although each of the major ideological manifestos of the period employed spiritual tropes and religious symbols as part of their appeal to the Chicano and Mexicano masses, they vilified church authority—and especially the overwhelmingly white European hierarchy of the institutional Catholic Church—as a source of the oppression and historical erasure of Chicanos in U.S. society.[11] Thus, from the point of view of these activists, as well as many ordinary people who shared their fervor, the adoption of Chicanismo, the strong new sense of cultural pride and solidarity that emerged at the time, required the rejection not only of the strategy of assimilation and the debilitating myth of the "melting pot" but also of constituted religious authority—particularly that of the Catholic Church.[12]

This was powerful and volatile stuff. But as important as the simultaneous engagement in bipolar identity politics, critique of religious authority, and the politics of knowledge production was at the time, the strident rhetoric tended to obscure the contradictions and elisions that were embedded in the ideologies and the foundational conceptual categories of the new Chicano "community." Indeed, even as Chicano activists and activist-scholars attempted to create and explore these new bases of individual subjectivity, collective solidarity, and political action, they were confronted almost immediately with some of the more glaring contradictions of their rhetoric and proposed agendas. The most serious challenge revolved around the question of the internal diversity of the Mexican-origin population and the increase of Mexican immigration that was unfolding at the precise moment when the Chicano movement reached its peak.

Indeed, the first flowering and early maturation of Chicano history and interdisciplinary Chicano studies in the 1970s and 1980s generated the following irony: the political moves that preceded and sparked these developments, while necessary to create the conditions for the emergence of these areas of inquiry in the first place, involved this first group of archivist-interpreters (and many of the younger scholars they subsequently trained) in a process of archiving and chronicling the passing of a historical epoch. Another era was beginning as mass migration from Mexico and Latin America dramatically remade the extant pan-Latino population of the United States. As the huge numbers of immigrants from Mexico and Latin America continued to climb in the 1970s, 1980s, and beyond, the subject of Chicano history, that is, the "Chicano community" itself, was being fundamentally transformed in myriad ways even as the field was being created and consolidated.[13]

The conceptual problems engendered by these developments can be seen most clearly simply by assessing the changing general demographic profile of the ethnic Mexican population between 1960 and 2000. In 1960, on the eve of the rise of Chicano militancy, the vast majority of the ethnic Mexicans in the United States—more than 86 percent—were U.S. citizens. Although Mexican migrants and immigrants had circulated through Mexican American communities in large numbers over the entire course of the twentieth century (with the notable exception of the Depression decade), the fact that so much of this migration was circular tended to keep their proportions of the permanent resident population comparatively low. As a consequence, the proportion of Mexican nationals as a component of the resident ethnic Mexican population dropped steadily between the censuses of 1930 and 1970. In 1929–30 the proportion of Mexican nationals in the resident ethnic Mexican population was at least 44 percent. By 1940 this proportion had fallen to 20 percent. By 1950 it had declined to 17 percent, and it reached historical lows of 14 percent in the censuses of both 1960 and 1970.[14]

After 1970, however, older patterns of labor migration from Mexico resumed to the point that by the turn of the twenty-first century the demographic structure of the ethnic Mexican population had reverted to a situation that strongly resembled that of the first decades of the twentieth century. Because of recurring economic crises in Mexico and the addiction to Mexican labor in the U.S. economy, by 1980 the proportion of Mexican nationals began to rise again, reaching 25 percent of the total in 1980, growing to 30 percent in 1990, and attaining a high of 41 percent in 2000. According to the latest available estimates, although the rate of population change appears to have slowed slightly by the middle of the first decade of the new millennium (and continues to slow because of the current economic contraction), as of 2010 Mexican nationals still constituted 35.6 percent of the nearly 33 million persons of Mexican heritage living in the United States.[15]

The magnitude of this ongoing demographic restructuring of the Mexican and pan-Latino population has created a variety of challenges for both historians and analysts of contemporary trends, but the most obvious is that this kind of population movement and population mixing has dramatically transformed and complicated the social, the cultural, and, crucially, the religious profile of the resident ethnic Mexican population. Whereas the population in 1970 was overwhelmingly composed of individuals who were born, raised, educated, and socialized in the United States, after 1970 the population became increasingly diversified by the massive influx of new immigrants from Mexico and by the entry into the mix of unprecedented numbers of Latin peoples from Central America, South America, and the Spanish-speaking Caribbean. The geographic dispersal of this population has also been unprecedented. In 1970 the vast majority of Latino groups were concentrated in a few regions of the United States, but in recent years the fastest rate of Latino population increase has occurred in the American South and Midwest, places that had seen only a very small Latino presence in the past. Again, although the overwhelming proportion of these migrants have been Roman Catholic, significant numbers also practice some form of Protestantism or various forms of syncretic indigenous religious traditions.[16]

⌘ Religious Studies and the Future of Chicano/ Mexicano Historiography

The tremendous diversification of the ethnic Mexican and pan-Latino populations of the United States since 1970 has stimulated a heated debate among Chicano and Latino studies scholars and other social analysts who have been scrambling to grapple with the implications of the explosive growth and unprecedented geographic dispersal of the putative subjects of their research. In Mexican American scholarship these trends have engendered a particularly fierce period of debate and, in some cases, bouts of recrimination. Much of this debate is based on long-simmering disputes about the politics of knowledge and knowledge production that have their roots in the heyday of the civil rights era.[17] Whereas most Chicano studies scholars of the 1970s and 1980s seemed at least tacitly to assume that Mexican immigrants would gradually be absorbed, by default, into extant Mexican American communities and thus also into patterns of political and cultural socialization that had characterized the post–World War II era, both the volume and the increasing heterogeneity of migration since then have raised

significant questions about the soundness of such assumptions. By extension, these shifting demographics have also raised important questions about
extant lines of the Chicano historiography and larger Chicano epistemes
produced during the height of the civil rights struggle.[18]

Indeed, in a perceptive and probing article that grapples with some of
these issues, the respected immigration sociologist Nestor Rodríguez suggests
that the resident ethnic Mexican and pan-Latino population has changed
so much in the past quarter century that many scholars—particularly those
trained in what he calls "Latino conflict theory" of the 1960s and 1970s—
have lost touch with the subjects of their research. Citing a combination of
growing differences in ideological frames of reference, language and translation issues (both linguistic translation and the larger issue of cultural translation and interpretation), and, perhaps most of all, the immense differences
in social class and potential class mobility that separate most Latino intellectuals from the Latino working masses, Rodríguez suggests that one of the
key challenges facing Latino studies researchers today is developing conceptual paradigms and analytical frameworks that will allow them credibly to
bridge the class and cultural chasms created by the increasing diversity and
cultural complexity of the nation's pan-Latino population. Although Rodríguez's article addresses the issue of religion and religiosity only in passing, his
emphasis on what he sees as a growing ideological gap between Latino intellectuals and the subjects of their research clearly foreshadows these arenas of
social life as potential areas of interpretive divergence and contradiction.[19]

The Chicana cultural critic Yolanda Broyles-González made much the
same point from a slightly different perspective in an article published in
2000, but with specific reference to some of the ways a religious studies approach might help address the epistemological and analytical challenges engendered by the persistence of older Chicano studies paradigms and frames
of reference. On one level, Broyles's insightful piece is a feminist meditation
on the life lessons instilled in her by her late grandmother, and more generally, on the role played by Latina/*indígena* women as teachers, mentors, and
generational transmitters of spiritual and cultural knowledge within families
and local communities. Broyles employs a potent mix of reminiscence and
autobiography to examine the different ways ordinary Latino working-class
women (who generally have had very low levels of formal education) nevertheless have used a wide range of alternative, spiritually infused sources of
knowledge to teach survival and living skills to those around them. The
article is also an exploration of the different ways ordinary people of very
modest means have confronted structures of power and authority in their
lives. Using her grandmother's life as a case study and object lesson, Broyles

focuses in particular on the extensive repertoire of spiritual practices, holistic curing traditions, herbalist techniques, and constantly shifting accommodations with the organs and representatives of organized religion (in this case, Roman Catholicism) that women like her grandmother have used historically in their communities. Broyles argues that each of these syncretic practices and sites of cultural knowledge production, defense, and contestation was a component of an elaborate meshwork of social strategies handed down over generations that served as important forms of self affirmation and survival for peoples perpetually marginalized in the capitalist economy, by organs and functionaries of the state, and by agents of institutionalized religion.

But like Rodríguez, Broyles also develops a critique of Latinos' own academic analyses and interpretations of such phenomena. Drawing on insights expounded by Mexican anthropologist Guillermo Bonfil Batalla on the significance of the survival and ongoing generational transmittal of ancient indigenous Meso-American cultural traditions, religious beliefs, and spiritual practices in Mexico, Broyles attempts to demonstrate just how strongly close attention to these kinds of enduring but largely invisible traditions and modes of cultural teaching can illuminate the complex cultural histories not only of indigenous populations in Mexico but also of the entire Mexican disapora, including working-class Mexican Americans and more recent Mexican and other Latino immigrants to the United States.[20] Thus, in the end, while primarily presenting something of a microethnography of her own family history, Broyles's intervention also serves as a critique of what she sees as overly narrow research agendas followed by too many Chicano and Latino scholars. She suggests that cultural and class differences in academe too often lead professional Latino studies scholars to come to abstract and reified findings, and she urges closer attention to deeper ethnographic and social-historical research that focuses on the dynamics of cultural expression and cultural practice as they actually exist in ethnic Mexican working-class communities. On a larger plane, she suggests that scholars seeking to analyze and interpret the Chicano/Latino experience would be well served by paying closer attention to nontextual traditions and spiritual practices—in this case, the realm of ongoing cultural/spiritual melding she calls "Indianized Catholicism or Catholicized native religion"—that clearly play a crucial role in ordering the daily lives, aspirations, and modes of survival used by ordinary Latinos, especially by many of the more recent immigrants from Mexico and Latin America.[21]

Broyles's and Rodríguez's arguments anticipated a growing trend of critical reassessment currently unfolding in Latino studies scholarship. Although scholars have not yet fully fleshed out a new, overarching research approach, agenda, or methodology that would allow historians and social scientists to make sense of the kaleidoscopic sociocultural heterogeneity of the pan-Latino population, there is an ongoing effort to take stock of the ways overly dichotomous epistemic assumptions and practices frame, for good or ill, the distant past as well as the contemporary moment. And it is here that religious studies scholarship may play an invaluable role in helping shape new research agendas and sophisticated new conceptual vocabularies equal to the task of dealing with the actual complexity of the pan-Latino population.

How does one best conduct basic social and historical analysis of these populations? On some levels, of course, this question is part of a larger debate well under way in the historical profession at large about how best to "do" social history in the context of the collapse of Fordist modes of production and the attendant rise of global neoliberal economic principles and in the aftermath of the so-called cultural turn in historical scholarship of the 1980s. In the face of structural changes that have rendered obsolete categories of analysis that emerged in earlier stages of capitalist development and human stratification, social historians have striven to develop new conceptual vocabularies and methodologies equal to this daunting task.[22]

In recent Chicano and Latino studies scholarship one of the most fruitful attempts to grapple with a similar set of issues has been to focus more explicitly on issues of religion and religiosity as windows into deeper forms of cultural and historical analysis, particularly in the increasingly multinational working-class majority. Drawing on insights from the work of Robert Orsi, David Carrasco, Timothy Matovina, and others, revisionist historians are beginning to rethink the trajectory of Mexican American and pan-Latino history from a vantage point that treats religion as a central, organic component of Latino society rather than as a discrete and separate arena of social and cultural life. As Orsi has argued, if one is interested in viewing the significance of religion in social history and in ordinary peoples' lives in the current moment, one must seek to understand religion as a crucial component of human beings' daily efforts to make sense of the world they live in. "'Religion' is best approached," he writes, "by meeting men and women at this daily task, in all the spaces of their experience." This requires "a redirection of religious scholarship away from traditions—the great hypostatized constructs of 'Protestantism,' 'Catholicism,' and so on—and likewise away from the denominational focus that has so preoccupied scholars of American religions, toward a study of how particular people, in particular places and times, live in, with, through, and against the religious idioms available to

them in culture—all the idioms, including (often enough) those not explicitly their 'own.'"[23]

The point is not simply to revivify U.S. religious history but to suggest
ways in which social historians might overcome the inherent problem all
conscientious ethnographic researchers face in any attempt to bridge the
existential and experiential chasm that almost always separates a university-
trained academic from the putative subject(s) of his or her research. Over
the course of his research into the meanings of everyday forms of devotion,
Orsi realized that the central methodological and epistemological questions
he faced centered on the challenge faced by any researcher in his or her attempt to re-create, interpret, and represent critical elements of social and
spiritual worlds that he or she does not, and probably cannot, occupy.

The lessons that can be drawn from Orsi's grappling with this fundamental question extend far beyond the study of religion or religiosity, per se, into
the broader realm of the social history of human consciousness and behavior. Indeed, social historians of all stripes—including, and perhaps especially, Latino studies scholars—should find Orsi's honest assessment of the
tortuous path he has taken in his effort to find what he calls an "intersubjec-
tive orientation" that actively and honestly engages "the dialectic of the
possible and the impossible" in religious studies research to be extremely
useful. How, for example, might we better grapple with lifeworlds in our own
"subject populations" that may show up in how individuals vote, decide to
join a political party or union, or decide to become, or choose not to become, naturalized citizens.[24]

Of course, such questions—particularly Orsi's focus on the vexed relationship of religious belief to what he calls the "normative teleology of
modernity"[25]—lie at the very heart of both the ethnographic endeavor and
that of social history. It seems clear that more systematic reengagement
with just this tension in both the recent history and the contemporary moment of the increasingly vast and internally complex ethnic Mexican and
pan-Latino populations in the United States may provide a much-needed
catalyst to rethink potential trajectories of both nineteenth- and twentieth-
century Chicano/Latino historiography in this moment of flux and uncertainty. The fruit of this kind of labor has already been seen in the fresh
analysis that scholars such as Gutiérrez, Matovina, Broyles, and Treviño have
brought to their reassessments of different dimensions of Mexican American
religious history. Although each of these scholars focuses on different themes
in very different times, locales, and specific historical contexts, each emphasizes the centrality of religious belief and practice in shaping peoples'

elemental senses of themselves as individuals and members of communities. Their focus on this relationship echoes what another religious studies scholar notes of Catholicism's historical influence in shaping Latinos' subjectivities when she describes Latino Catholicism as "a militant faith so fully interwoven with what we now consider to be secular issues such as identity and citizenship that it was impossible to untangle the different strands."[26]

By providing sophisticated analytical matrices that go beyond engagement with more readily apparent and accessible political and social topics, this kind of careful historical reconsideration might break through some of the deeply ingrained presuppositions under which many Latino scholars (including this author) labor. By exploring the effects on daily behavior in grassroots Latino populations of the often hidden intersections of emotion, desire, mythology, and faith, as the best of this recent work has attempted to do, the mapping of these intersections and interactions accomplishes more than charting the terrain of religious consciousness and specific spiritual rituals and practices. It also models an effective approach to analyzing some of the most pressing and inherently controversial current lacunae in the praxis of Chicano and Latino social history today. These new vectors of analysis force engagement with historical subjects more directly on their own terms rather than through the prism of received categories of analysis and frames of reference.

The work of Luis D. León, especially his sweeping synthetic monograph *La Llorona's Children* (2004), is among the best of the religious studies projects that make imaginative interventions in the service of comprehending the evolving and overlapping Latino cultural systems at the grassroots level in the Western Hemisphere.[27] León demonstrates the possibilities inherent in the careful exploration of the elemental question of how grassroots Latino Catholicism and related forms of religiosity play central roles in "how people survive and make meaning under conditions of discrimination, poverty, and degradation."[28] Inspired by the reflections on the relationship between Latino spirituality and "everyday forms of resistance" provided by pioneering Latino religious studies scholars such as Virgilio Elizondo, Enrique Dussel, and Davíd Carrasco and, on a broader cultural plane, by prominent Latino postcolonial and borderlands theorists such as Renato Rosaldo, Gloria Anzaldúa, José Saldívar, Jorge Klor de Alva, Walter Mignolo, Fernando Coronil, and Laura Pérez, León's central project is to recuperate from dismissal and stereotype the significance of an ethnic Mexican "religious ecology" that encompasses a wide range of disparate beliefs and practices.

Thus, rather than focusing exclusively on the sacraments and rituals of institutional Roman Catholicism, León takes seriously the panoply of sacred practices manifest among Mexicans and Mexican Americans. He argues that these practices and manifestations of faith include everything from attending Mass and participating in traditional, sanctioned Catholic sacraments to both folk-based and officially sanctioned veneration of the Virgin Mary, the practice of *curanderismo* (traditional techniques of "folk healing"), and the common Mexican cultural practice of individuals punishing images of the saints by scolding them, standing them on their heads in the dark recesses of dresser drawers or closets, or, at the extreme, smashing or burning them. Pointedly rejecting critiques of this kind of folk religious observance (and the complex belief systems that underlie and inform such deeply rooted cultural phenomena), León argues, like Orsi, that the symbolic universe these beliefs and practices manifest is a key component of an ever-evolving series of tactics and strategies designed to confront and "manage the crisis of everyday life" and, as such, must be taken seriously in any analysis of Chicano and Mexicano social reality.[29]

León's work is emblematic of a wave of revisionist scholarship that is now providing new lines of analysis and insight into the cultural dynamics of the ethnic Mexican population and the process of community formation and definition as they actually exist. He takes seriously the variety and density of religious belief and expression that includes everything from *curanderismo* to mainline Catholic and Protestant affiliation and practice, membership in tiny storefront Protestant evangelical churches, and the practices of spiritualism and *brujería* (witchcraft, usually of a benign sort) as organic components of a broader cultural repertoire and symbolic universe. Such practices enable individuals to adapt, adjust, and assert agency within a society that often scorns and rejects them (even as it recruits them to work). Thereby the daunting multiplicity of cultural forms and dynamics within an increasingly heterogeneous and stratified population is laid bare. Moreover, León's insistence on treating such folk practices as part of a larger Mexican and Chicano tradition of *rasquachismo*—that working-class repertoire of social pastiche, improvisation, cultural experimentation, and cultural melding critically analyzed with great verve some years ago by Tomás Ybarra-Frausto[30]—rather than as manifestations of persistent Mexican cultural "backwardness" and superstition is a fruitful way to plot the historical trajectory of more recent Mexican (and Latino) immigrants and their children and to structure comparisons with more remote periods of Chicano, Mexicano, and Latino history. He also reminds us, crucially, that ethnic Mexicans, like other groups of people, define themselves as members of multiple communities simultaneously; consequently, the place of religion (or any other form of individual and group identity and affiliation) may shift and relocate in response to social structural constraints and a variety of local circumstances. It may play a greater or lesser role in different contexts.

Although this last point is not explicit in León's analysis, it highlights another important issue raised in scholarship that takes religion and spiritual practices seriously. Whereas earlier models of Chicano scholarship tended to engage in their own form of hypostatizing by assuming that most members of the "Chicano community" were in tune with the broad progressive social and militant political objectives espoused by Chicano activists and activist-scholars in the 1960s and 1970s (or at least that they could be persuaded to be over time), recent scholarship has emphasized the broader range of opinion—and ideological conflict—that has always existed and continues to characterize politics in the ethnic Mexican population. This range of opinion is documented in two polls, one taken in 2003 and the other in 2006, among Latinos about their religious orientations and practices. Conducted among several thousand Latino respondents, the Hispanic Churches in American Public Life Survey and a similarly ambitious survey conducted by the Pew Forum on Religion and Public Life and the Pew Hispanic Center provide provocative insights into the nature of Latino religiosity.

In some ways the general findings of the two surveys are not terribly surprising and seem to comport with similar studies done in earlier eras.[31] For example, the surveys reveal that strong majorities of the pan-Latino population are significantly religious; that they remain strongly affiliated with the Roman Catholic Church; and that they tend to remain clustered in ethnically concentrated congregations. Logically enough, religious affiliations and practices are strongly correlated to nativity, education levels, and language preferences and proficiencies. Finally, given the depth of the demographic shift that has occurred over the past thirty to forty years, it is also not surprising that Latinos now constitute fully one-third of all U.S. Catholics and increasing proportions of various Protestant denominations. Owing to the aging of the U.S. native population and the relative youthfulness of the ethnic Mexican and Latino population, these trends will probably continue into the foreseeable future.

But when the two surveys are examined more closely and taken together, they provide striking details about the extent to which some of the most basic assumptions of even so-called experts about the defining characteristics of both the ethnic Mexican and larger pan-Latino populations may be deeply flawed. One of the most compelling of the surveys' cumulative findings is the extent to which the Latino population differs from that of the "non-Latino white" English-speaking population of the country. As one would expect, the surveys find important areas of difference that distinguish the United States' non-Hispanic white population from Latinos, especially with regard to aggregate socioeconomic indicators like education, income, job skill levels, linguistic preferences and proficiencies, fertility patterns, and specific cultural practices. With regard to general questions of religiosity and specific forms of religious practice, however, there are remarkable areas of overlap, similarity, and convergence that bind these otherwise disparate populations. For example, although nearly two-thirds of those Latinos surveyed identified themselves as Catholic, nearly one-third of Latino Catholics and 70 percent of those Latinos who are affiliated with other Christian denominations described themselves as being "born again" or "evangelical." Among ethnic Mexicans, nearly seven in ten identify as Catholic, but half of those identifying their affiliation in this way also self-identify as "spirit filled," born again, or evangelical. In addition, attendance at weekly or monthly services is comparable among Latinos and non-Latinos, similar proportions of both groups say that they pray on a daily basis, and increasing percentages of Latinos say that they read the Bible every week.[32]

Although more site- and group-specific research would be essential to any effort to explore fully the political and social implications of such general findings about populations that become more internally diverse and complicated with each passing day, the polls' results reveal some of the contradictory trends that have emerged in the pan-Latino population in recent years. On the one hand, the polls seem to indicate that religiosity continues to provide a foundation for a range of progressive civic activism among some Latinos, continuing a tradition that extends well back into the twentieth century. On the other hand, however, for all the recent hysteria about hemispheric migration and the revolutionary demographic and supposed cultural transformation of the United States, ethnic Mexicans and other Latinos often exhibit deeply conservative social tendencies and attitudes not unlike those displayed by other religious Americans. On issues such as (U.S.) patriotism, military service, same-sex marriage, and abortion and reproductive rights, there is general agreement across these ethnic categories.

This insight is just one more example of the ways in which the rapid demographic transformation of virtually every subpopulation of Latinos raises questions not only about commonly held stereotypes about Latinos but also about the continued viability of historical and social science paradigms in Chicano and interdisciplinary Latino studies scholarship that were framed in a very different historical era. Indeed, to cite a playful and provocative recent example, a team of political scientists studying the correlation between religious orientation and political behavior among Latinos came away posing the rhetorical question whether "Latinos are Republicans and just don't know it."[33]

Although most researchers (including this particular team) have concluded that it is premature to jump to such categorical conclusions at this time, the fact that such a question can be raised at all reflects the extent to which the ongoing demographic revolution in the United States challenges the old civil rights paradigm that sprang from the Chicano and other Latino political struggles of the 1960s.[34] In short, post-1970s Mexican immigrants (and their children) seem unlikely to follow political and social pathways similar to those established by previous generations of migrants and their offspring in the 1940s and 1950s.

To be sure, it is important to note that not all analysts accept the validity of recent polls on Latino religiosity. For example, some scholars have raised serious methodological questions about the Pew survey and similar polls. In addition, questions have been raised about whether the Pew survey's findings accurately reflect the direction of change in the Latino population—particularly with regard to the question of the degree of declension from Catholicism and the adoption of charismatic or evangelical practices, as well as the extent to which these shifts mark a movement toward conservative social positions. These questions are particularly salient because other polling data, such as those published in 2008 by researchers who reexamined the findings of UCLA's famous 1970 Mexican American Study Project, indicate that the children and grandchildren of the original study's sample population seem to be drifting away from formal religion over time.[35] The disparities underscore that such research findings remain suggestive rather than definitive, and that we need more detailed work on the linkages between Latino religiosity and political and social behavior.[36]

⮾ Religion and Gender

The study of women, gender, and gendered relations provides another broad arena of inquiry in which religious studies scholarship has helped expose old contradictions and provide new insights into the complex recent history of the Mexican-origin and pan-Latino populations. Of course, as Ramón Gutiérrez pointed out some years ago in his pathbreaking work on the history of transplanted Spanish Christian traditions, which focused on marriage and the family and the general evolution of structured social hierarchy on the Spanish colonial frontier, women have always held a central, if deeply ambiguous, position in Iberian and colonial Hispanic Christianity.[37] On the one hand, sexual anxiety about women and a deeply rooted tradition of what Robert Orsi has called "Catholic misogyny" led to their marginalization within the structure of the traditional patriarchal Hispanic family and to their exclusion from the Catholic clergy and hierarchy.[38] On the other hand, however, largely due to the veneration of the Virgin Mary and other female saints in that same pan-Hispanic Christian tradition, women have displayed a profound capacity for piety and moral agency. In addition, they have been teachers and transmitters of culture within families, and they often served as de facto anchors of faith in pan-Hispanic culture, whether as formal members of faith communities or, more commonly, as fervent keepers of various forms of devotional culture.

The Latino theologian Orlando Espín has argued that

> Latino popular Catholicism is foundationally dependent for its existence on the entire community, on the families within the community and, especially, on the older women within the families. The ministers of Latino Catholicism are primarily the older women. They are deemed wiser and usually in possession of greater personal and spiritual depth than men. Women are the center and pillars of the families, and Latino popular Catholicism is definitely woman-emphatic. . . . And so this explains . . . the Latino inclination to imagine and explain the divine and the religious through feminine symbols and categories, and through women-led rites.[39]

Exploration of gender tensions and contradictions in Latino religious life has proved fertile ground for revisionist historical analysis. Indeed, since the heyday of the Chicano and Latino civil rights movements, critical thinking by Latina women about the relationship of religion and religious institutions to gender inequality has often run parallel with the evolution of a feminist critique of sexism within their own communities and in the larger society. Thus, for example, early Chicana feminist critics such as Marta Cotera, Adelaida del Castillo, Sonya López, Gloria Anzaldúa, and Cherríe Moraga explicitly or implicitly implicated the patriarchal dimensions of Catholicism and the Christian legacy—particularly those elements that overlapped with and helped reinforce sexist ideologies and practices within Chicano and Mexicano culture—as key culprits in the general subordination of Chicanas and Mexicanas.[40] Coming to this conclusion was a decisive step in the ideological developments of the Chicano movement in that it marked a widening of the basis of feminist social critique from a primary or even exclusive focus on Chicana/"white" relationships to a much broader and more portentous stance that now encompasses analysis of the deeper sources of sexism, female subordination, violence against women, and deeply rooted, almost normative homophobia within Mexican, Mexican American, and pan-Latino cultures.[41] On the other hand, however, other Mexican American women, as well as many ethnic Mexican men, ultimately balked at rejecting their religious traditions and instead drew on the message of equality and emancipation in the Gospels as animating features of their evolving demands for social justice and democratization.[42]

Critical exploration in Chicano and Latino studies scholarship of the ambiguous and often tense relationship between religion and gender continues to the present day and has added nuance to the interpretation of women and structures of gender in Mexican American history. For example, in an important study of the establishment of Las Hermanas, a broad coalition of Chicana and Latina nuns and laywomen that emerged during the Chicano movement, Lara Medina provides insight into the complex ways in which the ethnic mobilizations of the 1960s and 1970s converged with Latinas' desire to reform the Catholic Church and to create a new sense among them of the possibility of achieving a more democratized institutional religion and greater freedom of religious practice.[43] Medina argues that Las Hermanas sought ways to achieve a "politicized spirituality" in the twenty years following the organization's founding. To this end it demanded reform from male church authorities and participated in a variety of social movements, including various local community-based initiatives, poor peoples' movements in Central and South America, and farmworkers' and other union struggles in the United States. Over time the work of Las Hermanas and other female religious activists also laid the foundations for the development of what has since become known as *mujerista* theology. Theorized as a synthesis of social and political activism, a religiously grounded system of feminist ethics, a positive gender-based sense of individual and communal ethnic identity, and perhaps most of all, a newly personalized relationship with God, mujerista theology evolved as a program designed to empower women within formal religious traditions and as a mechanism for developing meaningful religious praxis in Latinas' everyday lives. But again, although Medina emphasizes the politically progressive nature of much of Las Hermanas' activities over time, she is also attentive to the internal conflicts and disputes that sometimes erupted in the membership about how to reconcile militant protest activity with Christian injunctions of modesty and obedience, and how best to deal honestly and respectfully with the perennial hot-button issues of birth control, abortion, homosexuality, and women's ordination.[44]

Kristy Nabhan-Warren provides another important example of critical religious studies scholarship that revolves around a focused analysis of gender and gendered systems at the family and community levels. A close ethnographic study of how an apparition of the Virgin Mary affected grassroots religious belief and practices in a Mexican American barrio in Phoenix, Arizona, *The Virgin of El Barrio* (2005) deftly surveys the ways religion is lived and used in an ordinary Mexican American family.[45] Nabhan-Warren's work is another example of a scholarly intervention that explores the dynamics of cultural reproduction, adaptation, and change in the ethnic Mexican population. Although the specifics of her case study are somewhat unusual in that they deal with the impacts of a putatively supernatural or "miraculous" series of events, she provides a highly convincing account of how this particular case of a Marian visitation reveals volumes about the nature of contemporary Mexican American religious faith and practice. Religiously skeptical readers (including this author) can raise questions about how best to deal empirically with the purportedly supernatural phenomena described in the study, but the author presents a subtle and credible analysis of the complex ways in which this particular family in this one ethnic neighborhood creatively combined elements of both formal and folk religious practices, aspects of formal Catholicism and Protestant-tinged evangelism, and a flexible sense of community as a constantly morphing strategy of cultural adjustment, spiritual healing, and grassroots activism for social change and social justice.

Perhaps more important, Nabhan-Warren uses her analysis of the complex interaction of these elements to demonstrate the unexpected ways in which they combined to influence and change gender roles, identities, and relationships among men and women in this family and in the extended community in which it is embedded. In the process this study, like León's and other revisionist work, presents a compelling view of some of the ways in which ordinary Latinos use powerful strategies of religious experimentation and constant improvisation to help navigate challenges in different spheres of their daily lives.

∽ Catholic Transnationalism

Finally, for similar reasons, religious studies scholars have also begun to make important critical contributions to the expansion of transnational scholarship of the Western Hemisphere in a manner that further questions and complicates old conceptual models of Chicano/Mexicano historiography grounded in the stark "us versus them" Anglo/Mexican dichotomies of the 1960s and 1970s. Indeed, a growing number of scholars have begun to use the study of Catholicism, religiosity, and religious change over time and space as prime vectors through which to explore both the phenomenon of globalization and transnationalism and the social and cultural evolution of various communities of migrants that are embedded in transnational networks and circuits. This is, of course, a natural connection to make, especially in light of the inherently transnational nature of Roman Catholicism, the claims to universality that Catholicism and many other religions have professed historically, and the ways in which certain indigenous belief systems and communities transcend current national borders across the hemisphere. Moreover, transnational scholars' inherent interest in the complex interaction between the local and the global, the particular and the universal, and in new communication technologies that allow compression of time and space also makes the study of situated and global religion and religiosity essential to understanding the many ways in which transmigrants use religion to adjust to new surroundings and to carve out what the sociologist Peggy Levitt calls new "boundaries of belonging."[46]

Of course, the most obvious example of the reciprocal relationship among religion, globalization, transnationalism, and the constant creation and reformation of "community" in the Americas can be found in religious activism that historically has extended outward from the United States in the form of missionary work by religious groups like the Catholic Maryknolls and other Catholic missionaries, the Mormons, and various Protestant organizations. At the other end of the spectrum, there is also a long history—and an obvious recent intensification—of religiously based political activism within the United States on behalf of Latin American migrants, refugees, and political exiles. Indeed, through their support of the immigrants' rights movement, religious and quasi-religious organizations have played central roles in advocating for the rights and protection of ethnic Mexicans and other Latinos threatened by political persecution and economic exploitation. Gutiérrez, Matovina, Treviño, and other scholars have explored these dynamics over the period from the earliest faith-based activism in the nineteenth century to the activities of immigrant settlement houses at the turn of the twentieth. In addition to contemporary questions such as immigrants' rights, they have explored religious/political mobilizations around the complex issues raised by the Bracero Program and domestic farm labor between the mid-1940s and the 1980s and the defense of South and Central American political refugees in the 1970s and 1980s.[47]

A number of groundbreaking studies demonstrate the promise of using analysis of religion as an additional tool to illuminate transnational phenomena. León's synthetic overview of religion in the U.S.-Mexican–Latin American borderlands takes for granted that "religion in Chicano communities is a continuation and radical modification of religion in Mexico, and religion in Mexico is inevitably affected by religious developments north of the border: the transnational movements of people back and forth across the border necessarily result in the two mutually reinforcing one another."[48] His analysis of the specific ways in which religious ideas and practices move in both directions across the international frontier is particularly effective in his interpretive treatment of transnational Marian cults and the practice of *espiritualismo* rooted in and transposed between Mexico City, the capital of the Mexican Republic, and East Los Angeles, the capital of Mexican America. His work suggests that it is also reasonable to expect similar dynamics in the dense social networks that link hundreds of other communities in the Mexican hinterland with satellite communities throughout the United States. Like the research conducted by migration scholars Jorge Durand and Douglas Massey, León provides detailed portraits of how belief systems, ritual, and daily religious practice evolve in Mexico, get translated to serve specific local circumstances at immigrant-receiving sites in the United States, and then get modified and retranslated by migrants returning to local communities through long-established transnational social networks and circuits.[49]

A number of other studies follow similar paths. For example, in *Globalizing the Sacred* (2003), Manuel A. Vásquez and Marie Friedman Marquardt develop case studies of transnational religious congregations' use of the Internet, the spread of Pentecostal networks between the United States and El Salvador, and the expansion of religious broadcasting in Latin America. The authors present these cases as windows into the ways in which religion and religiosity help individuals involved in transnational networks establish alternative cartographies that actively and organically meld the material and the spiritual in peoples' lives. Like León, Vásquez and Marquardt demonstrate how religious faith and evolving practice allow members of transnational religious communities on both sides of the international frontier to collectively "deal with the existential predicaments [and dislocations] generated by globalization."[50] They argue that participation in such religious sodalities offers transmigrants and their families a strong new sense of community rooted not simply in nation, region, or locale but rather in faith and a shared sense of religious community. Such transnational institutions generated at the grassroots level enable congregants to cope with the bewildering changes unfolding around them both at "home" and "abroad." The authors suggest that these new forms of religious organization are likely to be durable not only because of their practical utility in meeting transmigrants' needs but also because they serve as ideal platforms for propagating various forms of religious belief and practice.

Not least, Vásquez and Marquardt propose that by exploring the process of religious experimentation, adaptation, and bricolage in situ (which, of course, in this case means at both ends of transnational networks and circuits), scholars can gain invaluable concrete knowledge about the praxis of religion and about other forms of transculturation—and about how religious subcultures "become the locus for multiple contestations . . . creative resistance, and appropriation."[51]

Other studies have pursued these themes to great effect. For example, as noted previously, Peggy Levitt uses a broadly comparative analysis of transnational religion to explore the evolution both of Latino religiosity and of other religious traditions. Insisting that the proliferation of different faiths in different contexts requires a profound reassessment of what is considered religiously normative in American society today, she builds a convincing argument regarding the dynamics of transnationalism and the changing nature of religion and religious practice in the United States.

Indeed, Levitt, the sociologist Robert C. Smith, and the anthropologist Lynn Stephen, among other scholars of transnationalism, are collectively building a compelling case that attention to the themes of religion and religiosity can help expose some of the most intimate social dynamics at work in the establishment and long-term functioning of transnational migration circuits and social networks in the United States and greater Latin America. Smith's study of the circuits linking local communities in Puebla, Mexico, with satellite communities in New York City and Stephen's analysis of migratory networks linking indigenous Zapotec and Mixtec regions of Oaxaca with California and the Pacific Northwest both focus extensively on the role religion and spirituality play in the migration process itself and in the dynamics of community maintenance at "home" and community formation "abroad." Both authors stress the ways in which religiosity serves as a stabilizing and organizing force for communities in almost constant flux, but they also offer keen observations about how the forces of globalization are simultaneously helping erode traditional forms of religion and religious life, thus encouraging further religious adaptation, creative syncretism, and/ or declension. For example, Stephen provides poignant glimpses of the erosion of deeply rooted local religious traditions and practices that has accompanied the scattering of *mixteco* populations over time. Whereas local communities had once been bound by powerful social ties rooted in local religious customs and observances and by an equally powerful tradition of communalism exemplified by a civil cargo system that required individuals to contribute their labor to local public works projects like road repair, irrigation and drainage improvement, and municipal construction, the physical absence over extended periods of people who have migrated has severely undermined these local practices. Smith makes similar observations about the effects of neoliberalism and migration on religious practices of sending communities in Puebla, particularly among the children of migrants who have to learn to adapt their own religious universes to the massive changes they experience in their travels between rural Mexico and New York City.[52]

Given the in-depth glimpses of the dynamics of cultural change provided by a sharp focus on religiosity in these excellent, critically acclaimed studies, it seems clear that explorations of the implications of transnational religion will become an even more important research trend among Chicano and Latino studies scholars in the years to come.

Recent historical and social science scholarship on Chicano/Mexicano religion and spirituality provides much food for thought about the general trajectory of both the past half century of Latino history and the effects these historical trends might have on the future of what León wryly calls the "Mexican Americas." Like the work of visionary and often controversial Latino public intellectuals and cultural critics such as Coco Fusco, Guillermo Gómez-Peña, Richard Rodríguez, Ilan Stavans, David Hayes-Bautista, Rubén Martínez, and others, revisionist religious studies scholars' meditations on the function of ethnic Mexican faith and spirituality as fundamental components of cultural change and adaptation have added crucial new insights into the massive social transformations that have roiled U.S. society in the past fifty years.

Explicitly rejecting the constellation of negative stereotypes and equivalences about Latinos that have been central features of the ongoing nativist backlash against the recent immigrants' rights movement, critical religious studies scholars have joined other cultural critics in soberly analyzing and, to a certain extent, simultaneously celebrating the ongoing Latinization of society. In the process, they have helped open a door to comprehending and interpreting often starkly contradictory social and political phenomena in the resident ethnic Mexican and pan-Latino populations in ways that simply do not comport with common stereotypes about them.

I have alluded to some of the apparent similarities in the basis of actual religious belief and practice between Catholic and religious Latinos and religious non-Latinos in American life—and to the comparatively conservative political implications these behaviors might hold in the future. Other trends, such as the steadily rising rates of naturalization and voter registration and the enthusiastic participation of both Latino citizens and noncitizens in the armed forces of the United States, exist in juxtaposition to the persistence of radical political tendencies in other grassroots elements of the Chicano/Mexicano/ Latino population. This reality should also give pause to those who continue to cling to outdated stereotypes, and help place into proper context the history of ethnic Mexicans and other Latinos over the past half century.

Given the richness of the critical historical and contemporary Catholic and comparative religious studies scholarship produced by Broyles, Gutiérrez, León, Matovina, Medina, and Treviño, other Latino studies scholars may soon come to recognize the importance of this conceptual and analytical approach as a lens through which to view the transformed and continually evolving ethnic Mexican (and, by extension, pan-Latino) population of the United States. The ultimate point of the ongoing effervescence of Latino religious history and interdisciplinary religious scholarship is not to provide either a unified theory of ethnic Mexican Catholicism or pan-Latino religion and religiosity or some kind of nostalgic return to the idealized and narrowly imagined community propounded by activists at the height of the movement. In the end, the point of much of this work is to insist that serious attention must be paid to religious faith and practice as objects of social study and as another crucial cultural characteristic of an increasingly heterogeneous population while also staying attentive to the instrumental uses, both "good" and "bad," to which these cultural strategies are applied in various aspects of social and political life.

However, some caveats and cautions should also be raised about these recent trends. Although it is clear that the field of interdisciplinary religious studies has much to contribute to the ongoing evolution of Chicano, Mexicano, and pan-Latino historiography and contemporary analysis, interpreters need to stay attentive to some of the inherent pitfalls and problems that arise from engagement with religion and notions of the divine. To return to an example prominently featured in this chapter, even though León's work breaks new ground in exploring a number of vital historical and contemporary questions in Chicano and Mexican studies, there are places in *La Llorona's Children* where the argument stressing the emancipatory and socially salutary effects of multivalent Mexican religious belief and practices seems to teeter on the edge of both positivism and romanticism.

The tendency toward romanticization and hagiography has been even more pronounced in some studies that have extolled the religious underpinnings of the efforts of messianic leaders such as Cesar Chavez, Reies López

Tijerina, and other prominent icons of Chicano and pan-Latino history. It remains important to recognize the centrality of religion and religiosity in informing the work of such individuals, but until very recently there has been an unfortunate tendency simply to recount those dimensions of the story while ignoring or diminishing the importance of less attractive aspects of the lives and activities of these leaders.[53] Thus, although the religious underpinnings of the activities of such individuals clearly need to be taken into account, we need also to balance analysis of religion and religiosity with honest assessment of the ways in which people like Chavez, Tijerina, and others also often seemed to betray their stated religious and philosophical principles in their treatment of women, in their often autocratic leadership styles, and in the positions they took on people deemed "outside" the movements they led.[54]

The ultimate point here is not to cast aspersions either on these historical figures or on the interpreters who use religion and religiosity as a lens through which to analyze them. The intent is simply to reiterate a point Orsi and others have been making for some time: the key to employing religious studies perspectives in ethnography and social history is to treat the study of religion as cautiously and carefully as one would engage the similarly slippery terrain of the histories of aesthetics, sensibility, or mentalité. Beyond this, honest engagement with the role of religion in social history requires that the conscientious scholar have the discipline to grapple with those areas of belief and practice that cause discomfort, embarrassment, or even anger. The trick is to commit, as Orsi has put it, to "studying and thinking about despised religious idioms, practices that make us uncomfortable, unhappy, frightened—and not just to study them but to bring ourselves into close proximity to them, and not to resolve the discomfort they occasion by imposing a normative grid."[55]

This is obviously easier said than done. As the historian Richard White quipped in summing up the challenge ethnographers and social historians continue to face in their daily work: "We are trying to reach our subjects. They are usually not trying to reach us."[56] The insights of Orsi and White serve as a caution to current would-be interpreters of the ethnic Mexican and Latino past. As I have tried to suggest in this chapter, this involves a strong commitment not to ignore the ideological underpinnings of our framing of Chicano and Latino historiography in the face of evidence that old models of conceptualization may not hold. It also involves making an equally strong commitment not to romanticize folk beliefs and practices because they appear in context to be examples either of everyday forms of resistance or more concerted forms of the subversion of power as constituted.

ᴄᴏ CHAPTER 6

The Catholic Moment in American Social Thought

WILFRED M. McCLAY

It is a cliché by now to say that one of the central preoccupations of American historiography in the past several decades has been the effort to be more inclusive of strands and elements of our history that have normally been pushed to the margins, but its being a cliché does not make it any less true. Part of the challenge is to decide just how much inclusion is right and just. Inclusion can come in the form of copious sidebars, inset panels, appendixes, and other marginalia and add-ons that augment the basic story without quite entering into it decisively, or it can have a more integral character that may alter the gravamen and texture of the central narrative. The Catholic element in the American story deserves far more of the latter kind of inclusion.

Perhaps one way to begin such inclusion would be by recovering a more vivid sense of the pervasive presence and influence of anti-Catholicism over the course of American history. It is startling to see how completely this theme has become submerged—a triumph for social harmony perhaps, but a defeat for historical memory. Such triumphs and defeats may serve larger goods than the professional training of historians allows us to admit. But there is no theme I find more difficult to make plausible to my students, even in teaching in the heavily Protestant South, so greatly has the situation changed since even fifty years ago. They find it impossible to comprehend the centrality of anti-Catholicism in early America or the nineteenth-century

United States; and although they are only slightly surprised to encounter frequent diatribes against "popery" in the sermons of New England Puritans, they are astonished to discover—whether in John Adams's declaration that "a free government and the Roman Catholick religion can never exist together in any nation or Country" or Thomas Jefferson's countless salvos against "monkish ignorance and superstition" and the oppressions endured by "priest-ridden peoples"—that the American founders and framers shared such negative sentiments.[1] If one thinks of the Adams-Jefferson correspondence as one of our richest and most indicative early dialogues about the meaning of the American experiment, then one needs to note that whatever the differences separating these two giants, they were in solid and unwavering accord about the evils of Roman Catholicism.

But that easy consensus does not close the question of influence, for there is nothing more formative, particularly in matters political, than a settled antagonism. Indeed, every powerful system of ideas is formed, in part, out of fear—as a mental line of defense against some perceived menace or mortal threat. Plato's fear of democracy, Hobbes's fear of anarchy, Tocqueville's fear of the tyranny of the majority, Hayek's fear of centralized economic control: all these examples point to the enduring importance of the negative reference group in the formation of systematic ideas.[2] Similarly, ancient fears about Catholicism lie at the origins and foundations of Protestantism, even if they are buried deeply or transmuted into such neighborly and sympathetic forms as to be unrecognizable.

These deep influences manifested themselves in various ways. It was not merely the alien quality of Catholicism but its status as Protestantism's opposite number, as the *summum malum* against which Protestants had defined themselves, that helped shape the peculiarly fraught character of much nineteenth-century U.S. immigration and gave the resultant nativism a moralistic edge of self-indictment, as if acquiescence in social change was also an act of religious betrayal. In other words, the Protestant-Catholic dynamic should be seen as something irreducibly different from, even if it is often conflated with, the larger array of ethnic, religious, racial, and national rivalries. Or consider Philip Hamburger's brilliant account of the evolution of the doctrine of separation of church and state, a story that, in his telling, is very far from being a linear deduction from the First Amendment but instead had a great deal to do with powerful cultural assumptions about the unfitness of Roman Catholicism for a leading role in U.S. public life and the strategies whereby the Catholic influence could be contained—an account of things without which the peculiar vehemence of controversies over Bible reading and prayer in public schools or public support for parochial schools is almost impossible to understand.[3] These examples suggest how the Catholic presence, even when it may have been operating unseen, has been an essential part of the narrative, in just the way in which an unseen gravitational field may determine the course of a visible planet.

Let me be clear that I am not advocating the systematic exhumation of old bones in order to construct a fresh victimization narrative. American historiography has enough of them already. Rather, I am arguing that the Protestant-Catholic relationship in American history, and particularly in American intellectual history, is best characterized not in terms of a Hartzian "fragment society," in which Protestantism was left free to develop apart from its Catholic/feudal/premodern antecedents, but as a kind of reciprocating engine in which the movement of one part is registered in the other.[4] That relationship has not remained static or unchanging, let alone invisible, and it seems to have come to an unprecedented juncture, a "moment" of both great opportunity and considerable peril. In selecting my title and using the word "moment" in it, I meant that word to evoke two well-known predecessors while serving as the carrier of yet a third significant meaning.

∞ Seizing the "Moment"

One of these predecessors is Richard John Neuhaus's influential book *The Catholic Moment*, published in 1987, just as Neuhaus was about to shift his religious affiliation from Lutheranism to Catholicism. "The Catholic moment" whose coming he was proclaiming represented the juncture in time "in which the Roman Catholic Church in the United States assumes its rightful role in the culture-forming task of constructing a religiously informed public philosophy for the American experiment in ordered liberty."[5] This rise to leadership did not take place in a vacuum; it was also a reflection of the steep decline of mainline Protestantism's cultural prestige and moral authority, and it certainly reflected the conviction that if Christianity was to have much of a future in the United States and the world and possess the institutional strength to stand up to its antagonists, it would have to derive leadership from the Catholic Church, which seemed to Neuhaus to be the sole remaining expression of Western Christianity that had the organizational strength and theological clarity to be equal to the task.

But this was not the only sense of "moment" that I had in mind. Less obviously, I was thinking how the term is used in J. G. A. Pocock's *Machiavellian Moment* (1975), a very different kind of book that employs the word "moment" especially to describe the point in the life of a republic when it becomes acutely self-conscious of its fragility and its liability to corruption and decay through the ravages of time.[6] Of course, the church is not a republic, but the dynamic Pocock examines is applicable to any institutional or organizational structure and any process of growth or decline. What Pocock describes is a sense of mortality, of struggle against time itself. This sense of "moment" is momentous in an entirely different way because it suggests that something large may be at stake and may even be endangered by the very ascent to cultural leadership that Neuhaus's "moment" described so enthusiastically.

There is also a third meaning of "moment" that I had in mind, drawn from physics, and I hope that it is not too recondite or gratuitous to be helpful. This additional sense of "moment" refers to a force applied from a distance, as with a simple machine like a lever. The image is worth pondering, I think, because of the elemental principle of physics that it illustrates. In such a machine the amount of force that is generated is directly proportional to the distance from the axial point. If you are using a board and a properly situated fulcrum to lift some heavy object, you will have greater success if you use a longer board, held farther away from the object, than you will with a short board held close to the object. The force that you can bring to bear grows with the distance, increasing your "mechanical advantage." I find in this third sense of "moment" a powerful way of thinking about how the subject of Catholic social thought can open new windows and offer fresh insights and illuminations for students of even the most familiar subjects in the American intellectual mainstream. The image suggests not only that this Catholic social thought might be possessed of significant moving force but also that it possesses such force precisely because it operates at a significant distance from the objects it ultimately would move.

In our own time, insights garnered from Catholic social thought have emerged, or are on the verge of emerging, as a force to be reckoned with as never before in the mainstream of American social thought. In other words, they have new and growing leveraging power. But they may lose the intellectual and spiritual equivalent of mechanical advantage—the fullest possible turning force—if they fail to base themselves at a sufficient distance from the objects they would move. They must be moving according to principles that are genuinely different from what the culture at large offers and operates under.

In saying this, I am in part giving expression to the central paradox of any robust pluralist social theory: a complex modern society is enlivened and enriched precisely by the sharp distinctness and vivid differentiation of its parts, and the many powerful cultural and political trends in the direction of assimilation and homogeneity, while perfectly natural and even inevitable, not to mention desirable for the sake of social harmony, also entail the risk of a loss of turning force. The powerful solvent of American culture is a central theme in the great American drama of immigration; there is no escaping that fact. But there is no element in recent American Catholic history that carries more irony, even pathos, than the myriad ways in which Catholics' social "success" has come at the expense of Catholic identity. The election of a Catholic president takes on an entirely different meaning if one believes that the noun was achieved entirely at the expense of the adjective. And it would be tragically mistaken for American Catholics to jettison an alternative vocabulary and alternative intellectual tradition by which some of the least attractive and most problematic features of American life—such as its near-maniacal commitment to a code of moral individualism—can be comprehensively critiqued, and alternative ways of imagining human affairs can be propounded. Such forfeiture will be not only a tragedy for Catholics but also an equal and opposite tragedy for the Protestantism-formed mainstream. That is precisely how the reciprocating engine of American culture works or can be brought to work.

Hence the general importance of attending to this important opportunity for a "Catholic moment" in American social thought, which has arisen simply because room has been made for it by the increasingly problematic character of the standard narrative against which it has always played the foil. That development now needs to be explored more fully.

There are several different ways in which one could identify the emergence of "Catholic social thought" as a player in mainstream American moral and political discourse. One of the strangest and most unexpected paths—and for that very reason one of the most indicative—has come through the words of Michael J. Gerson, longtime chief speechwriter for George W. Bush, both as governor of Texas and as president. A former senior editor at *U.S. News and World Report*, Gerson was a graduate of überevangelical Wheaton College in Illinois and a thoroughgoing evangelical Protestant working for a vocally and visibly conservative evangelical Protestant governor and then president.

Gerson seems not to have been tempted to conversion, but in interviews, speeches, op-ed columns, and finally in a book, he consistently identified Catholic social thought as the central influence on his own thinking on matters of political and social organization and the moral demands of politics. What he specifically had in mind were the twin principles of solidarity and subsidiarity, which for him entailed "a rejection of libertarian and traditional anti-government ideology" in favor of a conservatism of "the common good, influenced by Catholic social thought." He committed himself to taking "the principles of solidarity with the poor and the weak seriously, both in issues of poverty and race, and pro-life issues," but he also took "the principle of limited government seriously, trying to both respect and strengthen mediating institutions as a primary goal of policy."[7]

Gerson went on to explain the reasons for his embrace of Catholic social thought:

> I am not a Catholic, for a variety of theological reasons. But I recognize that my own theological tradition, just emerging from decades of cultural isolation and anti-intellectualism, has not developed a compelling philosophy of public engagement. The Catholic Church, after a history of suspicion toward democracy, has become its most insightful defender in the modern world— and its most courageous defender, given the Cold War leadership of Pope John Paul II. Catholic teaching on these issues does not require assent to Catholic theological distinctives; it summarizes the best of the Christian tradition, and is addressed to all people of goodwill.[8]

In another interview Gerson elaborated further:

> But there are so many evangelicals like me who went to Capitol Hill and were casting around for a construct to explain what it means to be a person of conscience in politics, and [we] came to John Paul II and the tradition of Roman Catholic social thought.[9]

Gerson's statements reflect the uncomplicated desire of someone of his religious background and political affiliations to identify himself publicly with a body of work (much of which was already articulated and in place) that anyone in his position would have shunned or even sprinted away from as recently as thirty years earlier. This fact, along with the fact that Gerson suffered not the slightest opprobrium from his evangelical confreres, is an indication that something going under the name of "Catholic social thought" had achieved a certain general public legitimacy.

Why, one wonders, did this "arrival" occur at this time and in this way? Surely some part of it was adventitious, even wildly counterintuitive. But Gerson's personal explanation also suggests a larger and more general one. As a morally serious Christian who found himself in the maelstrom of Washington politics, Gerson naturally first reached back into his evangelical heritage, hoping to find there resources sufficient unto the day. But although he found a great deal of wisdom about dynamics of personal salvation and the cultivation of individual piety, he found little or nothing that could prepare him to think systematically as a Christian about the large issues of public policy that he faced as a high-ranking White House official. Nor was there any sure guidance on how one might link those issues together in a comprehensive moral vision that was grounded in a Christian understanding of the human person.

Although Gerson's dilemma reflected the particular difficulties of an American evangelical, I argue that it also reflected something more pervasive. It offered an indication of the extent to which the ideals that constituted the standard narrative shape of American intellectual history in general, and the traditions of American social thought in particular, were losing their commanding force and buckling under their own contradictions and incapacities. Such a crisis, which had been long but steady in coming, provided a perfect opening for something dramatically different.

∞ The Self-Governing Protestant Individual

During the heyday of the American studies movement in the years after World War II, when the larger meaning of "America" was (as it is becoming once again today) a vital and hotly debated topic, it was still possible for serious thinkers to regard the American nation as the lengthened shadow of certain Protestant and Enlightenment ideas, often occurring in amalgamated form. Nineteenth-century American history was, in this view, a "progressive" story of a New Zion set down in the virgin wilderness, a fresh beginning for the human race that would follow its manifest destiny westward toward the earthly realization of God's kingdom. The narrative of American social thought, like that of American intellectual history, secularized this story but did not alter its fundamental shape. The American tradition was a liberal one, leading consistently in the direction of ever more fully realized and more autonomous individuals.[10]

As for the notion that Catholic ideas or thinkers might have contributed anything essential to the nation's meaning—well, that seemed too far-fetched even to require refutation. As John Ibson wittily expressed it, students of American life saw little reason to "explore the possibility that for some nineteenth-century Americans the Virgin Mary was of more consequence than the Virgin Land."[11] Even a brilliantly eccentric figure like Henry Adams, who seemed to defy that pattern, in fact merely confirmed it, for it was not the real church in real time (or, for that matter, the real Virgin) that he loved but an idealized medieval Catholicism, chiefly designed to function as an opposite number to a modern world he had come to loathe and fear.[12]

But Adams provides a clue regarding the complex operation and direction of the reciprocating machine. His liking for the twelfth-century cathedrals of France did nothing to warm his view of the nineteenth-century Boston Irish Catholics whom he described with such subtle disdain in *The Education of Henry Adams*, and there may have been something deliberately ludicrous about his halfhearted efforts to reduce human history to diagrammatic propositions in physics, as if he were trying to make modernity look even worse than it was. But his dissent echoed a theme that had far more cogency. As Catholic immigrant groups were enduring the wrenching process of modernization and Americanization, those among the native-born who were already modernized and Americanized found themselves moving in the opposite direction, badly needing some of the very things that immigrant Catholics were in danger of abandoning in their quest for assimilation.

The native-born dissenters like Adams were perhaps, whether they knew it or not, also affected by the lingering presence of preliberal social ideals that had once been far more salient in American life. Political scientist Barry Alan Shain's book *The Myth of American Individualism* argues that it was not liberalism but a very constrained form of communitarian Reformed Protestantism that best represented the dominant social and political outlook of eighteenth-century America.[13] More generally, communitarian critics of rights-based liberalism argue that until the twentieth century America's public philosophy was largely based on the "republican" assumption that the polity had a formative, prescriptive, "soulcraft" function to perform in matters of the economy, the family, church-state relations, personal morality, free speech, constitutional law, privacy, productive labor, and consumption.[14] That assumption has been so completely undone by the hegemony of individualistic rights-based liberalism of our own day that we have forgotten that it was ever there.

But it is the expansive, mid-nineteenth-century voices of men such as Ralph Waldo Emerson and Walt Whitman, romantic American nationalists and prophets of the unconstrained self, that have had the better end of the debate, sounding the liberatory yawp that has resounded over the rooftops and resonated through the streets of the American imagination even to the present day. It was Emerson who declared famously that a society is a "conspiracy against the manhood of every one of its members," and that "nothing is at last sacred but the integrity of your own mind."[15] And it was Whitman who declared that "the Great Idea" was "the idea of perfect and free individuals," and that "nothing, not God, is greater to one than one's-self is."[16] Although both men lived long enough to become deeply disillusioned by the crass economic opportunism and material acquisitiveness that took hold of American society in the post–Civil War years, one could hardly deny that such driving, self-interested ambition was a logical corollary to the spirit of unrestrained self-development. So, too, was the unforgettable image of Mark Twain's Huckleberry Finn, the seminoble, semisavage boy "lighting out for the territory" rather than face any more of the pinched and morally questionable rigors of "sivilization."

Nor should one imagine that such an outlook is restricted to freewheeling secular intellectuals. Instead, it reflected the evangelical Protestant emphasis on the ultimate value of the self-governing individual. Nineteenth-century American reformers held up as a social ideal the freely choosing individual who was constrained (and thereby made genuinely free) by the disciplining influences of education, religion, and formative moral training. From the time of the founding up to the end of the nineteenth century, the ultimate goal of social reform was the creation of the optimal conditions for what historian Daniel Walker Howe calls "the construction of the self."[17] It was an era that still unabashedly extolled the "self-made" man, in which "self-improvement" was regarded as a moral imperative, and in which the concept of "individualism" was understood not as a synonym for narcissism or footloose irresponsibility but rather as a highly desirable condition—a condition, though, that could not be properly understood or sustained apart from the existence of an objective moral order. And it was not enough for those constraints to be applied externally, like so many fences and leashes. They needed to be completely internalized as well. The responsible democratic self would need the help of institutions—family, church, neighborhood, and polity—with an interest in character formation. But the goal was not to remain in a state of tutelage but to become transformed internally in the direction of self-sufficiency and thereby become autonomous or self-constrained.

The relationship between the self-governing polity and the self-governing soul appears again and again—for example, in the thought of public-education pioneer Horace Mann, who saw the role of education as that of implanting the tools of self-regulation so that naturally anarchic individuals would be fit for the task of self-control and self-direction. The clergyman William Ellery Channing, whose 1838 lecture "Self-Culture" became a classic brief for the endless human capacity for self-improvement, argued that God had endowed the human race with the extraordinary power "of acting on, determining, and forming ourselves." As Howe has put it, the essence of the evangelical commitment was that it was "undertaken voluntarily, consciously, and responsibly, by the individual for himself or herself," by those "who have consciously decided to take charge of their own lives and identities," and who are willing to embrace a discipline that is "at one and the same time liberating and restrictive."[18]

This ideal of the self-governing individual stands behind many of the great reform movements of pre–Civil War America—temperance, women's rights, health faddism, and, of course, antislavery. That ideal is at the heart of the evangelical Protestant moral critique of slavery. Slavery was a systemic affront to the ideal of self-governance. It not only prevented slaves from being self-governing and fully realized individuals, but it also just as surely prevented masters from achieving that same status. It corrupted both and in the process had a corrupting effect on all who came into contact with them, a contention that the economically backward state of the South seem to prove. This critique went back as far as Thomas Jefferson's *Notes on the State of Virginia*, but it took a religious movement to provide the energy to act on it.

As the example of Huck Finn suggests, American thought and expression has always been rich in figures of heroic individuality and correspondingly poor in convincing and binding representations of community or social obligation. Whether one considers our accounts of the great colonial religious controversies, such as those involving rebels Roger Williams and Anne Hutchinson, or the moral fables embedded in our popular culture, such as that offered in the movies *One Flew over the Cuckoo's Nest* and *The Dead Poets Society*, or in protean idols of unfettered sexuality and perpetual self-invention like Madonna, we seem to have a boundless appetite for fables of personal liberation. And as the example of Madonna suggests, many American Catholics have embraced this mythic pattern with particular enthusiasm, having come to see their Catholic identity as a place of confinement rather than a place to stand.

If anything, the language of individual rights and the tendency to regard individual men and women as self-contained, contract-making, utility-maximizing, and values-creating actors who accept only those duties and obligations they elect to accept have grown steadily more powerful and pervasive in recent years. The recourse to individual rights, whether expressed as legal rights, voting rights, expressive rights, reproductive rights, sexual rights, membership rights, or consumer rights, remains the near-invincible trump card in most debates regarding public policy. The fundamental commitment to what Whitman called the "solitary self" has never been stronger.

ᑲThe Common Good?

Yet it is entirely conceivable that these seeming fixities of American culture are proving unsustainable and might yield to a greater concern with the common good. Both push and pull factors point in this direction. Economic distress in the wake of the financial crisis of 2008 and its aftershocks has given a rebuke to the insouciant presumption that economic growth is automatic and perpetual. The excitement surrounding Barack Obama's 2008 presidential campaign seemed to betoken a breakthrough in public sentiment, the sign of a widespread yearning for a more communitarian and less conflict-ridden approach to American public life. The ubiquity of the pronoun "we" in Obama's rhetorical appeals betokened a return—how enduringly is yet to be clear—of something that had been repressed.

Indeed, there have always been counterexamples and signs of contradiction amid the pervasive celebration of autonomous individuality. Tocqueville was not the only observer of American culture to see individualism as a potentially disastrous problem. The immense human suffering and dislocation wrought by nineteenth-century industrialization led to a rash of utopian novels, perhaps best exemplified by Edward Bellamy's fabulously best-selling 1888 fantasy *Looking Backward*, an effort to imagine a perfected postindustrial Boston, reconstituted as a socialist cooperative commonwealth in the year 2000. Far from celebrating individualism, Bellamy openly reviled it, proposing in its place a quasi-Christian "religion of solidarity" that would radically deemphasize the self and instead promote social bonds over individual liberty. The huge popularity of Bellamy's book—it was, second only to *Uncle Tom's Cabin*, the best-selling book of the nineteenth century and gave rise to innumerable "Bellamy clubs" across the nation, where the reform-minded gathered and dreamed together—showed how many Americans were hungry for such alternative ideas. Many of the most "progressive" forces of the day, whether one thinks of the cooperation-minded Knights of Labor, the theological advocates of a modernist "social gospel," or such Progressive reformers as Herbert Croly, Jane Addams, and John Dewey, admired and emulated Bellamy's spirit.[19]

The Progressive movement itself advanced, at least in some of its manifestations, a new corporate or collectivist ideal that sought to downplay individualism and instead to defend and preserve "the public interest" in the face of industrial capitalism's enormous and unprecedented coercive power. In some iterations this ideal had a distinctly communitarian tinge. In the hands of a sophisticated thinker like John Dewey and some of his followers, a case was made that the values of community and individuality, far from being in opposition, are mutually supporting and mutually sustaining, particularly in an age dominated by immense asymmetries of wealth and power and vast impersonal networks of interdependency. It was pointless, in their view, to attempt to restore the small-scale community of days past. The forces of economic and social modernity had rendered such community, with its personal bonds and face-to-face business transactions, obsolete. The task ahead was the creation of something new, which Dewey called "the Great Community," a systematically reconstituted social order that, it was hoped, would adapt the best features of the old community forms to the inexorable realities of the new economy and society.[20]

The new corporate/communitarian ideal made only limited headway. Although American life in the twentieth century steadily became more corporate, more organized, more standardized, and more interdependent, Americans' stubbornly individualistic self-conception did not follow suit. That is not to deny the cumulative effects of the deprivations of the Great Depression, the mildly socializing policies of the New Deal, and the solidarities induced by participation in World War II. But the rise of the totalitarian regimes of Europe, which served as the ultimate negative reference point by which American democracy would define itself, tended to cast doubt on the intentions, let alone the efficacy, of any system that would emphasize the group over the individual, however nuanced emphasis and sensible the reasoning.

The concerns generated thereby ramified in every imaginable direction, decisively shaping both the liberalism and the conservatism of the postwar years. Libertarians like Ludwig von Mises and Friedrich Hayek, not to mention the novelist and cult figure Ayn Rand, liberals like David Riesman, Lionel Trilling, and Reinhold Niebuhr, and even conservatives like Robert Nisbet and Russell Kirk all feared the Leviathan state, the corporate ideal, and the oppressive conformism of an intrusive and nannying culture. Dewey and other Progressives had argued consistently that individual men and women were morally improved by the society of others, but the postwar generation believed something closer to the opposite: moral man, immoral society. Accordingly, the social and political thought of postwar America revolved around a different ideal: the fierce protection of the autonomous self.

Riesman's *Lonely Crowd* warned against the conformism of "other-direction" in the American personality, and William Whyte's *Organization Man* deplored the predominance of a "social ethic" in America's white-collar classes.[21] Ayn Rand's wild pop-Nietzschean novels celebrated the autonomy of the individual creative genius and reviled the dullness of hoi polloi. Neo-Freudian psychology concerned itself with the problems of the ego, and such leading psychological theorists as C. G. Jung and Erik Erikson focused obsessively on the problem of individuation.

Even the emergence of a New Left movement in the early 1960s, which purported to rebel against the complacency of its liberal forebears, did little to alter this trend, since the movement's scattered communitarian tendencies were no match for its commitment to a radical, near-anarchic standard of behavioral and expressive liberty in speech, dress, sexuality, drug use, and other areas. As much, it provides a textbook illustration of the difficulty entailed in pursuing the politics of progressive reform while remaining programmatically suspicious of any and all sources of authority and value outside the self.

It also perhaps indicates the difficulty that arises when the "communitarian" is so easily confused with, conflated with, and subsumed under the "corporate." Corporatist remedies for radical individualism, in which the individual is absorbed into and given meaning by the larger organizational structure, may merely restate the problem of the disconnected person rather than resolve it since they substitute manufactured solidarities for those arising in uncoerced ways out of the "natural" solidarities of family, neighborhood, and church. Such mechanical vacillation between the unsatisfactory poles of individualism and corporatism is precisely the dilemma that Catholic social thought seemed tailored to address by introducing a whole different way of conceptualizing the problem, grounding it ultimately in a different way of affirming the individual.

These difficulties represented, and still represent today, a serious obstacle not only to radical reform but also to the reform aspirations of both liberalism and conservatism in contemporary times, since each of these ideological camps contains within itself anarcho-libertarian elements that, although undeniably popular, work against the establishment and sustenance of any stable conception of the common good or the public interest. For conservatives, the obstacle stems from an ideological commitment to economic liberty; for liberals, it arises out of an equally rigid commitment to moral and expressive liberty. In crucial ways, both ideological camps have in common an unwillingness to accept the need for an authority, a tradition, or an institutional nexus that is capable of superseding individual liberty in the name of social cohesion and the common good—precisely the values that Michael J. Gerson hoped to find in Catholic social thought.

∞The Catholic Moment

In the age of modernity and postmodernity the self has become the chief source of moral value. The term "self," which has had an amorphous history, has nevertheless evolved into something crucially different from the term "soul." It is a psychological term, largely stripped of metaphysical implications. The "self" is understood as the seat of personal identity, the source of mental cohesiveness and psychological integrity—the vanishing point, as it were, where all lines of psychological energy converge in the life of a "healthy" and "integrated" individual. The word "soul" maintains a link to the transcendent realm and is suggestive of an imperishable essence distinct from the bodily state. But the "self" is immanent, secular, worldly, transitory, adaptive, and pragmatic. "Soul" is a word that rarely crosses the lips of modern thinkers unless they employ it in a deliberately rhetorical or fanciful way, as do the neo-Jungian advocates of "soul-making" or the authors of books proclaiming the "lost soul" of this or that wayward entity. "Souls" are judged by the vanished God of faith; "selves" by the all-too-present God of health. By way of compensation, though, there remains a lingering ambiguity about "self"—some residue of the romantic "authentic" self always lurking in the corners of psychotherapeutic discourse, promising a kind of God experience, although one that is free of creedal, dogmatic constraints. The "authentic" self may well be drawn toward "spirituality," but not toward conventional organized "religion."[22]

But we have come to a point where this reliance on the self is clearly unsustainable. Absent an objective moral order on whose existence solid mid-Victorians could still rely, the self soon becomes unable to generate the solidarities necessary for large and sustained sacrifices and commitments or to provide nonarbitrary justifications for the fundamental building blocks of the social order. In the end, the freestanding self simply cannot bear the weight placed on it by modern life; it flies apart into a hundred pieces.

René Descartes inaugurated modernity with the assumption that the "I" is the most fundamental building block in our apprehension of reality, the unitary still point at the center of a moving world. Now it appears that the self, far from being foundational, is elusive and variable. The postmodern self is not a unitary thing but an ever-shifting ensemble of social roles—a disorderly venue in which the healthy ego functions less as a commander in chief than as a ringmaster.

The "disappearance of the subject" may have been a great publishing opportunity for academics, but it has been a calamity for liberalism, which relies on the objective reality of the world, the givenness of the individual person, and the possibility of genuinely voluntary, uncoerced action as the basis of everything else it deduces and proposes. Yet it is precisely at this point of crisis, in the breakdown of the axiomatic principles of the liberal individualist order, that Catholic social teaching finds its signal opportunity—its moment.

The road to a point where the church could take advantage of that opportunity was long and winding, however. Roman Catholicism first had to overcome the Protestant disposition to see it as antithetical to American democracy. The success of Paul Blanshard's *American Freedom and Catholic Power* (1949), lauded by many of the lions of American progressive thought, was indicative of the entrenched force of that resistance.[23]

The pivotal figure in the Catholic response was Father John Courtney Murray, SJ, whose *We Hold These Truths* (1960), although made up of previously published material, was published in part as a rejoinder to Blanshard.[24] Murray battled both entrenched Protestant prejudices and his own church hierarchy to produce an interpretation of the relationship between Catholicism and American democracy that seemed to reconcile the two by arguing for the compatibility of American political institutions with the Catholic understanding of the human person and society. Murray's argument succeeded to the point that it decisively influenced church doctrine regarding religious liberty, but the ultimate meaning of that success proved ambiguous. Was Murray merely engaged in an elaborate exercise to justify the ways of Catholics to Protestants, and vice versa, while fudging crucial theological differences for the sake of harmony and social progress? Or did his work represent a genuine breakthrough in the discovery or creation of genuine common ground?

It would require a monumental misreading of Murray to attribute to him anything like a full-scale capitulation to contemporary American political and cultural life. On the contrary, as Kenneth Grasso points out, Murray was searingly critical of midcentury American culture, declaring it to be "the quintessence of all that is decadent in the culture of the Western Christian world."[25] Murray argued for a compatibility between Catholicism and American democracy, but not an identity of premises or goals. His approval of the American founders was always guarded: their philosophy was "good" but "not good enough" because its reliance on "the rationalism, voluntarism, secularism, and individualism of 18th-century England and America" separated it from the more ancient sources of the liberal tradition, the true sources of "individual dignity and liberty," and thus rendered it unsustainable in the long run.[26] Sources even deeper and older than the founders would be needed to provide the means to sustain the American democratic experiment.

In other words, Murray's Catholicism came first. Rather than trim Catholicism's sails to fit American democratic sensibilities, he argued for the possibility that one could affirm American democratic institutions on a basis entirely faithful to the Catholic distinctives—one that might constitute a deeper and more satisfactory basis for that affirmation and aim not to destroy the founders' work but to fulfill it by addressing its inadequacies.

Because *We Hold These Truths* appeared at roughly the same time as the election of John F. Kennedy as the first Catholic president of the United States, it is perhaps irresistible to connect the two events, but they may be more useful as a point of contrast. Kennedy's famous speech to the Greater Houston Ministerial Association on September 12, 1960, in which he attempted to reassure nervous Protestants that he would not take political instruction from the pope, is notable for many reasons, but certainly its most striking feature is the near-total extent to which his outlook conformed to the strict-separationist doctrines of the Southern Baptists to whom he was speaking. This way for Catholicism to move into the mainstream is much more open to the charge of accommodation than the one Murray proposed. Indeed, after the work on pluralism and religious liberty done by Murray, and after the Second Vatican Council had settled fully into the life of the church, the path seemed more open than ever before to brisk intellectual commerce. The reciprocating engine of Protestant-Catholic relations had entered a new phrase of activity.

And not a moment too soon, because mainline Protestant thought seemed unable to offer fresh and compelling ideas about the sources of human solidarity other than identification with the causes of secular politics. The vacuum created thereby was tailor-made for the pontificate of John Paul II, which saw itself not as reversing modernity but as "saving modernity from itself."[27] The result was the self-conscious emergence into wider public view of a century's worth of the church's social teaching, running from *Rerum Novarum* in 1891 to *Centesimus Annus* in 1991, a remarkably coherent body of moral reflection that, although it had emerged piecemeal, had addressed itself with remarkable cogency to "the signs of the times" in industrial and postindustrial society.

The basic tenets of Catholic social thought have been summarized variously, and no single inventory is regarded as definitive. But these tenets include such principles as respect for the dignity of the human person, the dignity of work, the dignity of community life grounded in respect for the common good, the dignity of the poor, the call to social justice and peace-making and solidarity with others, and the call to care for the created order. All these desiderata and more are grounded in an anthropology that insists on a deeply communitarian understanding of the human person and on the primacy of the natural family as the "first and fundamental structure," or "the first and essential cell of human society."[28]

It is hard to overestimate the extent to which this understanding of the human person challenged the deepest assumptions of the general American culture. But does Catholic social thought really have the capacity to introduce something genuinely new and different into the national bloodstream? Or will mainstream American culture prove stronger, causing the inherent tensions within Catholic social thought to break down along the lines of typical preexisting American political divisions, for example, between conservatives who stress the constraints inherent in a demanding personal (and particularly sexual) morality, on the one hand, and progressives who emphasize the constraints imposed by a serious and thoroughgoing pursuit of economic and social justice, on the other? Can Catholic social thought realign American politics? Or has it, as some critics argue, already been changed and neutralized by America, turned into nothing more than a prop for the status quo or a slogan invoked by speechwriters and politicians? Can it be invoked piecemeal as conditions warrant? Or is its seamlessness and its grounding in Catholic anthropology part and parcel of whatever authority it enjoys, so that one must either accept the whole fabric or utterly violate the fabric's integrity by tearing it in accord with one's own predilections?

The difficulties expressed here can be seen vividly in the anomalous relationship of American Catholics to the hardest divisions operating in American politics—divisions that Catholic social teaching tends to cut across, which is why Catholic voters find themselves divided between the two major political parties. The fact that many of the leading figures in current American political life, whether in Congress or in the Supreme Court, are self-identified Catholics only makes the problem more acute and inescapable. Within the structure of Catholic social teaching, both the absolute dignity of every human life, which necessitates the prohibition of abortion, and the pursuit of the common good, which encourages the vigorous use of government to pursue common ends, are principles that hold an honored place. Yet American political issues are so understood and debates are so structured that few Catholic politicians feel able to give the same weight to both imperatives. In the various congressional debates over President Obama's health-care proposals in the fall of 2009, the vexing question of abortion coverage within a "public option" again and again brought this dilemma to a head for

Catholic politicians, and particularly Democratic ones. The protection of innocent life is a Catholic imperative, but so too is the widest possible provision for the common good.

Like it or not, the issues are framed in a way that makes it very difficult for Catholic politicians on either side to be entirely obedient to what Max Weber would call "an ethic of conviction." The dilemma is general and deeply felt, and its persistence is a sign of how difficult it may be for nonselective, nonpiecemeal, and therefore truly integral and truly revolutionary application of Catholic social thought to American politics to occur. Indeed, the persistence of the dilemma may be a sign that despite all efforts to the contrary, everything distinctive and challenging about Roman Catholicism is destined either to be hopelessly marginalized or to be fudged, cornercut, reinterpreted, and finally dissolved by and absorbed into the great solvent of mainstream American culture.

In Charles E. Curran's important account of Catholic social teaching from 1891 to 2002, the author concludes by asserting that "Catholic social teaching has little or no visibility in the wider philosophical or political science discussions and writings in the United States."[29] So much for Catholic moments in American social and political thought! Curran goes on to argue that (a) the handful of books that have dealt in a sophisticated and thoughtful way with Catholic social teaching and its relationship to liberalism are all written by Catholics, and (b) the most influential secular liberal thinkers, such as John Rawls, have had no serious interest in the work of Catholic thinkers, such as Murray.

Curran's gloomy outlook seems warranted, although he admits that communitarians like Robert Bellah constitute an exception—a rather important and spacious exception, I should think. But it certainly jibes with my own experience as a mainline Protestant academic working in secular institutions, in which I have found that a favorable mention of Catholic social thought is often greeted in much the same manner as a favorable mention of astrology or phrenology or, more darkly, with the suspicion that what one is "really" talking about is the church's position on such litmus issues as abortion or same-sex marriage. The barrier between secular and nonsecular perspectives may be highest in the academy, far higher than it is in the rest of the world.

There is an element of insight behind these rather automatic reflexes. The more general interest in Catholic social teaching has come, perhaps not entirely coincidentally, at a moment when the teaching authority of the church is at a low ebb, and Catholics feel free to set aside church doctrine (particularly relating to the teachings of *Humanae Vitae* and other aspects of human sexuality: contraception, abortion, divorce, and homosexuality) whenever it pleases them to do so. It is hard to see how the genie of self-assertion can be summoned back into the bottle. Although we still occasionally see Catholic politicians being forced to wrestle painfully and publicly with the conflicts between their faith and their secular duties, no such wrestling seems to be required anymore for lay Catholics in the conduct of their private lives. Even the most conservative Catholics now seem to carry one or two asterisks in their back pockets, to be used as self-administered dispensations whenever the painful and difficult conditions of life lead them to choose heterodoxy as an uncategorical and provisional imperative.

To do so is, of course, a tacit commentary on those human frailties from which none of us is exempt. But it is also a commentary on the relative weakness of the church's teaching authority. It is an enormous paradox that as the fullness of the church's social-teaching message has waxed, the respectfulness and attentiveness of its audience has waned. When Catholic social teaching is proposed in general terms, emphasizing the dignity of the human person, the common good, subsidiarity, peacemaking, care for the poor, and the like, everyone applauds because it is so enormously attractive—more attractive, one might argue, than most of the secular alternatives on offer. When such teaching begins to be applied to concrete social, economic, and political issues, however, it quickly becomes the case that Catholics insist on making up their own minds no matter what the interpreters of Catholic social teaching have to say, and the seamless fabric is soon rendered into a thousand pieces.

Does this mean that we are seeing the Pocockian version of the Catholic moment, meaning that to the extent to which Catholicism has been permitted to rise to a kind of national prominence, even political predominance, it has done so at the expense of itself and is now confronted with an existential threat to its continued existence as a robust and meaningful source of moral direction for Catholics and for the nation? Has the frankly accommodationist example of John F. Kennedy proved more enduringly influential than the careful reasonings of John Courtney Murray, which sought to bring Catholicism and America into alignment without sacrificing the one to the other? And, to bring the question back to where I began, are we at a point where American Catholicism, in losing its grip on meaningful structures of authority, has also lost its principal mark of distinctiveness in relation to the individualistic American value system? Does the "mechanical advantage" of the Catholic difference—the "Catholic moment" in the third sense—still operate meaningfully in the authority-free conditions of present-day American Catholicism? And if not, can it be restored in ways that do not forfeit the gains that Catholics have made in American culture and on terms that will make their contribution to that culture even more meaningful than they are today?

◌Implications for American Historians and American History

One need not accept all of the Catholic Church's claims for itself to recognize that the steady erosion of its independent authority cannot continue indefinitely; if the past is prologue, one must weigh the fact that the church has faced and survived many far more parlous moments in its incomparably long institutional history. Its resistance to change is, in the longer view, a source of resilience, a way of laying aside provisions for the day that no one now anticipates. Yet two hundred years ago no one could have anticipated that, as Murray recognized, the Enlightenment project on which the United States was founded would lose its élan, and deeper roots would have to be found to sustain the Republic.

In keeping with this awareness of Catholicism's resilience in U.S. and global history, one might consider the conclusion of Curran's aforementioned study, which respectfully cites the Protestant historian William Lee Miller's thoughts about previous and potential Catholic contribution to public life in America:

> Something like such a personalistic communitarianism is the necessary base for a true republic in the interdependent world of the third century of this nation's existence. And the Roman Catholic community is the most likely single source for it—the largest and intellectually and spiritually most potent institution that is the bearer of such ideas.[30]

If Miller is correct, then the first sense of "moment," Neuhaus's sense, is still operative. The time is still right, and the need remains unaddressed, especially in the world of ideas. But I think it important also to stress the other two senses of "moment." There is the real possibility that as Catholic social thought becomes more prominent, its integrated and radically cross-cutting character will be broken down into something that cannot stand for extrapolitical sources of value and orientation. Hence the importance of the third sense of "moment," the importance of resisting assimilation into the general ethos and of maintaining a distance—not a large and gaping distance, not a hostile or sectarian distance, but a principled and respectful distance—as the necessary condition of effectual influence.

There is, in fact, something quite American about this distancing. As Murray argued, one of the sources of proper Catholic loyalty to America flows from the fact that full membership in the American system does not, in the end, demand the sacrifice of one's more fundamental Catholic identity. This is, of course, the deepest principle animating the American conception of pluralism: the notion that being an American need not, and should not, take precedence over all other sources of personal and group identity. But, as I have tried to indicate, the Protestant-Catholic dyad—the reciprocating engine of American religious history, albeit one that has often been overlooked in the historiography—has a special role to play in American life, and moreover has proved to be far more formative of the American experience than anyone could have anticipated at the outset. The Protestant interest in Catholic social thought is only the latest iteration of this creative antagonism. There may be many more such surprises in the road ahead.

How would the more widespread recognition among American historians of an ongoing Catholic social sensibility, trailing the Protestant rise and decline like the tail of a comet, change the way in which we conceptualize the American past? Will we have to rewrite the textbooks in accordance with some new foundational insight? Or do we just further burden them with a whole new list of names, books, events, and concepts added on top of the others?

The problem is in some ways similar to the problem of incorporating women's history or any of a number of other histories of ignored or marginalized groups. And the answer in nearly all cases is the same: such efforts at integration will succeed if they bear in mind the fact that the new histories are best understood when they are placed in creative and constructive relationship with the old ones. The solution is neither simply deconstructive nor simply additive but instead involves the recognition of a dynamic element that had formerly been hidden or forgotten.

There is something irretrievably artificial about a history of women that prescinds from considering the fact that women have generally lived in proximity to men; and there is something gratuitous about a history of women that is simply tacked on to the standard accounts of male-dominated public life. Alas, it may not always be possible to do better than that. But where the subject matter and sources permit it—for example, in accounts of the marriage of John and Abigail Adams—the result is a clear advance in our historical understanding and an account of the past that is richer and, in a real sense, more accurate than one that treats the marital union as a fact of, literally, no account. Yet it is an accuracy that depends on the kinds of questions we wish to put to the past; and such questions would not have been of general interest two hundred years ago—certainly not to the extent they are today.

This model can be fruitfully applied to the Protestant-Catholic dyad, mutatis mutandis, if we think of it as a narrative of both mutual antagonism and mutual dependency. Such a narrative would be built on the knowledge that for most of American history the Catholic "other" lurked conspicuously, and not merely incidentally, in the imagination of leading Americans. It would be candid about the virtues and vices of both parties and would trace the flow of events whereby the "other" made its way to center stage. And it would treat the reversal of places, the crises of confidence, and other ironies and surprises that have been sketched in this chapter. Such a narrative would, in the end, lift American history out of its insular place and cause one to see the Protestant-Catholic dynamic in a fresh way, as a key element in the larger drama of American history—and, indeed, of Christian history and the history of the West. Compared with such a sweeping perspective, the Progressive-Protestant paradigm would seem small and pinched. Building such a narrative would no doubt require a rethinking of some of the familiar lines of twentieth-century American social, political, and religious history. But it just might be worth trying.

Conclusion: The Forgotten Americans?

R. Scott Appleby

On first blush it seems odd, at best, to refer to Roman Catholics as "forgotten" Americans. How could any student of the United States in the twentieth century have overlooked the nation's largest religious body, whose members constituted nearly one-quarter of the population? Catholics built powerful political machines in Chicago, Boston, and New York and wielded social, economic, and political influence in Philadelphia, Baltimore, New Orleans, San Francisco, Providence (Rhode Island), St. Paul (Minnesota), and many other American cities. By the century's end there were more Catholics serving in the U.S. Congress than members of any other denomination.[1] During the course of the century Irish American Catholics became the second most prosperous ethnoreligious minority after American Jews. Catholic Americans created the largest private school system in the nation (and in the world) and built a network of hospitals, orphanages, and charitable organizations; this vast social infrastructure provided essential services that eased the load of overburdened public institutions. To call Catholics "forgotten," "marginalized," or "overlooked" smacks of hubris and risks offending the millions of truly disadvantaged racial and ethnic minorities, women, and the working poor, all of whom suffered from the various forms of discrimination that accompanied second- or third-class social and economic status in the United States.

Yet one who scans the most popular history textbooks assigned in public schools and universities, as well as the "mainstream" historical research and monographs on which they are based, will see nary a reference to the distinctive presence and agency of Catholics as Catholics in the workforce and especially in labor unions, where they often accounted for sizable portions of the membership and a disproportionate percentage of union leadership.[2] Nor will one find plausible accounts in most of the otherwise-perceptive, fine-grained social histories, of how one-quarter of the population negotiated gender relations, raised children, thought about war and peace, navigated the marketplace, or imagined their place in the national myth of origins and ends.

The contributors to this volume include distinguished American historians of race, politics, social theory, labor, and gender who acknowledge in their respective chapters—confession being good even for the non-Catholic soul—that they have largely overlooked Catholic narratives in their previous work, to its detriment. Impressively, Thomas Sugrue, Lizabeth Cohen, Wilfred McClay, David Gutiérrez, and R. Marie Griffith evince more than a passing familiarity with at least some of the historiography produced by the relatively small and somewhat isolated group of historians of Catholicism in the United States, the majority of whom are Roman Catholic or from a Catholic background. By drawing critically and constructively on this body of scholarship as a resource for their own research and writing, the contributors to this volume have become inadvertent pioneers in the American Historical Association.

This is encouraging news for participants in the Cushwa Center's project, "Catholicism in Twentieth-Century America," which is dedicated to promoting Catholic remembering and to remembering Catholics, for it reflects a growing awareness that the omission of Catholics qua Catholics is not a minor lacuna but a gaping hole in the literature. Compensatory and integrative efforts to bridge what Griffith calls "the Catholic divide" seem crucial to the larger, ongoing disciplinary drive to weave from the available historical evidence a richer tapestry of the breathtakingly diverse sets of experiences, memories, practices, cultures, and societies that together constituted "twentieth-century America."[3]

∞ Comprehending "the Catholic Thing"

The authors of this volume indicate something of what has been lost in the previous failures to examine Catholics on their own terms. Doing so, I will argue, is not merely a matter of considering the impact of Catholics on twentieth-century politics, culture, and society—although, of course, charting the agency of historical actors is central to the historian's task—but also of striving to understand the relation between agency and the internal dynamics of Catholic thought, practice, belief, and behavior. The theologian Rosemary Haughton has referred to that "organic whole" as "the Catholic thing"—the capacious sacramental religious imagination that operates by analogy rather than linear logic and perceives virtually everything human (including the body and sexual love) as an occasion for a graced encounter with the divine mystery.[4]

In the opening chapter Robert Orsi, one of a handful of scholars of Catholic life whose work has gained a wide audience in the larger academy, maps major features of what might be called the alternative cosmos of Catholic Americans—their construal of American origins as a tale of sacralization of the land and its peoples through martyrdom, backbreaking labor, and piously endured poverty and oppression, all imagined as a recurring recapitulation of the salvific self-sacrifice of Christ; their deeply sacramental valorization of the world as it is, a world accepted in faith as an already-graced arena of divine mercy; and the inclination to interpret waves of nativist persecution and social exclusion as vindication of both their own sense of chosenness and their "church militant" pugnacity toward outsiders.

Orsi writes so engagingly and evocatively of this American Catholic sensibility that his body of work could be taken as an unhelpful move to exoticize a subculture whose "foreignness" was used to justify the very marginalization under scrutiny in this volume. But he deftly avoids that trap by illuminating the irony that Catholics' insistence on sustaining their own "strange" cosmos and accompanying religious imaginary was also the psychological and spiritual source of their equally ardent desire to become fully American and to be accepted as such. Noting that "the civic traditions [of U.S. Catholics] were American in their aspirations, whereas the sacred narrative sought to transform America into a Catholic reality," he argues that "it is the uneasy synthesis of the two in various patterns over time that constitutes American Catholic historical consciousness and civic motivation." Historians seeking to complicate their previous accounts of "the American character," the evolution of national identity and civic culture alongside burgeoning religious and cultural pluralism, or the social and psychological foundations of nationalism will find a resource-rich environment in U.S. Catholicism as it is being reconstructed by Orsi and others who, in explaining the behaviors and sensibilities of Catholics, rightly privilege their religious consciousness.

∞ Explaining Change over Time

Orsi, citing the French anthropologist and social theorist Bruno Latour, contends that the process of becoming modern requires "purifying" memory of the supernatural past—a particularly challenging requirement for Catholics, but one that many Irish, Italian, Polish, and other European-heritage U.S. Catholics seem to have achieved at some point during the course of the American Century. The timing and shape of that achievement varied, however, across and even within Catholic ethnic groups and subcultures, producing disparate consequences in the American social and political order.

In his closely reasoned chapter on what he sees as the flawed historiography of the 1960s, Thomas Sugrue tackles the daunting challenge of plotting change over time. He recruits Catholics as confirming evidence of his thesis that the conventional interpretation of the period as a moment of cultural revolution that seemingly came out of nowhere, stimulated almost exclusively by the convulsions of Vietnam, civil rights, the New Morality, and the other usual suspects, needs major revision in light of "the long process of social, cultural, and political change that remade the United States." Indeed, Catholics started forgetting their own past well before the "Me" decade. Like other Americans, they refashioned their sense of time and space to accommodate the rhythms of the modern white-collar workplace, and they learned to obey the imperatives of the bureaucratic state. Like other Americans, their experience of service in the U.S. armed forces during the world wars forged for them a bond with their countrymen and deepened their sense of national ownership, patriotism, and citizenship. And, as Sugrue points out, Catholics, too, were subject to the postwar ideological shifts in political consciousness, including the emergent antiliberalism that was partly a response to the perceived "socialism" of Franklin Roosevelt's New Deal legislation, the early phases of the civil rights movement, and the power of organized labor.

Yet Catholics exhibited striking differences within the general pattern of change. After World War II marriage across Catholic ethnic divides became commonplace, but interfaith or "mixed" marriages remained rare until the 1970s, when the numbers began to grow.[5] More significantly, the mode of public presence that Catholics had developed as an immigrant church, characterized by interest-group, ethnic-bloc politics lodged in the Democratic Party, remained the preference of the U.S. bishops, as well as the members of the rank and file whose allegiance they still commanded, until another revolution in sociopolitical mores occurred in the 1980s—the one inspired by President Reagan. While professing to be aloof from politics, bishops and other church leaders still occasionally used their perceived (and thus actual) political clout to seek aid for parochial schools, to resist permissive birth-control legislation, and to protect Catholic interests on social welfare and educational issues. Moreover, the immigrant style was reinvigorated in the 1970s and beyond with the arrival in the United States of hundreds of thousands of working-class and poor Latino Catholics.[6]

Similarly, Catholics lagged behind Protestants in treading paths that some worried might lead to "indifferentism," a code for secularization.[7] The GI Bill of 1944 is generally seen as a trigger of postwar assimilation for U.S. Catholics, who had not previously attended public universities in significant numbers; the subsequent migration from inner-city enclaves and ethnic parishes to ecumenical suburbia nudged the process along. Sugrue quotes the sociologist and priest Andrew Greeley, who in 1959 pronounced the suburban arrival of upwardly mobile Catholics "a profound social revolution."

So Catholics changed, but they did so at their own pace and in their own ways—not entirely distinct from the "mainstream" middle-class population, but not quite in step with it either. A dimension of the story to which Sugrue merely alludes is actually crucial in accounting for the "unmeltable" Catholic exceptions to the patterns of political reconfiguration he is exploring. The endurance of political patterns and affiliations from the immigrant era notwithstanding, it is true that Catholics were not exempt from the ideological restructuring of postwar American religion along roughly "liberal" and "conservative" lines, and eventually they, too, arrived at various places on the political spectrum alongside their respective Protestant and Jewish counterparts.[8] U.S. Catholics also began to adopt the opinions of the majority of Americans on controversial social issues to such a degree that by the 1970s it was difficult to differentiate their attitudes on the morality of artificial birth control, divorce, and premarital sex from those of most mainline Protestants. Yet the Catholic journey to this familiar American religious-communal experience of internal fragmentation—that is, to various and sometimes clashing political and social destinations—was sui generis. Understanding its dynamics seems crucial to grasping the subtle but consequential differences that continued to set Catholic teachers, politicians, health-care providers, college and university faculty and administrators, and social workers apart from their non-Catholic professional colleagues to the end of the century and beyond.

Those dynamics were driven by internal as well as external factors working in synergy. Sugrue acknowledges that Catholics of the 1960s experienced two "shocks to the system, one endogenous, the other exogenous." The first was the Second Vatican Council, "which launched a period of intense theological debate, a rethinking of the role of the church in the world, a reconceptualization of clerical authority, and a reconfiguration of rite, ritual, and devotion." But it is the second—"the impact of the political, social, and cultural changes in U.S. society writ large during the 1960s, which reinforced and compounded the tectonic shifts in everyday life, belief, and religious practice among Catholics"—that claims his attention in placing Catholics within the longer, pre- and post-sixties trajectory of political transformation.

Sugrue criticizes the account of the sixties provided by historians of American Catholicism for reinforcing the "exceptionalist" interpretation of the decade and for depicting Catholics and their church "as the objects of change, not the agents of change." These Catholic historians, he charges (correctly, in my opinion), focus too exclusively on the internal changes in Catholic belief and practice, an emphasis that "ignores the profound role that Catholics played in the reconfiguration of U.S. politics and society in the mid-twentieth century . . . and . . . downplays or overlooks the ways in which Catholics set the terms for debates about public policy that would remake the United States over the last third of the twentieth century." Sugrue's remedy is to list to the other extreme by privileging the external dynamics of Catholic political affiliation, policy decisions, and social behavior. But this solution obscures the important relationship between the contours of the Catholic religious imagination at a given moment and Catholics' sense of the world that they inhabit and their moral agency within it. To ignore the interplay between theology and politics, sacramental ecclesiology and public presence, is to overlook the roots of Catholic difference within similarity and thus to miss a key feature of twentieth-century American political history.

Lizabeth Cohen's chapter sketches a strategy for avoiding this particular pitfall of the attempt to integrate Catholics into the narratives of American history. That strategy depends on appreciating the symbiosis between the endogenous and the exogenous forces that were shaping Catholic sensibilities at midcentury. At the center of Cohen's project on the rebuilding of American cities after World War II stands Edward J. Logue, a pioneer of urban renewal who found it necessary to build an alliance with Boston's powerful Catholic Church and the archdiocese that governed it. Although Cohen does not aim to provide an Orsi-like immersion in the religious world of Cardinal Cushing, Monsignor Francis J. Lally, Mayor John Hynes, and other Catholic Bostonians who loom large in her study, she does explore the ecclesial, the institutional, and even something of the theological impact of the Second Vatican Council in shaping Catholic sensibilities, from the fiery resistance of antibusing lay Catholics who took the council's call to greater lay responsibility as a warrant for situational dissent from unpopular episcopal leadership, to the priests and bishops who saw urban renewal as an occasion for the embrace of the social justice apostolate and the acceptance of racial and religious diversity.

Cohen's delving into the depths of ecclesiastical politics, contested conciliar reforms, and lived theology—terrain previously uncharted by most non-Catholic historians—lends to her account of urban politics and conflictual social change an important explanatory dimension grounded in internal Catholic dynamics. In this regard her study of the postwar rebuilding of urban American environments may well provide a useful model for other first-time Catholic integrationists.

∽Whose Norms? Whose Values?

Incorporating Catholics faithfully, so to speak, is first to acknowledge that their attitudes, beliefs, and practices, especially the contrary or countercultural ones, should not be taken as merely odd or scandalous or trivial phenomena to be suppressed or explained away. It is not surprising, perhaps, that an American religious historian who has specialized in the study of women of faith, R. Marie Griffith, takes the conversation a step further in this direction by pushing back against the tendency to assume that the theories currently favored in the secular academy should constitute the default mode in analyzing and evaluating the beliefs and behaviors of Catholic (or other religious) women and men.

On matters of interpretation regarding gender, sex, sexuality, family, and women's agency, Griffith appreciates elements of the reigning academic orthodoxy, certainly, but she admits that her own scholarly projects and methodological approaches have more in common with those of certain Catholic scholars than with those of some of the more radical gender theorists whose main lines of analysis they reject. Griffith's chapter on rethinking aspects of the historiography of sex and gender draws on her research into the twentieth-century confrontations between Catholic moralists and liberal reformers Margaret Sanger, Alfred Kinsey, and the sex-education advocate Mary Steichen Calderone. In coming to terms with these widely divergent Catholic, Quaker, Protestant, liberal, and secular perspectives without giving short shrift to any side, Griffith concludes, strikingly, that "Catholic studies' usual occupation of a more traditional wing of gender scholarship makes fairly good sense for historians, if not necessarily for activists."

Implied in Griffith's reflections is the notion that historians are at their best when they try to inhabit the lives of, and develop a measure of empathy for, those historical figures they might find most disagreeable, misguided, or even repulsive. This is hardly a new or radical thought, but it becomes a formidable challenge when it is applied to the religious "other," to those antimoderns who stubbornly refused to forget their contrary, supernaturalist past and to join the liberal celebration of an easy universalism. Liberal, "enlightened," post–Vatican II Catholics are less of a problem, of course, at least to the extent to which they join the broad liberal consensus. The eminent intellectual historian David Hollinger ruefully admits as much:

> In the name of universal capacity for spiritual experience, religious ecumenists aimed to neutralize sectarian conflict through the claim that "we all believe in the same God," who turned out, of course, to be the God of liberal Protestantism.
>
> To resist the extravagant universalism discernible in the scientific, social-scientific, humanistic, religious, and political discourse of the generation represented by the Kinsey reports is to belong to the sprawling cohort I am here calling "we." We history-conscious members of the generation experiencing the end of the century—and of the millennium—realize that Kinsey's generation was far from the first to conflate the local with the universal, but the legacy of this mid-twentieth-century American generation presents a special challenge for us. Not only have our Kinseys and Willkies and Steichens been close at hand; their universalism was often directed against certain particularisms we still take to be evil.

These "still-troubling particularisms," Hollinger adds, "include . . . nationalist chauvinism, religious bigotry and obscurantism, and a host of provincial taboos."[9]

How far should historians go, then, in taking Catholicism seriously? This question lingers over many of the passages in David Gutiérrez's instructive chapter, which reviews the work of the most influential scholars who have gone quite far down this road. Gutiérrez, who describes himself as "a secular, religiously skeptical Chicano historian," is candid about his previous reluctance to integrate the sometimes troubling particularism of religion into his work. But he welcomes signs in Latino American scholarship over the past twenty years that "the divide between secularist scholars and religious studies specialists is beginning to be bridged," and he notes that the massive influx since the 1970s of immigrants from Mexico, Central America, South America, and the Spanish-speaking Caribbean virtually requires the development of expertise in the dynamics of transnational Catholicism, Protestantism, and indigenous/syncretic religions. Moreover, Gutierrez is generous in his appraisals, applauding Luis D. León, for example, for exploring "the variety and density of religious belief and expression" that enables evangelicals, Catholics, and folk healers alike to "adapt, adjust, and assert agency within a society that often scorns and rejects them (at the same time at which it recruits them to work)." In a similar vein, he quotes historian and religion scholar Virginia Garrard-Burnett in appreciation of her recognition of the power of Catholicism, in its "militant" Latino context, to shape Latinos' subjectivities and their resulting notions of identity, citizenship, and social agency.

Yet Gutierrez does not entirely abandon his hesitations about "handling religion" (my phrase, not his). Like many other secular scholars, he seems to perceive religion primarily as a subset of culture; it is admittedly an important but also a dependent variable in determining attitudes and behaviors. In his words, religious beliefs and expressions are "organic components of a broader cultural repertoire and symbolic universe." Elsewhere, perhaps revealing his own affinity for a "normative teleology of modernity" not shared by many of the religious subjects studied by León and others, Gutierrez worries about a world in which religion serves as more than a functional component of something else, a world in which "messianic leaders such as Cesar Chavez, Reies López Tijerina, and other prominent icons of Chicano and pan-Latino history . . . also often seemed to betray their stated religious and philosophical principles in their treatment of women, in their often autocratic leadership styles, and in the positions they often took on people they deemed 'outside' the movements they led." In what could be taken as a modest victory for the project of integrating these sometimes troubling Americans of intense faith into the historical narratives, Gutierrez does not suggest that even the messy messianic types, much less the ardent "average" practitioners/ believers, are disqualified from serious coverage, analysis, and, yes, fair-minded scrutiny by secularist historians.

⌒ The End of Catholic Difference?

The closing chapter, in which Wilfred McClay asks both whether the present moment in American political history might be ripe for a sustained intervention by Catholic public philosophy and whether it might already be too late for Catholics to take advantage of the opportunity, revisits several themes of this volume from the perspective of a historian, social philosopher, and cultural critic. Whereas Orsi emphasizes Catholic difference by drawing attention to the cult of martyrdom and redemptive suffering and to Catholic myths of the nation's origins in supernatural heroism, McClay retrieves the Catholic roots of American natural-law philosophy in order to underscore what he sees as the surpassing relevance of Catholic traditions to the possibility of a renewal of American civic virtue and national purpose. The countercultural character of Catholic social values and public presences, which Griffith explores with regard to abortion, birth control, and gender relations, is taken by McClay to be a much-needed resource to combat the moral decay visited on the nation by Protestant-secular relativist liberalism. Whereas Sugrue charts the convergence of Catholic, Protestant, and secular processes of internal fragmentation that leads to surprising coalitions in a plural public square, McClay offers at least a qualified hope that Catholic social teaching may provide a political center for pro-life, pro-justice Americans of whatever religious or secular orientation.

But McClay, like Griffith, Gutiérrez, and Orsi, faces squarely the erosion of Roman Catholicism's alternative cosmology and the severe weakening of the church's moral authority, in part as a result of dissent from the ban on artificial birth control (the controversy over *Humanae Vitae*, which McClay mentions) and the sexual-abuse scandals (emphasized by Griffith). "It is an enormous paradox that as the fullness of the church's social-teaching message has waxed, the respectfulness and attentiveness of its audience has waned," he writes. "When Catholic social teaching is proposed in general terms, emphasizing the dignity of the human person, the common good, subsidiarity, peacemaking, care for the poor, and the like, everyone applauds because it is so enormously attractive—more attractive, one might argue, than most of the secular alternatives on offer. When such teaching begins to be applied to concrete social, economic, and political issues, however, it quickly becomes the case that Catholics insist on making up their own minds no matter what the interpreters of Catholic social teaching have to say, and the seamless fabric is soon rendered into a thousand pieces."

This now-familiar lament raises the question whether twentieth-century Americanization served as a powerful passage toward secularization as well. McClay worries that the "frankly accommodationist" example of the first Catholic U.S. president ultimately prevailed over efforts, such as those of John Courtney Murray, to reconcile Catholicism and America "without sacrificing the one to the other." Are we now at a point, McClay asks, where "American Catholicism, in losing its grip on meaningful structures of authority, has also lost its principal mark of distinctiveness in relation to the individualistic American value system?" Or, to recall Orsi's explication of two strategies for being Catholic in America, has "Catholic otherness" been eclipsed by "Catholic modern"?

⌒The Contribution of Catholic Historians

Catholics have been "forgotten," then, by Protestant, secular, and Catholic historians alike. Let us take these culprits one by one. A few of the authors of this volume occasionally conflate "Protestant" and "secular," implying that so-called mainline Protestants adapted so thoroughly to—their religious critics would say, rather, "surrendered to"—post-Enlightenment, liberal, technoscientific habits of mind that they became essentially "postreligious." One can imagine both serious Protestants and serious secularists objecting to this conflation. And certainly Protestants qua Protestants, who in the nineteenth and early twentieth centuries dominated the American historical profession, had their own reasons for marginalizing Catholic interpretations of and (constructive) roles in American history, just as agnostic and irreligious and postreligious secularists qua secularists had their own reasons for muting Catholic voices. Griffiths and McClay sketch and critique aspects of the Protestant motivations and strategies, while Gutierrez and Hollinger (quoted earlier) refer to the secularist disdain of religious hypocrisy and religious fanaticism, respectively.

But how did Catholic historians contribute to the forgetting of Catholics? The vast majority of Roman Catholic "church historians," as they were called until the 1980s, inhabited the Catholic world they studied; whatever their critical distance from "the alternative cosmology" in which they had been immersed as children and teens, they were formed by "Holy Mother Church" and took for granted the existence of saints and the supernatural, sin and miracles, authority and (sanctified) community.

As suggested earlier, empathy with one's subjects can be an asset in the writing of insightful and genuinely critical history, but it can also blind the historian to what is actually distinctive, odd, or scandalous about one's own tribe. Catholic historians until recently were too preoccupied with their own story, however, to integrate it fully into synoptic American narratives or to observe with a wry detachment and curiosity, and write insightfully about, the Protestants, Jews, and secularists who also had made American history. Instead, for most historians of Catholicism in the United States, it has been difficult to adopt a disinterested stance toward "the Catholic Thing," the memories of which (and continued participation in) evoke sympathy here, anger and resentment there, ambivalence everywhere, and sometimes all of these in the same individual.

It is just that kind of professional engagement, marked by detachment and disinterest, however, that Cohen, Sugrue, and their colleagues in the mainstream of the profession can contribute to Catholic self-understanding and to the writing of history by Catholics themselves. That is, sympathetic "outsiders" might provide the kind of "moment" that McClay describes (referring, instead, to what Catholics can provide to the mainstream), namely, "a force applied from a distance, as with a simple machine like a lever . . . [such that] the amount of force that is generated is directly proportional to the distance from the axial point." Their studiously naïve perceptions can generate fresh insights and provide new directions for research rich in potential for "mainstreaming."

I do not mean to suggest that historians of Catholicism in the United States have engaged primarily in apologetics. Hardly: Catholic historians have been sufficiently critical of Catholic institutions, practices, and leaders and nimble, by and large, in importing methods and theories from anthropology, sociology of religion, critical theory, postmodernism, and other disciplines in the service of rendering plausible and contextualizing the various forms of Catholic "difference." Applying these tools, Catholic historians have portrayed with remarkable care and skill the thick web of Catholic parishes, neighborhoods, schools, colleges, seminaries, devotions, material culture, and ethnoreligious practices, from Father Peyton's Rosary Crusade to the Day of the Dead. They have mapped the contours of public Catholicism, that is, styles of Catholic activism and political organizing; and they have vividly conveyed the sensibilities of cradle Catholics and converts, nuns and priests, politicians and educators. In short, Catholic historians have been preoccupied with making sense of the inner rhythms and meanings of the Catholic subculture. Mainstream historians who are wondering whether and how to incorporate Catholic sensibilities into their work, Griffith suggests, might find inspiration in the idea that taking Catholics seriously would help "subvert and supplant the imperialist trappings of Protestant scholarship that claims to be more broadly 'American.'" Subversion, like confession, can be beneficial to the academic's soul.[10]

Catholic scholars have now explicitly invited mainstream U.S. historians into the conversation. That these colleagues have already begun to think alongside and with some Catholic historians is evident from this volume. In order for U.S. historians to integrate the rich Catholic experience—at once familiar and unrecognizable—into their narratives, they need not have had that experience themselves. But in order to reshape American political, economic, cultural, and social history to incorporate the ubiquitous Catholic presences, they must come to comprehend something of the inner world of Catholic Americans—the alternative cosmology of the Catholic imaginary.

In this they have a marvelous array of guides and interlocutors, including Robert Orsi, Timothy Matovina, Jay Dolan, Margaret McGuinness, and James McCartin, among others, on the "alternative cosmology" and its saints, devotions, prayers and sacraments; John McGreevy, Patrick Allitt, David O'Brien, and James T. Fisher, among others, on the public presences of Catholic Americans; Evelyn Stern, Mary Wingerd, Paula Kane, and Timothy Kelly on "place"—the variety of state and urban Catholicisms; Kathleen Sprows Cummings on the "new women" of the Progressive Era and Leslie Woodcock Tentler on Catholics and contraception; Suellen Hoy, Carol Coburn, and Amy Koehlinger on the twentieth-century spiritual, institutional, theological, and social trajectories encompassing "nuns," "sisters," and "women religious"; Joseph Chinnici, on "the history of suffering" across the middle decades of the twentieth century; Una Cadegan and Paul Elie on the "cultural work" accomplished by Catholic literary culture of the interwar years and beyond; James O'Toole on the laity; and Philip Gleason on Catholic higher education.[11]

The works of these gifted Catholic historians are landmarks along the way toward a nuanced appreciation of the internal Catholic psychological-cultural-institutional dynamics—the web of Catholic signs, symbols, practices, and sensibilities that provided form and structure to the historical experiences of Catholic Americans. These elements, we are now called to remember, are also constitutive elements of the historical experiences of all Americans. We eagerly await the new American histories to be written in the wake of this remembering.

⌒Notes

Introduction

1. I rely on Alan Brinkley's superb book *The Publisher: Henry Luce and His American Century* (New York: Farrar, Straus and Giroux, 2010), 432–33, 438–39. Also see Ralph G. Martin, *Henry and Clare: An Intimate Portrait of the Luces* (New York: Putnam, 1991), 259, 348; and Emmet John Hughes, "A Man for Our Season" (1969), folder 1288, box 28, John Courtney Murray Papers, Georgetown University Archives.

2. "To Be Catholic and American," *Time* (December 12, 1960), http://www.time .com/time/magazine/article/0,9171,871923,00.html (accessed February 19, 2012).

3. Murray to Fr. Vincent McCormick, July 22, 1958, file 151, box 1, John Courtney Murray Papers; Brinkley, *Publisher*, 421–28.

4. Joseph A. Komonchak, "The Silencing of John Courtney Murray," in *Cristianesimo nella storia: Saggi in onore di Giuseppe Alberigo*, ed. Alberto Melloni (Bologna: Il Mulino 1996), 692, 695.

5. Fr. Francis Connell to Fr. Joseph Fenton, November 22, 1960, Church-State Writings file, Francis Connell Papers, Redemptorist Archives–Baltimore Province, Brooklyn, New York.

6. John Courtney Murray, *We Hold These Truths: Catholic Reflections on the American Proposition* (New York: Sheed and Ward, 1960), 12, 41.

7. Brinkley, *Publisher*, 371–84, 438–39; "To Be Catholic and American."

8. Henry Luce, "The American Century" (1941), in *The Ambiguous Legacy: U.S. Foreign Relations in the "American Century,"* ed. Michael Hogan (Cambridge: Cambridge University Press, 1999), 11–29.

9. Murray, *We Hold These Truths*, 27.

10. Richard Linkh, *American Catholicism and European Immigrants, 1900–1924* (New York: Center for Migration Studies,1975), 109; Leslie Woodcock Tentler, *Seasons of Grace: A History of the Catholic Archdiocese of Detroit* (Detroit: Wayne State University Press 1990), 3.

11. Fr. Nicholas Accolti, SJ, to James McMaster, May 8, 1874, I 2 a, Manuscripts and Archives, University of Notre Dame.

12. For example, J.P. Daughton, *An Empire Divided: Religion, Republicanism, and the Making of French Colonialism, 1880–1914* (New York: Oxford University Press, 2006).

13. John Tracy Ellis, *The Life of James Cardinal Gibbons: Archbishop of Baltimore, 1834–1921* (1952; repr., Westminster, Md.: Christian Classics, 1987), 308.

14. John Thomas, quoted in Peter McDonough, *Men Astutely Trained: A History of the Jesuits in the American Century* (New York: Free Press, 1992), 435.

15. The anti-Catholic and deeply Protestant character of North Atlantic nation building in the late seventeenth and eighteenth centuries is now a dominant theme in the literature. See, for example, Steven Pincus, *1688: The First Modern Revolution* (New Haven, Conn.: Yale University Press, 2009); and Thomas Kidd, *The Protestant Interest: New England after Puritanism* (New Haven, Conn.: Yale University Press, 2004). On how Catholic Marylanders nonetheless became American patriots, see Maura Jane Farrelly, *Papist Patriots: The Making of an American Catholic Identity* (New York: Oxford University Press, 2011).

16. Brinkley, 393; George Barry O'Toole, "Translator's Preface," in *The Liberal Illusion*, by Louis Veuillot (Washington, D.C.: National Catholic Welfare Conference, 1939), 19; Benjamin Masse, SJ, *Economic Liberalism and Free Enterprise* (New York: America Press, 1944), 8; more broadly, James Terence Fisher, *The Catholic Counterculture in America, 1933–1962* (Chapel Hill: University of North Carolina Press, 1989).

17. Leslie Woodcock Tentler, *Catholics and Contraception: An American History* (Ithaca, N.Y.: Cornell University Press, 2004).

18. Evelyn Savidge Sterne, *Ethnic Politics and the Catholic Church in Providence* (Ithaca N.Y.: Cornell University Press, 2004); Mary Lethert Wingerd, *Claiming the City: Politics, Faith and the Power of Place in St. Paul* (Ithaca, N.Y.: Cornell University Press, 2001).

19. Joshua M. Zeitz, *White Ethnic New York: Jews, Catholics, and the Shaping of Postwar Politics* (Chapel Hill: University of North Carolina Press, 2007).

20. Barry A. Kosmin and Ariela Keysar, "American Religious Identification Survey (ARIS), 2008" (Hartford, Conn.: Trinity College, 2009).

21. Vincent Viaene, "International History, Religious History, Catholic History: Perspectives for Cross-Fertilization, (1830–1914)," *European History Quarterly* 38 (2008): 578–607.

22. Peter R. D'Agostino, *Rome in America: Transnational Catholic Ideology from the Risorgimento to Fascism* (Chapel Hill: University of North Carolina, 2004); John Connelly, *From Enemy to Brother: The Church and the Jews in the Twentieth Century* (Cambridge, Mass.: Harvard University Press, 2012); Matthew Connelly, *Fatal Misconception: The Struggle to Control World Population* (Cambridge, Mass.: Harvard University Press, 2008).

23. David Schultenover, SJ, ed., *The Reception of Pragmatism in France and the Rise of Roman Catholic Modernism, 1890–1914* (Washington, D.C.: Catholic University Press 2009).

24. John O'Malley, *What Happened at Vatican II* (Cambridge, Mass.: Harvard University Press, 2008). The recent debate over the council's interpretation is persuasively analyzed in Joseph A. Komonchak, "Benedict XVI and the Interpretation of Vatican II," in *The Crisis of Authority in Catholic Modernity*, ed. Michael J. Lacey and Francis Oakley (New York: Oxford University Press, 2011), 93–110. Benedict XVI's remarks on the Second Vatican Council and its interpretation are reprinted in "Remarks on Interpreting the Second Vatican Council," in Lacey and Oakley, *Crisis of Authority in Catholic Modernity*, 357–62.

25. D'Agostino, *Rome in America*; John T. McGreevy, *Catholicism and American Freedom: A History* (New York: W. W. Norton, 2003); Michael Pasquier, *Fathers on*

the Frontier: French Missionaries and the Roman Catholic Priesthood in the United States, 1789–1870 (New York: Oxford University Pres, 2010); Gerald McKevitt, *Brokers of Culture: Italian Jesuits in the American West, 1848–1919* (Stanford: Stanford University Press, 2007); Timothy Matovina, *Guadalupe and her Faithful: Latino Catholics in San Antonio from Colonial Origins to the Present* (Baltimore: Johns Hopkins University Press, 2005). In French, Florian Michel, *La pensée catholique en Amérique du nord: Réseaux intellectuels et échanges culturels entre l'Europe, le Canada et les Etats-Unis (années 1920–1960)* (Paris: Desclée de Brouwer, 2010); Tangi Villerbu, "Faire l'histoire catholique e l'Ouest américain au 19 siècle. Une terre de missions a reevaluer," *Revue d'Histoire Ecclesiastique* 101 (2006); 117–42. In German, Michael Hochgeschwender, *Wahrheit, Einheit, Ordnung: Die Sklavenfrage und der amerikanische Katholizismus, 1835–1870* (Paderborn: Ferdinand Schöningh, 2006). In Italian, Matteo Sanfilippo, *L'affermazione de cattolicesimo nel Nord America: Elite, emigranti e Chiesa cattolica negli Stati Uniti e in Canada, 1750–1920* (Viterbo: Sette città, 2003).

Chapter 1

1. For a sociological account of the great success story of post–World War II Catholicism in the United States, see Andrew M. Greeley, *The American Catholic: A Social Portrait* (New York: Basic Books, 1977). Father Greeley has been the strongest proponent of the view that by the 1960s Catholics had moved into the American mainstream. *The De-Romanization of the American Catholic Church* was written by Edward Wakin and Father Joseph F. Scheuer (New York: New American Library, 1966); quote from 309. I have written about the American Catholic sense of time and history in this era in " 'The Infant of Prague's Nightie': The Devotional Origins of American Catholic Memory," *U.S. Catholic Historian* 21, no. 2 (Spring 2003): 1–18. The guide for Catholic parents mentioned in the text is James DiGiacomo and Edward Wakin, *We Were Never Their Age (A Guide for Christian Parents)* (New York: Holt, Rinehart and Winston, 1972). Full disclosure: I was among the adolescents at Fordham Prep School in the Bronx who served as Father DiGiacomo's research base on modern adolescence, which certifies that I too was never the age of the Catholics about whom I am writing. For images of the Catonsville action, see the extraordinary website, "Fire and Faith: The Catonsville Nine File," under the auspices of the Enoch Pratt Library, State Library Resources, City of Baltimore; content by Marilyn Julius, http://c9.mdch.org.

2. Warren Goldstein argues that the Berrigans did not make much sense to non-Catholics in *William Sloane Coffin, Jr.: A Holy Impatience* (New Haven, Conn.: Yale University Press, 2006). For an account of Philip Berrigan's bloodletting before the action at the U.S. Customs House in Baltimore, October 1967, see Murray Polner and Jim O'Grady, *Disarmed and Dangerous: The Radical Lives and Times of Daniel and Philip Berrigan, Brothers in Religious Faith and Civil Disobedience* (New York: Basic Books, 1997), 174. "Phil [stabbed] his arm so many times in an attempt to improve the suction that the others begged him to stop."

3. For Bishop John Carroll's "synthesis," see Joseph P. Chinnici, OFM, *Living Stones: The History and Structure of Catholic Spiritual Life in the United States* (New York: Macmillan, 1989), 3.

4. My understanding of the place of forgetting in the making of the modern owes much to David Gross, *Lost Time: On Remembering and Forgetting in Late Modern Culture* (Amherst: University of Massachusetts Press, 2000); see also Gross, *The Past in Ruins: Tradition and the Critique of Memory* (Amherst: University of Massachusetts Press, 1992). On forgetting and the making of liberal nation-states, see Anthony W. Marx, *Faith in Nation: Exclusionary Origins of Modern Nationalism* (New York: Oxford University Press, 2003). Also helpful to me were the essays in Michael P. Steinberg, ed., *Walter Benjamin and the Demands of History* (Ithaca, N.Y.: Cornell University Press, 1996), and three essential novels: W. G. Sebald, *Austerlitz*, trans. Anthea Bell (New York: Modern Library, 2001); Steve Stern, *The Angel of Forgetfulness* (New York: Viking, 2005); and Antonio Muñoz Molina, *Sepharad*, trans. Margaret Sayers Peden (New York: Harcourt, 2003). Bruno Latour discusses "purification" in *We Have Never Been Modern*, trans. Christine Porter (Cambridge, Mass.: Harvard University Press, 1993), passim.

5. Two examples of the awareness of the danger of forgetting from the Catholic popular press are Catherine Walsh, "Half-Breeds in the New Church," *U.S. Catholic* 31 (May 1965): 55–57, and Phyllis B. Simpson, "The Learned Laity vs. Parish Old-timers," *Information* 76 (May 1962): 17–23. The date of modernity's end is clearly a contested matter, as is the exact nature of what followed it, but there is wide agreement that the political, technological, and cultural transformations of the 1970s and 1980s marked a decisive break with what came before in terms of ways of living and of understanding the self and the world. See, for example, Perry Anderson, *The Origins of Postmodernity* (London and New York: Verso Books, 1998). The same forces that made for postmodernity globally had an impact on Catholics too, of course, and changed their lives along with everyone else's. But among Catholics the seismic shifts of the era were felt most intimately in their changed relationship with the supernatural following the implementation of the mandates of the Second Vatican Council. The institution of new ways of being in relationship with Jesus, Mary, and the saints (and with one another in the context of these transformed bonds, as in new understandings of the priesthood) were accompanied in the United States by the movement of the descendants of European Catholic immigrants out of the industrial working class into postindustrial service and professional occupations. Mexican Americans who had been in the United States for decades by the 1970s experienced the era much as other Catholics did, and this is true of Puerto Rican Catholics as well. But as the numbers of migrants from Mexico and elsewhere in South and Central America grew exponentially in this decade and afterward, Latino and Latina Catholics brought into the American Catholic mix ways of prayer and worship, such as the charismatic and evangelical Cursillo movement, that revived the spirit of preconciliar piety, but in new forms. This migration contributed fundamentally to the shape of American Catholicism after the council.

6. On two of the three sites of Mary's appearance in the modern United States mentioned in this paragraph, Necedah and Bayside, see Sandra Zimdars-Swartz, *Encountering Mary: From La Salette to Medjugorje* (Princeton, N.J.: Princeton University Press, 1991); also relevant on Necedah in the context of this chapter is Thomas Kselman and Steven M. Avella, "Marian Piety and the Cold War in the United States," *Catholic Historical Review* 72 (1986): 403–24. John McGreevy discusses the

immediate post–World War II apparition in the Bronx in "Bronx Miracle," *American Quarterly* 52, no. 3 (September 2000): 405–43. My understanding of Catholicism's active engagement with the challenges of the modern world was influenced by the work of Joseph Komonchak, especially "Modernity and the Construction of Roman Catholicism," *Cristianesimo nella storia* 18 (1997): 353–85, and "The Enlightenment and the Construction of Roman Catholicism," *Annual of the Catholic Commission on Intellectual and Cultural Affairs*, 1985, 31–59. The locus classicus of the identification of Protestantism and modernity is Max Weber, *The Protestant Ethic and the Spirit of Capitalism*, trans. Talcott Parsons (New York: Charles Scribner's Sons, 1958). Weber published an initial version of his thesis in 1904–5.

7. For a contemptuous account of Catholic devotions as out of place in a modern, sophisticated democracy after World War II (when, again, Catholics were becoming mainstream), see two books by Paul Blanshard, *American Freedom and Catholic Power* (Boston: Beacon Press, 1949) and *Communism, Democracy, and Catholic Power* (Boston: Beacon Press, 1951). The best book on American philo-Catholicism as the obverse of its anti-Catholicism is, in my judgment, Jenny Franchot, *Roads to Rome: The Antebellum Protestant Encounter with Catholicism* (Berkeley: University of California Press, 1994). Ahlstrom made his comment to me in conversation when I was his student at Yale University in the mid-1970s.

8. Luce's phrase about America's "special dispensation" is quoted in Robert E. Herzstein, *Henry R. Luce: A Political Portrait of the Man Who Created the American Century* (New York: Charles Scribner's Sons, 1994), 177; the information about Luce's ancestor and his parents is from chapter 2 of this volume. Herzstein discusses the preparation and reception of Luce's article on 179–85. The text of Luce's famous clarion call is in Henry R. Luce, *The American Century* (New York: Farrar and Rinehart, 1941).

9. On the four chaplains, see "The Brotherhood of Soldiers at War: The True Story of the Four Chaplains," http://www.homeofheroes.com/brotherhood/chaplains.html, and the Four Chaplains Memorial Foundation, http://www.fourchaplains.org/. On U.S. Catholics generally during World War II, see James Hennesey, SJ, *American Catholics: A History of the Roman Catholic Community in the United States* (New York: Oxford University Press, 1981), 271–83.

10. Marx, *Faith in Nation*, 29–30, 182, 183.

11. Daniel Walker Howe, *What God Hath Wrought: The Transformation of America, 1815–1848* (New York: Oxford University Press, 2007), 194. There is a large literature on antebellum anti-Catholicism; see, for example, Ray A. Billington, *The Protestant Crusade, 1800–1860* (New York: Quadrangle, 1962); and on the riots in Philadelphia, Michael Feldberg, *The Philadelphia Riots of 1844: A Study of Ethnic Conflict* (Westport, Conn.: Greenwood Press, 1975).

12. On the war in the Philippines, see Stuart Creighton Miller, *"Benevolent Assimilation": The American Conquest of the Philippines, 1899–1903* (New Haven, Conn.: Yale University Press, 1982). On Anglo-Saxonism, see also Matthew Frye Jacobson, *Barbarian Virtues: The United States Encounters Foreign Peoples at Home and Abroad, 1876–1917* (New York: Hill and Wang, 2000). Thomas T. McAvoy, CSC, briefly discusses the significance of the American war in the Philippines for U.S. Catholics in the context of the unfolding Americanist controversy in *A History of the Catholic*

Church in the United States (Notre Dame, Ind.: University of Notre Dame Press, 1969), 342–44. My discussion of Catholics and the Spanish-American War also relies on Frank T. Reuter, *Catholic Influence on American Colonial Policies, 1898–1904* (Austin: University of Texas Press, 1967). Reuter discusses the buildup to war on 3–19 and McKinnon on 74. The story about soldiers digging up priests' graves is on 75.

13. Reuter discusses the anti-imperialism turn among U.S. Catholic prelates in *Catholic Influence on American Colonial Policies*, 117–19; the quote from the *New York Freeman's Journal* is on 113.

14. A good survey of Catholicism in the United States in these years is Charles R. Morris, *American Catholic: The Saints and Sinners Who Built America's Most Powerful Church* (New York: Times Books, 1997). On the subject of the campaign in Rome and in the United States to protect the city from Allied bombing, see James Hennessey, SJ, "American Jesuit in Wartime Rome: The Diary of Vincent A. McCormick, S.J.," *Mid-America* 56 (1974): 32–55; for anxious defenses of Catholics' loyalty, see "The Bombing of Rome," *America* 69 (July 31, 1943): 463–64, and "Rome," *Commonweal* 38 (July 30, 1943): 360–61. On the response to Clark's nomination, see F. William O'Brien, SJ, "General Clark's Nomination as Ambassador to the Vatican: American Reaction," *Catholic Historical Review* 44 (1958/1959): 421–39. The essential historical study of relations between the Holy See and the United States in this period is Gerald P. Fogarty, SJ, *The Vatican and the American Hierarchy from 1870 to 1965* (Stuttgart: Anton Hiersemann, 1982). On Catholics and Franklin Roosevelt, see George Q. Flynn, *Roosevelt and Romanism: Catholics and American Diplomacy, 1937–1945* (Westport, Conn.: Greenwood Press, 1976); David J. O'Brien, *American Catholics and Social Reform: The New Deal Years* (New York: Oxford University Press, 1968); and Frederick L. Broderick, *The Right Reverend New Dealer: John A. Ryan* (New York: Macmillan, 1963).

15. The quote about the purpose of Columbus's mission is from *The Church in United States History: America's Debt to Catholics* (Huntington, Ind.: Our Sunday Visitor, n.d.), second page of the unpaginated introduction. A reference in the book's first sentence dates the volume to 1937–38. On Shea's contribution to the study of American Catholic history, see Peter Guilday, *John Gilmary Shea: Father of American Catholic History, 1824–1892* (New York: United States Catholic Historical Society, 1926). Shea's thesis about the endurance of Native peoples among whom Catholic missionaries had worked is from John Gilmary Shea, *Catholic Missions among the Indian Tribes of the United States* (New York: P. J. Kenedy Publishers to the Holy Apostolic See, 1899), 15.

16. Joseph Moreau, "Rise of the (Catholic) American Nation: United States History and Parochial Schools, 1878–1925," *American Studies* 38, no. 3 (Fall 1997): 67–90. This article was of great assistance to me in preparing the middle sections of this chapter. On the ambitions of American Catholic educators in the key period after the turn of the century, see Timothy Walch, *Parish School: American Catholic Parochial Education from Colonial Times to the Present* (New York: Crossroad, 1996), 67–133. Walch sums up the situation of parochial schools at the end of the 1920s: "Even though American Catholic schools remained distinct from the public schools in one important area—intensive religious instruction—they became increasingly similar in other areas" (75). For the Commission on American Citizenship, see *Bet-*

ter Men for Better Times (Washington, D.C.: Commission on American Citizenship and Catholic University of America, 1943); also George Johnson, "The Commission on American Citizenship of the Catholic University of America," *Journal of Educational Sociology* 16, no. 6 (February 1943): 380–85; and John L. Elias, "Education in Time of War: George Johnson and the Commission on American Citizenship of the Catholic University of America," http://www.religiouseducation.net/member/06_rea_papers/Elias_John.pdf. The commission created the popular and widely distributed Catholic comic book *Treasure Chest of Fun and Fact*, which was published in the years 1946–72. The full text of *Treasure Chest* can be found online, in full color, through the website of the American Catholic Research Center and University Archives, Catholic University of America, at http://www.aladin.wrlc.org/gsdl/collect/treasure/treasure.shtml.

17. Moreau, "Rise of the (Catholic) American Nation," 83.

18. The quote from *The Church in United States History* is on the fifth page of the unpaginated introduction. A popular biography of Noll is Ann Ball, with Father Leon Hutton, *Champion of the Church: The Extraordinary Life and Legacy of Archbishop Noll* (Huntington, Ind.: Our Sunday Visitor Publishing Division, 2006).

19. Egan is quoted in *The Church in United States History* on the first page of the unpaginated introduction. The comment about Protestantism not existing when America was discovered is quoted in Moreau, "Rise of the (Catholic) American Nation," 75, as is Sister Mary Celeste, 84. On the broader intellectual context of the American Catholic assertion of the Catholic roots of American political culture, see John T. McGreevy, *Catholicism and American Freedom: A History* (New York: W. W. Norton, 2003), 19–42 and passim.

20. Allan Greer, *Mohawk Saint: Catherine Tekakwitha and the Jesuits* (New York: Oxford University Press, 2005), 193–94.

21. P. F. X. de Charlevoix, "Catherine Tegahkouita: An Iroquois Virgin" (1744), in *The Jesuit Relations: Natives and Missionaries in Seventeenth-Century North America*, ed. Allan Greer (Boston: Bedford/St. Martin's, 2000), 172–85; quotes on 182. Also quoted in this paragraph is Greer, *Mohawk Saint*, 195, 199.

22. On Father Marquette's suffering in the wilderness, see "The Old Faith in a New World," *Treasure Chest of Fun and Fact* 8, no. 6 (November 20, 1952): 26–32, http://dspace.wrlc.org/view/ImgViewer?url=http://dspace.wrlc.org/doc/manifest/2041/27654. This is part of an extended series with that title. See also "God's Frontiersman: Father Jacques Marquette," *Treasure Chest of Fun and Fact* 13, no. 6 (November 21, 1957): 11–16.

23. Jérôme Lalement, "How Father Isaac Jogues Was Taken by the Iroquois, and What He Suffered on His First Entrance into Their Country" (1647), in Greer, *Jesuit Relations*, 157–71; quotations on 157 and 163.

24. Brébeuf's comment about baptism is quoted in Greer, *Mohawk Saint*, 6; on Columbus as a suffering figure, see Moreau, "Rise of the (Catholic) American Nation," 77. Moreau writes, "The experiences of Columbus, [Father Andrew] White [apostle of Maryland], and numerous martyrs serve as metaphors for the hardships endured by all steadfast Catholics in the New World."

25. Spalding's account of Nerinckx's mortifications is from Martin J. Spalding, *Sketches of the Life, Times, and Character of Rt. Rev. Benedict Joseph Flaget* (Louisville,

Ky.: Webb and Levering, 1852), 89–91. I thank Matthew Cressler for bringing this passage to my attention.

26. Rev. William Joseph Howlett, *Life of Rev. Charles Nerinckx, Pioneer Missionary of Kentucky and Founder of the Sisters of Loretto at the Foot of the Cross* (Techny, Ill.: Mission Press, SVD, 1915), 238. Nerinckx undertook at times literally to bear Christ's cross in the New World in public processions, which he introduced to encourage prayer for the souls in purgatory.

27. The last two paragraphs of this section depend on Moreau, "Rise of the (Catholic) American Nation," for the description of the martyrdom of Lalement and Brébeuf (73–74) and of Rasles (78); for the story of the Irish woman killed as a witch (78); and for the reference to the history by William H. J. Kennedy and Sister Mary Joseph. Moreau's comment about Catholics' spiritual claim to the land is on 74. The quote from Shea is from *The Church in United States History*, first page of the unpaginated introduction.

28. Brother Philip, FSC, "The Teaching of Religion and the Formation of Character," *Bulletin of the National Catholic Educational Association*, 1940, 400–409; quote on 404.

29. Thomas B. Chetwood, SJ, *Tony* (St. Louis: Queen's Work, 1933), 19, 21.

30. Ibid., 23–24, 27–28.

31. Pietro di Donato, *Christ in Concrete* (New York: Bobbs-Merrill, 1939); on Ralph Fasanella, see Patrick Watson, *Fasanella's City: The Paintings of Ralph Fasanella with the Story of His Life and Art* (New York: Knopf, 1973); Paul S. D'Ambrosio, *Ralph Fasanella's America* (Cooperstown, N.Y.: Fenimore Art Museum, 2001).

32. I discuss Catholic competitive suffering in *Thank You, Saint Jude: Women's Devotion to the Patron Saint of Hopeless Causes* (New Haven, Conn.: Yale University Press, 1996), 71, 85–88; see also Leslie Woodcock Tentler, *Catholics and Contraception: An American History* (Ithaca, N.Y.: Cornell University Press, 2004).

33. I referred to a collection of Dooley's works, *Dr. Tom Dooley's Three Great Books: Deliver Us from Evil, The Edge of Tomorrow, The Night They Burned the Mountain* (New York: Farrar, Straus and Cudahy, 1960). The quotation in the text is on 129. On what Catholics made of Dooley's cancer, see James Terence Fisher, *The Catholic Counterculture in America, 1933–1962* (Chapel Hill: University of North Carolina Press, 1989), 187. On Dooley, see James Terence Fisher, *Dr. America: The Lives of Thomas A. Dooley, 1927–1961* (Amherst: University of Massachusetts Press, 1997); see also James Monahan, ed., *Before I Sleep: The Last Days of Dr. Tom Dooley* (New York: Farrar, Straus and Cudahy, 1961).

34. John F. Donovan, *The Pagoda and the Cross: The Life of Bishop Ford of Maryknoll* (New York: Charles Scribner's Sons, 1967), 194, 210. The comparison between Catholic and Protestant missionaries is on 64.

35. Rev. Harold W. Rigney, SVD, *4 Years in a Red Hell* (Chicago: Henry Regnery Company, 1956). The holy card was included in the volume I purchased on the Internet.

36. The Cardinal Mindszenty Foundation is discussed in Donald T. Critchlow, *Phyllis Schlafly and Grassroots Conservatism: A Woman's Crusade* (Princeton, N.J.: Princeton University Press, 2005), 80–83. See also Carol Felsenthal, *Phyllis Schlafly: The Sweetheart of the Moral Majority* (Chicago: Regnery Gateway, 1981), 167–68.

37. Buchanan's high-school years are discussed in Joseph Scotchie, *Street Corner Conservative: Patrick J. Buchanan and His Times* (Alexander, N.C.: Alexander Books, 2003); the phrase "God's marines" is on 15. Fred Garel's wonderful memoir is *Lighting the Lamps* (New York: Xlibiris, 2002); quote on 68. The story about Bing Crosby and "Big Jim" is from his brothers' memoir, Ted Crosby and Larry Crosby, *Bing* (Los Angeles: Bolton Printing Co., 1937), 31. On the draft riots, see Iver Bernstein, *The New York City Draft Riots: Their Significance for American Society and Politics in the Age of the Civil War* (New York: Oxford University Press, 1990). The Catholic contribution to antiabortion violence can be approached via three excellent works: James Risen and Judy L. Thomas, *Wrath of Angels: The American Abortion War* (New York: Basic Books, 1998); Cynthia Gorney, *Articles of Faith: A Frontline History of the Abortion Wars* (New York: Simon and Schuster, 1998); and William Saletan, *Bearing Right: How Conservatives Won the Abortion War* (Berkeley: University of California Press, 2004). On McCarthy, I consulted Thomas C. Reeves, *The Life and Times of Joe McCarthy: A Biography* (New York: Stein and Day, 1982); David M. Oshinsky, *A Conspiracy So Immense: The World of Joe McCarthy* (New York: Oxford University Press, 2005); and Donald F. Crosby, *God, Church, and Flag: Senator Joseph R. McCarthy and the Catholic Church, 1950–1957* (Chapel Hill: University of North Carolina Press, 1978). On Father Coughlin, see Donald I. Warren, *Radio Priest: Charles Coughlin, the Father of Hate Radio* (New York: Free Press, 1996); Mary Christine Athans, *The Coughlin-Fahey Connection: Father Charles E. Coughlin, Father Denis Fahey, C.S.Sp., and Religious Anti-Semitism in the United States* (New York: P. Lang, 1991); Marcus Sheldon, *Father Coughlin: The Tumultuous Life of the Priest of the Little Flower* (Boston: Little, Brown, 1973); and Alan Brinkley, *Voices of Protest: Huey Long, Father Coughlin, and the Great Depression* (New York: Knopf, 1982).

38. Clerical noir is a huge genre. It includes novels and memoirs, stories in the many U.S. Catholic popular periodicals (for adults and children), and comic books, and it also found its way into the movies. The hard-boiled priest is a standard figure of writings for and about altar boys. The trope goes back at least to the 1920s, when class differences among American Catholics were becoming more pronounced. One of the aims of the tough-guy-priest tale was to show that priests crossed class differences among Catholics in the United States and could speak to the poorest as well as to the richest Catholics. An early example is Martin J. Scott, SJ, *A Boy Knight* (New York: P. J. Kenedy and Sons, 1921). The life of Bishop Sheil discussed in this paragraph is Roger L. Treat, *Bishop Sheil and the CYO* (New York: Julian Messner, 1951); quotations from 8 (gun down the throat), 4 (rough towels and vigorous calisthenics), and 36–37 (dying boy). Another example of this genre is Peter V. Rogers, OMI, *Tragedy Is My Parish: Working for God in the Streets of New Orleans* (New York: Macmillan, 1979). For an interesting example of how these tropes of clerical noir contributed to the cast of clerical social activism, see Margery Frisbie, *An Alley in Chicago: The Ministry of a City Priest* (Kansas City: Sheed and Ward, 1991), about Monsignor John Egan of Chicago.

39. For Pat Buchanan's political and religious story, see Pat Buchanan, *Right from the Beginning* (Washington, D.C.: Regnery Gateway, 1990). Buchanan's judgment that the business of America is not business (6) is true to the American Catholic criticism of American affluence. He presents himself as a voice for this perspective

among conservatives whose vision is narrowly economic, in his view, referring to the United States as "this materially rich but morally confused country of ours" (15). It is a Catholic who makes this judgment. Buchanan's account of his childhood relentlessly emphasizes, with pride and approbation, its violence. On Clarence Thomas, see his autobiography, *My Grandfather's Son* (New York: HarperCollins, 2007), and Kevin Merida and Michael A. Fletcher, *Supreme Discomfort: The Divided Soul of Clarence Thomas* (New York: Doubleday, 2007). For Scalia, I referred to Richard A. Brisbin Jr., *Judge Antonin Scalia and the Conservative Revival* (Baltimore: Johns Hopkins University Press, 1998). L. Brent Bozell's memoir is *Mustard Seeds: A Conservative Becomes a Catholic* (Front Royal, Va.: Christendom Press, 2001). Bozell's role in Barry Goldwater's political life is discussed in Rick Perlstein, *Before the Storm: Barry Goldwater and the Unmaking of the American Consensus* (New York: Hill and Wang, 2001).

40. Harvard Sitikoff, ed., *Perspectives on Modern America: Making Sense of the Twentieth Century* (New York: Oxford University Press, 2001). Leaving Catholics almost completely out is one way of not being historically heretical, a risk that historians, among all academics, seem to fear the most.

41. See Jon Butler, "Historiographical Heresy: Catholicism as a Model for American Religious History," in *Belief in History: Innovative Approaches to European and American History*, ed. Thomas Kselman (Notre Dame, Ind.: University of Notre Dame Press, 1991), 286–309.

Chapter 2

1. Lizabeth Cohen, *Making a New Deal: Industrial Workers in Chicago, 1919–1939* (New York: Cambridge University Press, 1990; 2nd ed., 2008); Cohen, *A Consumers' Republic: The Politics of Mass Consumption in Postwar America* (New York: Alfred A. Knopf, 2003); David M. Kennedy, Lizabeth Cohen, and Thomas A. Bailey, *The American Pageant*, 11th, 12th, 13th, and 14th eds. (Boston: Houghton Mifflin, 1998, 2002, 2006, 2011); Lizabeth Cohen, *Saving America's Cities: Ed Logue and the Struggle to Renew Urban America in the Suburban Age*, in process.

2. Samuel Eliot Morison and Henry Steele Commager, *The Growth of the American Republic*, 4th ed., 2 vols. (New York: Oxford University Press, 1950).

3. Ibid., 2:372.

4. Ibid., 1:537; see through to 538; Jonathan Zimmerman, "'Brown'-ing the American Textbook: History, Psychology, and the Origins of Modern Multiculturalism," *History of Education Quarterly* 44, no. 1 (Spring 2004): 46–69.

5. Samuel Eliot Morison and Henry Steele Commager, *The Growth of the American Republic*, 5th ed., vols. 1 and 2 (New York: Oxford University Press, 1962), 524–27 on slavery; 966–71 on civil rights.

6. Ibid., 777, 787, 790.

7. Samuel Eliot Morison, Henry Steele Commager, and William E. Leuchtenburg, *The Growth of the American Republic*, 7th ed., vol. 2 (New York: Oxford University Press, 1980), 451, 688.

8. Leslie Tentler, *Wage-Earning Women: Industrial Work and Family Life in the United States, 1900–1930* (New York: Oxford University Press, 1979); Robert Orsi, *The*

Madonna of 115th Street: Faith and Community in Italian Harlem, 1880–1950 (New Haven, Conn.: Yale University Press, 1985); David Gutiérrez, *Walls and Mirrors: Mexican Americans, Mexican Immigrants, and the Politics of Ethnicity* (Berkeley: University of California Press,1995); John T. McGreevy, *Parish Boundaries: The Catholic Encounter with Race in the Twentieth-Century Urban North* (Chicago: University of Chicago Press, 1996); Thomas Sugrue, *The Origins of the Urban Crisis: Race and Inequality in Postwar Detroit* (Princeton, N.J.: Princeton University Press, 1992); R. Marie Griffith, *God's Daughters: Evangelical Women and the Power of Submission* (Berkeley: University of California Press, 1997); Jacqueline Dowd Hall et al., *Like a Family: The Making of a Southern Cotton Mill World* (Chapel Hill: University of North Carolina Press, 1987); Gary Gerstle, *Working-Class Americanism: The Politics of Labor in a Textile City, 1914–1960* (New York: Cambridge University Press, 1989); and George Chauncey, *Gay New York: Gender, Urban Culture, and the Making of the Gay Male World, 1890–1940* (New York: Basic Books, 1994).

9. Christina Klein, *Cold War Orientalism: Asia and the Middlebrow Imagination, 1945–1961* (Berkeley: University of California Press, 2003); Sarah E. Igo, *The Averaged American: Surveys, Citizens, and the Making of a Mass Public* (Cambridge, Mass.: Harvard University Press, 2007).

10. The literature on "whiteness" is extensive. The two founding texts are David Roediger, *Wages of Whiteness* (London: Verso, 1991), and Noel Ignatiev, *How the Irish Became White* (New York: Routledge, 1995). Other important works in the field thereafter include Matthew Frye Jacobson, *Whiteness of a Different Color: European Immigrants and the Alchemy of Race* (Cambridge, Mass.: Harvard University Press, 1998); George Lipsitz, *The Possessive Investment in Whiteness: How White People Profit from Identity Politics* (Philadelphia: Temple University Press, 1998); Eric Arnesen, "Scholarly Controversy: Whiteness and the Historians' Imaginations," *International Labor and Working-Class History* 60 (Fall 2001): 1–92; Bruce Nelson, *Divided We Stand: American Workers and the Struggle for Black Equality* (Princeton, N.J.: Princeton University Press, 2001); Peter Kolchin, "Whiteness Studies: The New History of Race in America," *Journal of American History* 89 (June 2002): 154–73; Thomas Guglielmo, *White on Arrival: Italians, Race, Color, and Power in Chicago, 1890–1945* (New York: Oxford University Press, 2003); David R. Roediger, *Working toward Whiteness: How America's Immigrants Became White; The Strange Journey from Ellis Island to the Suburbs* (New York: Basic Books, 2005).

11. Joan Wallach Scott, "Gender: A Useful Category of Historical Analysis," *American Historical Review* 91 (December 1986): 1069, 1074.

12. Linda Gordon, *Pitied but Not Entitled: Single Mothers and the History of Welfare, 1890–1935* (New York: Free Press, 1994); Gail Bederman, *Manliness and Civilization* (Chicago: University of Chicago Press, 1995); Alice Kessler-Harris, *In Pursuit of Equity: Women, Men, and the Quest for Economic Citizenship in 20th-Century America* (New York: Oxford University Press, 2001), 5–6, 18, 45, 63, 146, 205–6, 291.

13. Cohen, *Consumers' Republic*; Grace Hale, *Making Whiteness: The Culture of Segregation in the South, 1890–1940* (New York: Pantheon, 1998); Lawrence Glickman, ed., *Consumer Society in American History: A Reader* (Ithaca, N.Y.: Cornell University Press, 1999); Jennifer Scanlon, ed., *The Gender and the Consumer Reader* (New York: New York University Press, 2000); and Meg Jacobs, *Pocketbook Politics:*

Economic Citizenship in Twentieth-Century America (Princeton, N.J.: Princeton University Press, 2005). For a useful review of the literature on consumer history, see David Steigerwald, "All Hail the Republic of Choice: Consumer History as Contemporary Thought," *Journal of American History* 93, no. 2 (September 2006): 385–403, followed by responses by T. H. Breen and Lizabeth Cohen, 404–13.

14. Nancy MacLean, *Behind the Mask of Chivalry: The Making of the Second Ku Klux Klan* (New York: Oxford University Press, 1994); Lisa McGirr, *Suburban Warriors: The Origins of the New American Right* (Princeton, N.J.: Princeton University Press, 2001); and Matthew D. Lassiter, *The Silent Majority: Politics in the Sunbelt South* (Princeton, N.J.: Princeton University Press, 2006).

15. See Stephen Tuck, "The New American Histories," *Historical Journal* 48, no. 3 (2005): 811–32, for an insightful review of active subfields in recent American history. On the state of twentieth-century American religious history, see Jon Butler, "Jack-in-the-Box Faith: The Religion Problem in Modern American History," *Journal of American History* 90 (2003): 1357–78; R. Marie Griffith and Melanie McAlister, eds., "Special Issue: Religion and Politics in the Contemporary United States," *American Quarterly* 59 (September 2007); Robert A. Orsi, "A New Beginning, Again," *Journal of the American Academy of Religion* 72 (September 2004): 587–602; Orsi, *Between Heaven and Earth: The Religious Worlds People Make and the Scholars Who Study Them* (Princeton, N.J.: Princeton University Press, 2005).

16. David O'Brien, *Public Catholicism* (New York: Macmillan, 1989); Mary Lethert Wingerd, *Claiming the City: Politics, Faith, and the Power of Place in St. Paul* (Ithaca, N.Y.: Cornell University Press, 2001); Evelyn Savidge Sterne, *Ballots and Bibles: Ethnic Politics and the Catholic Church in Providence* (Ithaca, N.Y.: Cornell University Press, 2003); Leslie Tentler, *Catholics and Contraception: An American History* (Ithaca, N.Y.: Cornell University Press, 2004); James T. Fisher, *On the Irish Waterfront: The Crusader, the Movie, and the Soul of the Port of New York* (Ithaca, N.Y.: Cornell University Press, 2009).

17. Orsi, *Madonna of 115th Street*; Robert A. Orsi, *Thank You, St. Jude: Women's Devotion to the Patron Saint of Hopeless Causes* (New Haven, Conn.: Yale University Press, 1996); Orsi, *God of the City: Religion and the American Urban Landscape* (Bloomington: Indiana University Press, 1999).

18. Thomas Bender, *A Nation among Nations: America's Place in World History* (New York: Hill and Wang, 2006), 6–7. For other discussions of a more internationalized American history, see Ian Tyrrell, "American Exceptionalism in an Age of International History," *American Historical Review* 96 (October 1991): 1031–55; Michael J. Hogan, "SHAFR Presidential Address: The 'Next Big Thing'; The Future of Diplomatic History in a Global Age," *Diplomatic History* 28, no. 1 (January 2004): 1–21; Thomas Bender, ed., *Rethinking American History in a Global Age* (Berkeley: University of California Press, 2002); and Tuck, "New American Histories," 813–15.

19. "Broadband," *Wikipedia*, http://en.wikipedia.org/wiki/Broadband.

20. John W. Briggs, *An Italian Passage: Immigrants to Three American Cities, 1890–1930* (New Haven, Conn.: Yale University Press, 1978).

21. Brenda Gayle Plummer, *Rising Wind: Black Americans and U.S. Foreign Affairs, 1935–1960* (Chapel Hill: University of North Carolina Press, 1996); Penny Von

Eschen, *Race against Empire: Black Americans and Anticolonialism, 1937–1957* (Ithaca, N.Y.: Cornell University Press, 1997); Robin Kelley, "'But a Local Phase of a World Problem': Black History's Global Vision, 1883–1950," *Journal of American History* 86, no. 3 (December 1999): 1045–77; Mary Dudziak, *Cold War Civil Rights: Race and the Image of American Democracy* (Princeton, N.J.: Princeton University Press, 2000); Thomas Borstelmann, *The Cold War and the Color Line: American Race Relations in the Global Arena* (Cambridge, Mass.: Harvard University Press, 2001); Carol Anderson, *Eyes off the Prize: The United Nations and the African American Struggle for Human Rights, 1944–1955* (New York: Cambridge University Press, 2003); Nikhil Pal Singh, *Black Is a Country: Race and the Unfinished Struggle for Democracy* (Cambridge, Mass.: Harvard University Press, 2004); Jonathan Rosenberg, *How Far the Promised Land? World Affairs and the American Civil Rights Movement from the First World War to Vietnam* (Princeton, N.J.: Princeton University Press, 2006); Ruth Feldstein, "'I Don't Trust You Anymore': Nina Simone, Culture, and Black Activism in the 1960s," *Journal of American History* 91, no. 4 (March 2005): 1349–79; and James Campbell, *Middle Passages: African American Journeys to Africa, 1787–2005* (New York: Penguin Press, 2006). I should note that some of this literature focuses on black elites, intellectuals, and social reformers.

22. Lawrence W. Kennedy, *Planning the City upon a Hill: Boston since 1630* (Amherst: University of Massachusetts Press, 1992), 167; Nancy Rita Anone, "Redevelopment in Boston: A Study of the Politics and Administration of Social Change" (Ph.D. diss., Massachusetts Institute of Technology, 1965), 10–24; John H. Mollenkopf, *The Contested City* (Princeton, N.J.: Princeton University Press, 1983), 142–46; "Boston: What Can A Sick City Do?" *Fortune*, June 1964, 132; Thomas H. O'Connor, *Building a New Boston: Politics and Urban Renewal, 1950–1970* (Boston: Northeastern University Press, 1993), 190.

23. My discussion of Vatican II and the Boston Church's experience with it and the city's urban renewal is based on the following sources: "The Unlikely Cardinal," in "Catholics in the U.S.: A Surge of Renewal," special issue, *Time*, August 21, 1964, http://www.time.com/time/printout/0,8816,876036,00.html; Xavier Rynne, "Letter from Vatican City," *New Yorker*, December 25, 1965, http://www.newyorker.com/archive/1965/12/25/1965_12_25_034_TNY_CARDS_000282451; Patrick Allitt, *Religion in America since 1945: A History* (New York: Columbia University Press, 2003), 67, 80–86, 107–11; John T. McGreevy, *Catholicism and American Freedom. A History* (New York: W. W. Norton, 2003), 205, 236–38, 256, 269, 283–84; Thomas H. O'Connor, *Boston Catholics: A History of the Church and Its People* (Boston: Northeastern University Press, 1998), 239–82; McGreevy, *Parish Boundaries*, 125–26, 128–32, 145, 151, 158–64, 178–80, 209; O'Connor, *Building a New Boston*, 13–14, 37, 42, 45, 49, 92–98, 102–6, 116, 127–31, 177, 196–97, 216–19; and J. Anthony Lukas, *Common Ground: A Turbulent Decade in the Lives of Three American Families* (New York: Alfred A. Knopf, 1985), 354–56, 385. For interesting evidence of Monsignor Lally's progressivism before Vatican II, which likely reflected Cushing's sentiments as well, see "A Mike Wallace Interview with Francis J. Lally," produced by the American Broadcasting Company in association with the Fund for the Republic, 1958, http://www.hrc.utexas.edu/multimedia/video/2008/wallace/lally_francis_t.html. Insight into Lally's views during the key urban-renewal era of the

1960s can be gleaned from Francis J. Lally, *The Catholic Church in a Changing America* (Boston: Little, Brown, 1962).

24. My discussion of the crisis of busing in Boston's Catholic communities is based on Lukas, *Common Ground*, esp. 358–404; Ronald P. Formisano, *Boston against Busing: Race, Class, and Ethnicity in the 1960s and 1970s* (Chapel Hill: University of North Carolina Press, 1991); O'Connor, *Boston Catholics*, 283–304; and D. C. Williams, "Militant Women or Concerned Mothers: Catholic Women, School Desegregation and Busing in Boston, 1974–1976" (paper for History 2601, January 12, 2007, in my possession). Two years into his archbishopship in Boston, Medeiros expressed his social vision, which included racial integration, in his published pastoral letter, *Man's Cities, God's Poor* (Boston: Daughters of St. Paul, 1972), particularly 61.

25. I am grateful for suggestions on possible future research projects from John McGreevy in his comments on my keynote presentation at the conference "Catholicism in the Twentieth Century" at the Cushwa Center for the Study of American Catholicism, University of Notre Dame, April 17, 2008. Timothy Matovina of Notre Dame has done important work on Mexican American Catholics; see Matovina and Gary Riebe-Eestrella, eds., *Horizons of the Sacred: Mexican Traditions in U.S. Catholicism* (Ithaca, N.Y.: Cornell University Press, 2002); and Matovina, *Guadalupe and Her Faithful: Latino Catholics in San Antonio, from Colonial Origins to the Present* (Baltimore: Johns Hopkins University Press, 2005). On global population-control policies, see Matthew Connelly, *Fatal Misconception: The Struggle to Control World Population* (Cambridge, Mass.: Harvard University Press, 2008); and Erez Manela, forthcoming book on global population policies. On American Catholic contraception practices, see Tentler, *Catholics and Contraception*.

Chapter 3

1. Philip Gleason, *Keeping the Faith: American Catholicism Past and Present* (Notre Dame, Ind.: Univ. of Notre Dame Press, 1987), 139.

2. Bernardin and others quoted in Joseph P. Chinnici, OFM, "The Catholic Community at Prayer, 1926–1976," in *Habits of Devotion: Catholic Religious Practice in Twentieth-Century America*, ed. James M. O'Toole (Ithaca, N.Y.: Cornell University Press, 2004), 9–11; Joseph Komonchak, "Interpreting the Council: Catholic Attitudes toward Vatican II," in *Being Right: Conservative Catholics in America*, ed. Mary Jo Weaver and R. Scott Appleby (Bloomington: Indiana University Press, 1995), 22.

3. Charles R. Morris, *American Catholic: The Saints and Sinners Who Built America's Most Powerful Church* (New York: Times Books, 1997), 255.

4. Benjamin DeMott, "The Sixties: A Cultural Revolution," *New York Times Sunday Magazine*, December 14, 1969, 30.

5. Rick Perlstein, "Who Owns the Sixties?" in *Quick Studies: The Best of Lingua Franca*, ed. Alexander Star (New York: Farrar, Straus and Giroux, 2002), 234–46.

6. Chinnici, "Catholic Community at Prayer," to take one example, offers an important corrective. And work on Catholic family history and contraception high-

lights the shift toward understandings of companionate marriage that were widespread in the modern United States.

7. Alan Matusow, *The Unraveling of America: A History of Liberalism in the 1960s* (New York: Harper and Row, 1984); Milton Viorst, *Fire in the Streets: America in the 1960s* (New York: Simon and Schuster, 1980); John Morton Blum, *Years of Discord: American Politics and Society, 1961–74* (New York: W. W. Norton, 1991); William O'Neill, *Coming Apart: An Informal History of America in the 1960s* (Chicago: Quadrangle, 1971).

8. Kim Phillips-Fein, *Invisible Hands: The Making of the Conservative Movement from the New Deal to Reagan* (New York: W. W. Norton, 2009), Lisa McGirr, *Suburban Warriors: The Origins of the New American Right* (Princeton, N.J.: Princeton University Press, 2001); Kevin M. Kruse, *White Flight: Atlanta and the Making of Modern Conservatism* (Princeton, N.J.: Princeton University Press, 2005); Rick Perlstein, *Before the Storm: Barry Goldwater and the Unmaking of the American Consensus* (New York: Hill and Wang, 2001).

9. Ira Katznelson, "Was the Great Society a Lost Opportunity?" in *The Rise and Fall of the New Deal Order,* ed. Steve Fraser and Gary Gerstle (Princeton, N.J.: Princeton University Press, 1988).

10. On grassroots antiliberalism, see Arnold R. Hirsch, *Making the Second Ghetto: Race and Housing in Chicago, 1940–1960* (New York: Cambridge University Press, 1983); Thomas J. Sugrue, *The Origins of the Urban Crisis: Race and Inequality in Postwar Detroit,* Princeton Classic ed. (Princeton, N.J.: Princeton University Press, 2005); and Robert O. Self, *American Babylon: Race and the Struggle for Postwar Oakland* (Princeton, N.J.: Princeton University Press, 2003). On the family and sexuality, see Stephanie Coontz, *The Way We Never Were: American Families and the Nostalgia Trap* (New York: Basic Books, 1992); Joanne Meyerowitz, ed., *Not June Cleaver: Women and Gender in Postwar America* (Philadelphia: Temple University Press, 1994); John D'Emilio, *Sexual Politics, Sexual Communities: The Making of a Homosexual Culture in the United States, 1940–1970,* 2nd ed. (Chicago: University of Chicago Press, 1998); and Marc Stein, *City of Sisterly and Brotherly Loves: Lesbian and Gay Philadelphia, 1945–1972* (Chicago: University of Chicago Press, 2000).

11. Doug Rossinow, *The Politics of Authenticity: Liberalism, Christianity, and the New Left in America* (New York: Columbia University Press, 1998); Daniel Bell, *The Cultural Contradictions of Capitalism* (New York: Basic Books, 1976); Terry Anderson, "The New American Revolution: The Movement and Business," in *The Sixties from Memory to History,* ed. David Farber (Chapel Hill: University of North Carolina Press, 1994); Thomas Frank, *The Conquest of Cool: Business Culture, Counterculture, and the Rise of Hip Consumerism* (Chicago: University of Chicago Press, 1997); Thomas Frank and Matt Weiland, eds., *Commodify Your Dissent* (New York: W. W. Norton, 1997).

12. Jacqueline Dowd Hall, "The Long Civil Rights Movement and the Political Uses of the Past," *Journal of American History* 91 (2005): 1233–63; Glenda Gilmore, *Defying Dixie: The Radical Roots of Civil Rights* (New York: W. W. Norton, 2008); Peniel Joseph, *Waiting 'til the Midnight Hour: A Narrative History of Black Power in America* (New York: Henry Holt, 2006); Thomas J. Sugrue, *Sweet Land of Liberty: The*

Forgotten Struggle for Civil Rights in the North (New York: Random House, 2008); Thomas F. Jackson, *From Civil Rights to Human Rights: Martin Luther King, Jr. and the Struggle for Economic Justice* (Philadelphia: University of Pennsylvania Press, 2007).

13. See Matthew Lassiter, *The Silent Majority: Suburban Politics in the Sunbelt South* (Princeton, N.J.: Princeton University Press, 2005); and various chapters in Kevin M. Kruse and Thomas J. Sugrue, eds., *The New Suburban History* (Chicago: University of Chicago Press, 2006).

14. James Fisher, "Clearing the Streets of the Catholic Lost Generation," in *Catholic Lives, Contemporary America*, ed. Thomas J. Ferraro (Durham, N.C.: Duke University Press, 1997), 86.

15. Only two textbooks on the 1960s spend more than a few paragraphs on religion. One dates from the early 1970s: O'Neill, *Coming Apart*; the other is more recent, Maurice Isserman and Michael Kazin, *America Divided: The Civil War of the 1960s* (New York: Oxford University Press, 1999), 241–60.

16. See Jackson Lee and John J. Carey, eds., *The Death of God Debate* (Philadelphia: Westminister Press, 1967).

17. Rossinow, *Politics of Authenticity*; Hugh Heclo, "The Sixties' False Dawn: Awakenings, Movements, and Postmodern Policy-Making," in *Integrating the Sixties: The Origins, Structures, and Legitimacy of Public Policy in a Turbulent Decade,* ed. Brian Balogh (University Park: Pennsylvania State University Press, 2004), 34–63; Amanda Porterfield, *The Transformation of American Religion: The Story of a Late Twentieth-Century Awakening* (New York: Oxford University Press, 2001), 90, 119–20.

18. Gleason, *Keeping the Faith*, 84.

19. Porterfield, *Transformation of American Religion*, 90, 119–20.

20. Elaine Tyler May, *Homeward Bound: American Families in the Cold War Era* (New York: Basic Books, 1988); Kathryn A. Johnson, "A Question of Authority: Friction in the Catholic Family Life Movement, 1948–1962," *Catholic Historical Review* 86 (2000): 217–41; Johnson, "The Home Is a Little Church: Gender, Culture, and Authority in American Catholicism, 1940–1962" (Ph.D. diss., University of Pennsylvania, 1997).

21. Leslie Woodcock Tentler, *Catholics and Contraception: An American History* (Ithaca, N.Y.: Cornell University Press, 2004), offers a superb overview of this topic.

22. Chinnici, "Catholic Community at Prayer," 9–87; Jay P. Dolan, R. Scott Appleby, Patricia Byrne, and Debra Campbell, *Transforming Parish Ministry: The Changing Roles of Catholic Clergy, Laity, and Women Religious* (New York: Crossroad, 1990); David J. O'Brien, *Public Catholicism*, 2nd ed. (Maryknoll, N.Y.: Orbis Books, 1996), 232.

23. Andrew M. Greeley, *Religion and Career* (New York: Sheed and Ward, 1963); Greeley, *The American Catholic: A Social Portrait* (New York: Basic Books, 1977).

24. One interesting account is Timothy Kelly, "Suburbanization and the Decline of Catholic Public Ritual in Pittsburgh," *Journal of Social History* 28 (Winter 1994): 311–30.

25. Joseph Fichter, SJ, quoted in R. Scott Appleby, "Present to the People of God: The Transformation of the Roman Catholic Parish Priesthood," in Dolan et al., *Transforming Parish Ministry*, 48; Andrew M. Greeley, *The Church and the Suburbs* (New York: Sheed and Ward, 1959), 33, 149, 47. For an excellent discussion of Catholic suburbanization, see Johnson, "Home Is a Little Church," 32–41.

26. Michael Clapper, "The Constructed World of Postwar Philadelphia Area Schools: Site Selection, Architecture, and the Landscape of Inequality" (Ph.D. diss., University of Pennsylvania, 2008), 149.

27. "Catholic Teachers Accuse Diocese of Fostering Racial Segregation," *Philadelphia Evening Bulletin*, July 31, 1973, cited in Clapper, "Constructed World," 149.

28. Greeley, *Church and the Suburbs*, 56.

29. R. Scott Appleby, "The Triumph of Americanism: Common Ground for U.S. Catholics in the Twentieth Century," in Weaver and Appleby, *Being Right*, 39.

30. For the importance of the Cold War in bringing Catholics and Protestants together, see Michelle Nickerson, "Women, Gender, and Conservatism in Cold War Los Angeles, 1945–1966" (Ph.D diss., Yale University, 2004).

31. On anti-Catholicism, see John Higham's classic, *Strangers in the Land* (New Brunswick, N.J.: Rutgers University Press, 1954); more recently, Mark S. Massa, *Anti-Catholicism: The Last Acceptable Prejudice?* (New York: Crossroad Press, 2003); quote from Michael Novak, *The Rise of the Unmeltable Ethnics* (New York: Macmillan, 1972), 71–72. Novak ignored the fact that many prominent advocates of civil rights in the urban North were priests and nuns. See Amy L. Koehlinger, *The New Nuns: Racial Justice and Religious Reform in the 1960s* (Cambridge, Mass.: Harvard University Press, 2007); Suellen Hoy, *Good Hearts: Catholic Sisters in Chicago's Past* (Urbana: University of Illinois Press, 2006), 125–54; and Patrick Jones, *The Selma of the North: Civil Rights Insurgency in Milwaukee* (Cambridge, Mass.: Harvard University Press, 2009).

32. James A. Sullivan, "Catholics United for the Faith: Dissent and the Laity," in Weaver and Appleby, *Being Right*, 107–37. On Bozell's influence on Barry Goldwater, see Thomas J. Sugrue, "In Your Guts You Know He's Nuts" [review of Barry Goldwater, *The Conscience of a Conservative*], *London Review of Books*, January 3, 2008, 29–31, and generally on Bozell and his milieu, Patrick Allitt, *Catholic Intellectuals and Conservative Politics in America, 1950–1985* (Ithaca, N.Y.: Cornell University Press, 1993).

33. Michael Novak, *The Spirit of Democratic Capitalism* (New York: Simon and Schuster, 1982).

34. George Weigel, "The Neo-conservative Difference: A Proposal for the Renewal of Church and Society," in Weaver and Appleby, *Being Right*, 150.

35. Shaun A. Casey, *The Making of a Catholic President: Kennedy vs. Nixon, 1960* (New York: Oxford University Press, 2009), esp. 163–76, 200–203.

36. Daniel Patrick Moynihan, *The Negro Family: The Case for National Action* (Washington, D.C.: U.S. Department of Labor, 1965). Few historians or commentators dwell on Moynihan's Catholicism. James T. Patterson, *Freedom Is Not Enough: The Moynihan Report and America's Struggle over Black Family Life from LBJ to Obama* (New York: Basic Books, 2010), 15, 226n13, and 232n28, only fleetingly mentions Moynihan's religious beliefs. There are some suggestive sentences here and there in Godfrey Hodgson, *The Gentleman from New York: Daniel Patrick Moynihan; A Biography* (Boston: Houghton Mifflin, 2004), esp. 78. Johnson, "Home Is a Little Church," offers a rich analysis of Catholic family values.

37. Allitt, *Catholic Intellectuals and Conservative Politics in America*; for my discussion of Bozell's influence on Barry Goldwater's *Conscience of a Conservative*, see Sugrue,

"In Your Guts You Know He's Nuts"; Donald Critchlow, *Phyllis Schlafly and Grassroots Conservatism: A Woman's Crusade* (Princeton, N.J.: Princeton University Press, 2005); Maurice Isserman, *The Other American: The Life of Michael Harrington* (New York: Public Affairs, 2000); Frederick John Dalton, *The Moral Vision of César Chávez* (Maryknoll, N.Y.: Orbis Books, 2003); the full text of the *Moynihan Report* with commentaries (silent on Moynihan's religion) can be found in Lee Rainwater and William L. Yancey, eds., *The Moynihan Report and the Politics of Controversy* (Cambridge, Mass.: MIT Press, 1967).

38. The classic example of this work is Lee Benson, *The Concept of Jacksonian Democracy: New York as a Test Case* (Princeton, N.J.: Princeton University Press, 1964).

39. Lizabeth Cohen, *Making a New Deal: Industrial Workers in Chicago, 1919–1939* (New York: Cambridge University Press, 1990); Gary Gerstle, *Working-Class Americanism: The Politics of Labor in a Textile City, 1914–1960* (New York: Cambridge University Press, 1989) (better than most on Catholicism); Sugrue, *Origins of the Urban Crisis*, 192, 213–17, 237–40. McGreevy's Stanford dissertation was published as *Parish Boundaries: The Catholic Encounter with Race in the Urban North* (Chicago: University of Chicago Press, 1997); Gamm's Harvard dissertation was published as *Urban Exodus: Why the Jews Left Boston and the Catholics Stayed* (Cambridge, Mass.: Harvard University Press, 1999). For works that examine Catholicism and politics in earlier periods, see Mary Lethert Wingerd, *Claiming the City: Politics, Faith, and the Power of Place in St. Paul* (Ithaca, N.Y.: Cornell University Press, 2001); and Evelyn Savidge Sterne, *Ballots and Bibles: Ethnic Politics and the Catholic Church in Providence* (Ithaca, N.Y.: Cornell University Press, 2004).

40. John T. McGreevy, *Catholicism and American Freedom* (New York: W. W. Norton, 2003), 265; *Bishops' Program of Social Reconstruction* (Washington, D.C.: National Catholic Welfare Conference, 1919); John A. Ryan, *Social Reconstruction* (New York: Macmillan, 1920); Zachary Ryan Calo, " 'The Ethical Aspect of Economic Doctrine': The Social Thought of John A. Ryan and the Making of American Catholic Liberalism, 1900–1940" (Ph.D. diss., University of Pennsylvania, 2007). Both Alice Kessler-Harris, *In Pursuit of Equity: Women, Men, and the Quest for Economic Citizenship in 20th-Century America* (New York: Oxford University Press, 2001), and Linda Gordon, *Pitied but Not Entitled: Single Women and the History of Welfare* (New York: Free Press, 1994), highlight the gendered limitations of the American welfare state but leave Catholicism out.

41. On the New Deal, see the classic by David J. O'Brien, *American Catholics and Social Reform: The New Deal Years* (New York: Oxford University Press, 1968); and Kenneth J. Heineman, *A Catholic New Deal: Religion and Reform in Depression Pittsburgh* (University Park: Pennsylvania State University Press, 1999). On the New Deal compromise, see Thomas J. Sugrue, "All Politics Is Local: The Persistence of Localism in Twentieth-Century America," in *The Democratic Experiment: New Directions in American Political History*, ed. Meg Jacobs, William Novak, and Julian Zelizer (Princeton, N.J.: Princeton University Press, 2003), 301–26.

42. On the campaign for free enterprise, see Elizabeth Fones-Wolf, *Selling Free Enterprise: The Business Assault on Labor and Liberalism, 1945–1960* (Urbana: University of Illinois Press, 1995). On the appeal of Republicans to Catholic voters, especially in the 1950s, see Joshua M. Zeitz, *White Ethnic New York: Jews, Catholics, and the*

Shaping of Postwar Politics (Chapel Hill: University of North Carolina Press, 2007). On Catholics and McCarthy, see the old but still-useful book of Donald Crosby, *God, Church, and Flag: Senator Joseph R. McCarthy and the Catholic Church, 1950–1957* (Chapel Hill: University of North Carolina Press, 1978). For a local case study of anticommunism—we need more—see Colleen Patrice Doody, "Anti-communism in America: Detroit's Cold War, 1945–1960" (Ph.D. diss., University of Virginia, 2005), chap. 2. On the growing legitimacy of free-enterprise rhetoric among Catholic intellectuals, see Allitt, *Catholic Intellectuals and Conservative Politics*. The most influential advocate of pro-capitalist Catholicism is Michael Novak. See his *Spirit of Democratic Capitalism* and *The Catholic Ethic and the Spirit of Capitalism* (New York: Free Press, 1993)

43. Peter J. Henriot, SSJ, "Political vs. Religious Liberalism among Catholics," in *Catholics/U.S.A.: Perspectives on Social Change*, ed. William T. Liu and Nathaniel J. Pallone (New York: John Wiley and Sons, 1970), 298.

44. On activism at La Salle University, St. Joseph's University, and Villanova University, see Paul Lyons, *The People of This Generation: The Rise and Fall of the New Left in Philadelphia* (Philadelphia: University of Pennsylvania Press, 2003), 73–87; on Fordham, see Zeitz, *White Ethnic New York*, 207–22.

45. Lawrence Wittner, *Rebels against War: The American Peace Movement, 1933–1983* (Philadelphia: Temple University Press, 1984); James Tracy, *Direct Action: Radical Pacifism from the Union Eight to the Chicago Seven* (Chicago: University of Chicago Press, 1996); Marian Mollin, *Radical Pacifism in Modern America: Egalitarianism and Protest* (Philadelphia: University of Pennsylvania Press, 2006).

46. For an excellent brief discussion of the Berrigans and radicalism, see David J. O'Brien, *The Renewal of American Catholicism* (New York: Oxford University Press, 1972), 194–230. Francine du Plessix Gray, *Divine Disobedience* (New York: Random House, 1969), remains the best biography of the Berrigans.

47. Daniel Berrigan, quoted in O'Brien, *Renewal of American Catholicism*, 200, 205–6; see also David O'Brien, "American Catholics and the Vietnam War: A Preliminary Assessment," in *War and Peace: The Search for New Answers*, ed. Thomas Shannon (Maryknoll, N.Y.: Orbis Books, 1981), 119–51.

Chapter 4

1. The term "Protestant" is problematic, of course, given the many varieties within the tradition, past and present, and I cannot give adequate definitional precision in this chapter without constantly disrupting the narrative flow to clarify exactly which American Protestants I mean in each case. Generally, by "liberal Protestants" I mean those in denominations within the National Council of Churches of Christ (formerly the Federal Council of Churches), and more specifically those who have leaned toward greater freedoms and civil rights for women, among other causes—those who take an egalitarian view of gender, in other words. By "conservative Protestants" I typically refer to fundamentalists and to those evangelicals who take a different view of gender; in this chapter these include those who have at various times opposed the birth-control movement, the sex reports of Alfred Kinsey, and comprehensive sex-education programs in the public schools. These are

clearly not in any way fixed categories; their usage here should be considered flexible and descriptive rather than rigid or prescriptive. Because evangelicals, like Catholics, have stood on all sides of these issues, I avoid using the term "evangelical" here, but certainly the conservative Protestants whom this chapter explores included many evangelicals.

2. John T. McGreevy, *Catholicism and American Freedom: A History* (New York: W. W. Norton, 2003); quote on 157.

3. Ibid., 95. Here he is quoting from "Christianity and Woman's Suffrage," *Woman's Journal*, August 24, 1878, 268; and T. W. E., "A Suffragist's Reply to a Roman Catholic Bishop," *Woman's Journal*, March 24, 1877, 93. As McGreevy shows, well into the twentieth century, many Protestant women's reform and rescue societies built successful fund-raising campaigns by describing in vivid detail Catholic ill-treatment of women and children.

4. I hasten to note that by "mainstream" here I mean simply the historical scholarship that is generally celebrated, read, and taught in the field of gender and sexuality studies outside Catholic (and perhaps other religious) circles.

5. John D'Emilio and Estelle B. Freedman, *Intimate Matters: A History of Sexuality in America*, 2nd ed. (Chicago: University of Chicago Press, 1997); for example, see 281–82, 344, 350. Only one paragraph is devoted to lay Catholics who have rejected the church's ban on birth control (252).

6. Beth Bailey, *Sex in the Heartland* (Cambridge, Mass.: Harvard University Press, 1999). Here again, even where Catholic leaders are shown to support liberal or progressive views on gender issues, they appear only as atypical exceptions (see, for instance, 115).

7. Jane Gerhard, *Desiring Revolution: Second-Wave Feminism and the Rewriting of American Sexual Thought, 1920 to 1982* (New York: Columbia University Press, 2001), 64.

8. For instance, George Chauncey, *Gay New York: Gender, Urban Culture, and the Making of the Gay Male World, 1890–1940* (New York: Basic Books, 1994).

9. Kathleen Sprows Cummings, *New Women of the Old Faith: Gender and American Catholicism in the Progressive Era* (Chapel Hill: University of North Carolina Press, 2009), 3. Cummings's work ruminates in sophisticated and illuminating ways on some of the issues I treat more briefly here.

10. In other words, I do not know of formal discussions or scholarly articles that have taken up this topic or argued in favor of omitting Catholics from a particular study of gender; reasons for the omission tend to be unspoken, but some, at least, seem fairly clear.

11. As a typical example, the website for Harvard University's Program in Studies of Women, Gender, and Sexuality states, "At the heart of this field is the assertion that gender and sexuality are fundamental categories of social organization and power that are inseparable from race, ethnicity, class, nationality, and other categories of difference" (http://www.fas.harvard.edu/~wgs/about/about.htm). Similarly, the University of California at Berkeley gives this description on its Gender and Women's Studies page: "The Department of Gender & Women's Studies offers interdisciplinary perspectives on the formation of gender and its intersections with other relations of power, such as sexuality, race, class, nationality, religion, and age"

(http://womensstudies.berkeley.edu/). The website for the Gender Studies Program at the University of Notre Dame, however, offers a less social-constructivist view of gender as chiefly an axis of power relations: "Gender Studies analyzes the significance of gender—and the cognate subjects of sex, sexuality, race, ethnicity, class, religion, and nationality—in all areas of human life, especially in the social formation of human identities, practices, and institutions. Gender Studies gives scholars the methodological and theoretical tools to analyze gender and its cognates in their chosen disciplines in the arts, humanities, social sciences, and natural sciences. Gender Studies also provides its students and alumni with an intellectual framework in which the analysis of gender and its cognates can be creatively and critically applied to their personal, familial, professional, and civic roles. In the context of the Catholic identity of Notre Dame, Gender Studies facilitates the study of the intersection of gender and religion in the shaping of ethics, culture, and politics. Alongside our diverse array of courses drawn from across the university, our summer internship and academic-credit internship programs emphasize the holistic and practical life applications of a Gender Studies education at Notre Dame" (http://www.nd.edu/~gender/).

12. I refer here to scholars such as Judith Butler, Eve Kosofsky Sedgwick, and Donna Haraway, to name a few of the most influential among many who argue against gender binaries. Gender, in this light, has been understood as a social construction (however malleable) but even more as performance, while sex has been redefined as a spectrum rather than a binary, thus upending the traditional categories of man and woman as well as the normative assumption of heterosexuality. See, for starters, Judith Butler, *Gender Trouble: Feminism and the Subversion of Identity* (New York: Routledge, 1990); Eve Kosofsky Sedgwick, *Epistemology of the Closet* (Berkeley: University of California Press, 1990); and Donna J. Haraway, *Simians, Cyborgs, and Women: The Reinvention of Nature* (New York and London: Routledge, 1991).

13. Numerous critics of the women and gender studies field have made this argument, including Christina Hoff Sommers, Elizabeth Fox-Genovese, and Daphne Patai. In no way should my description of the field suggest sympathy with the exaggerated, distorted depictions each of these writers has painted.

14. Aline H. Kalbian, *Sexing the Church: Gender, Power, and Ethics in Contemporary Catholicism* (Bloomington: Indiana University Press, 2005).

15. See, for example, Mary J. Henold, *Catholic and Feminist: The Surprising History of the American Catholic Feminist Movement* (Chapel Hill: University of North Carolina Press, 2008).

16. Among numerous examples that could be cited here are the following: Carol K. Coburn, *Spirited Lives: How Nuns Shaped Catholic Culture and American Life, 1836–1920* (Chapel Hill: University of North Carolina Press, 1999); Suellen Hoy, *Good Hearts: Catholic Sisters in Chicago's Past* (Urbana: University of Illinois Press, 2006); Amy Koehlinger, *The New Nuns: Racial Justice and Religious Reform in the 1960s* (Cambridge, Mass.: Harvard University Press, 2007); and Sarah McFarland Taylor, *Green Sisters: A Spiritual Ecology* (Cambridge, Mass.: Harvard University Press, 2007).

17. Henold, *Catholic and Feminist.*

18. Robert A. Orsi, *The Madonna of 115th Street: Faith and Community in Italian Harlem, 1880–1950* (New Haven, Conn.: Yale University Press, 1985); Julie Byrne,

O God of Players: The Story of the Immaculata Mighty Macs (New York: Columbia University Press, 2003).

19. Leslie Woodcock Tentler, *Catholics and Contraception: An American History* (Ithaca, N.Y.: Cornell University Press, 2004). This is in no way to denounce those other studies, many of which are extremely valuable and important; it is simply to note that gender as a category of analysis is not of great significance in them. See, for instance, James Terence Fisher, *The Catholic Counterculture in America, 1933–1962* (Chapel Hill: University of North Carolina Press, 1989); Peter R. D'Agostino, *Rome in America: Transnational Catholic Ideology from the Risorgimento to Fascism* (Chapel Hill: University of North Carolina Press, 2004); and McGreevy, *Catholicism and American Freedom.*

20. Paula Kane, "General Introduction," in *Gender Identities in American Catholicism,* ed. Paula Kane, James Kenneally, and Karen Kennelly (Maryknoll, N.Y.: Orbis Books, 2001), xix, xxvii.

21. Ibid., xxvi.

22. Several scholars of Catholicism who write in a much more radical vein and who align more with queer theory than with women's history come to mind, above all, the ethicist Mark D. Jordan. See Jordan, *The Silence of Sodom: Homosexuality in Modern Catholicism* (Chicago: University of Chicago Press, 2000).

23. Cummings, *New Women of the Old Faith,* 13, 160.

24. Tentler, *Catholics and Contraception,* 46. McGreevy also writes extensively about battles over birth control as well as abortion in *Catholicism and American Freedom,* although with less detail than Tentler.

25. The denunciations have often focused on Sanger's eugenic views while forgetting how many other Americans, including Catholic leaders, shared in the Progressive Era eugenic craze before reconsidering its horrific possibilities.

26. See, for instance, Angela Franks, *Margaret Sanger's Eugenic Legacy: The Control of Female Fertility* (Jefferson, N.C.: McFarland, 2005); George Grant, *Killer Angel: A Short Biography of Planned Parenthood's Founder Margaret Sanger,* rev. ed. (Nashville: Cumberland House, 2001), esp. 90. Grant is a fundamentalist Protestant who has cooperated with right-wing Catholics such as Randall Terry on issues relating to sexuality and reproduction.

27. David M. Kennedy, *Birth Control in America: The Career of Margaret Sanger* (New Haven, Conn.: Yale University Press, 1970); Ellen Chesler, *Woman of Valor: Margaret Sanger and the Birth Control Movement in America* (1993; repr., New York: Simon & Schuster, 2007).

28. Kathleen A. Tobin, *The American Religious Debate over Birth Control, 1907–1937* (Jefferson, N.C.: McFarland & Company, 2001).

29. Kathleen A. Tobin, "Catholicism and the Contraceptive Debate, 1914–1930," in *Reconciling Catholicism and Feminism? Personal Reflections on Tradition and Change,* ed. Sally Barr Ebest and Ron Ebest (Notre Dame, Ind.: University of Notre Dame Press, 2003), 202–16; quotes on 210.

30. Ibid., 211.

31. Alfred C. Kinsey, Wardell B. Pomeroy, and Clyde E. Martin, *Sexual Behavior in the Human Male* (Philadelphia: W. B. Saunders, 1948); Alfred C. Kinsey, Wardell B. Pomeroy, Clyde E. Martin, and Paul H. Gebhard, *Sexual Behavior in the Human*

Female (Philadelphia: W. B. Saunders, 1953); Donald Porter Geddes and Enid Curie, eds., *About the Kinsey Report: Observations by 11 Experts on "Sexual Behavior in the Human Male"* (New York: New American Library, 1948), 17; "Sheehy Attacks Kinsey Report," *Washington Post* (November 14, 1948), M19.

32. Bill Condon, director, *Kinsey* (20th Century Fox, 2004), DVD. On opening day Stuart Shepard, a correspondent for Focus on the Family, warned potential moviegoers that "the film's trailer only begins to hint at how foul it actually is." Shepard cited the indefatigable anti-Kinsey writer Judith Reisman as an authority on Kinsey's support of pedophilia and quoted her unsubstantiated description of Kinsey as "a man who organizes the rapes of hundreds, if not thousands of children, infants included, 2 months of age"; http://www.family.org/cforum/fnif/news /a0034534.cfm. Focus on the Family also launched an anti-Kinsey website called the Kinsey Impact Project, an initiative "to counter the film's misleading message" that remained online long after the film's shift from theater to rental store. The broader contemporary anti-Kinsey campaign is too expansive to detail here. See, e.g., Susan Brinkmann, *The Kinsey Corruption: An Exposé on the Most Influential "Scientist" of Our Time* (West Chester, Penn.: Ascension Press, 2004), 1, 4. Brinkmann's book is based on the book *Kinsey: Crimes and Consequences* by Dr. Judith Reisman (Crestwood, Ky.: Institute for Media Education, 1998). Ascension Press is the publishing arm of Catholic Outreach, a lay-run ministry that vigorously supported Mel Gibson's 2004 film *The Passion of the Christ*. The foreword was penned by Christopher West, the conservative Catholic author of such books as *Good News about Sex and Marriage* and various commentaries on Pope John Paul II's *Theology of the Body*.

33. Elizabeth and William Genné, *Christians and the Crisis in Sex Morality* (New York: Association Press, 1962), 16–17, 77. The Gennés authored this popular trade book in the wake of the First North American Conference on Church and Family in 1961, convened by the Canadian and National (U.S.A.) Councils of Churches and held at Green Lake, Wisconsin. The conference attracted over five hundred delegates who represented thirty-three denominations and fifty-seven states and provinces. For five days participants took part in plenary sessions presenting sex research from a wide range of research specialists, response panels from church leaders, lengthy discussion groups, and a number of special events devoted to issues relating to sex and sex education. The Gennés edited the conference proceedings, titled "Foundations for Christian Family Policy: The Proceedings of the North American Conference on Church and Family," April 3—May 5, 1961 (New York, 1961), and published this second book for a wider audience. I have analyzed Kinsey's enormous impact on liberal Protestant rethinking of sexual morality in "The Religious Encounters of Alfred Kinsey," *Journal of American History* 95 (September 2008), 349–77.

34. "Pandering to Prurience," *America*, January 3, 1948, 371–72.

35. "Kinsey Report Hit in Catholic Group," *New York Times*, September 15, 1948, 20.

36. "News Release on the Kinsey Report," issued by Loyola University, Chicago (January 15, 1948).

37. George Gallup, "Kinsey Survey of Sex Habits Is Widely Approved by Public," *Washington Post*, February 21, 1948, 11. The poll did not strongly distinguish between liberal and conservative Protestants.

38. "Sheehy Attacks Kinsey Report," *Washington Post*, November 14, 1948, M19.

39. John Chapple to Kinsey, telegram, August 21, 1953, Binder 72, p. 102, Media Responses to Kinsey collection (Kinsey Institute).

40. The only study of religious responses to Kinsey is Robert Cecil Johnson, "Kinsey, Christianity, and Sex: A Critical Study of Reaction in American Christianity to the Kinsey Reports on Human Sexual Behavior" (Ph.D. diss., University of Wisconsin, 1973).

41. The sources on Kinsey's childhood religion cited by both Gathorne-Hardy and Jones all come from interviews with Kinsey's wife and children that were completed long after Kinsey's death. This tale of dour Methodists, replete with Gathorne-Hardy's own comments on the "absolutely appalling" strictures imposed by Methodism's founder, John Wesley, is surely no disinterested account, but it has become a widely accepted story of Kinsey's relation to religion. Jonathan Gathorne-Hardy, *Sex the Measure of All Things: A Life of Alfred C. Kinsey* (Bloomington: Indiana University Press, 1998), 7, 8; James H. Jones, *Alfred C. Kinsey: A Public/Private Life* (New York: W. W. Norton, 1997), 13, 14, 15. Subsequent scholars have simply taken this narrative for granted. For example, the historian Philip J. Pauly writes, "James Jones's recent comprehensive biography has emphasized how Kinsey's private passions—in particular, his desire to overcome his sexually repressed adolescence and his interest in justifying his homosexual desires—led him to investigate human behavior beginning in the late 1930s," and shortly thereafter notes the "kind of puritan repression that Kinsey was determined to overcome." Pauly, *Biologists and the Promise of American Life: From Meriwether Lewis to Alfred Kinsey* (Princeton, N.J.: Princeton University Press, 2000), 233.

42. Regina Markell Morantz, "The Scientist as Sex Crusader: Alfred C. Kinsey and American Culture," *American Quarterly* 29 (Winter 1977): 566.

43. Condon, *Kinsey*.

44. Calderone to Sister Mary Nora, June 26, 1956, Schlesinger Library, Cambridge, Mass. MC179/M-125, Box 12, Folder 203.

45. Calderone to Jack Heber, June 3, 1958, Schlesinger Library MC179/M-125, Box 12, Folder 203.

46. Mary Steichen Calderone, Phyllis Goldman, and Robert P. Goldman, *Release from Sexual Tensions: Toward an Understanding of Their Causes and Effects in Marriage* (New York: Random House, 1960), 238, 102, 220, 214, 38, 93.

47. Ibid., 214, 221, 220.

48. She actually wrote this pamphlet, she notes in an interview with Mary Steichen Calderone, M.D., August 7, 1974, Schlesinger-Rockefeller Oral History Project, 23.

49. Calderone to Father John C. Knott, February 23, 1962, Schlesinger Library MC179/M-125, Box 12, Folder 203; Calderone to Knott, April 19, 1962, ibid.

50. Calderone to Knott, June 1, 1962, ibid.

51. Henry V. Sattler to Calderone, June 29, 1962, Schlesinger Library MC179/M-125, Box 12, Folder 203; Calderone to Sattler, March 7, 1962, ibid. If Calderone responded to Sattler's cordial if candid letter, her reply has not been preserved.

52. Calderone to H. H. Neumann, May 6, 1963, Schlesinger Library MC179/M-125, Box 12, Folder 203; Neumann to Calderone, May 20, 1963, ibid.

53. Interview with Mary Steichen Calderone, M.D., August 7, 1974, Schlesinger-Rockefeller Oral History Project, 31.

54. John L. Thomas, SJ, "The Catholic Position on Population Control," *Daedalus* 88 (Summer 1959): 444–53; quotes on 445.

55. George Hagmaier, *Counselling the Catholic: Modern Techniques and Emotional Conflicts* (New York: Sheed and Ward, 1959), 9.

56. Mary S. Calderone, "Report on: Colloquium on the Sexuality of Woman," typescript, John T. McGinn, C.S.P. Papers, Paulist Archives, Washington, D.C. (uncataloged). I am very grateful to Leslie Woodcock Tentler for bringing this fascinating document to my attention and giving me a copy.

57. John L. Thomas, "The Road Ahead," in *Sexuality and Human Values*, ed. Mary S. Calderone (New York: Association Press, 1974), 132–52. Interview with Mary Steichen Calderone, M.D., August 7, 1974, Schlesinger-Rockefeller Oral History Project, 28, 34, 42.

58. Calderone's speech at Notre Dame received positive coverage in the student newspaper; Pat Gafney, "Sex Is Sex Is Sex," *Observer*, March 15, 1968, 2.

59. Mary S. Calderone, "Human Sexuality—Battleground or Peaceground?" in *Progress in Sexology: Selected Papers from the Proceedings of the 1976 International Congress of Sexology*, ed. Robert Gemme and Connie Christian Wheeler (New York: Plenum Press, 1977), 587–93; quotes on 589, 591, 592, 593.

60. Mary Breasted, *Oh! Sex Education!* (New York: New American Library, 1970); Janice M. Irvine, *Talk about Sex: The Battles over Sex Education in the United States* (Berkeley: University of California Press, 2004; Jeffrey P. Moran, *Teaching Sex: The Shaping of Adolescence in the 20th Century* (Cambridge: Harvard University Press, 2000).

Chapter 5

1. As will be made clear in the body of the text, the question of ethnic and national labeling involves complex, intertwined processes of self-definition, ascription, and juridical status. However, for the purposes of making very broad distinctions between and among population groups discussed in this chapter, I use the terms "Chicano" or "Chicana" to refer to individuals who use or have used these markers as signs of both cultural identity and critical political positioning; "Mexican American" to refer to U.S. citizens of Mexican descent or heritage; "Mexican national," "Mexican immigrant," *Mexicano*, or *Mexicana* to refer to citizens of Mexico, regardless of their ethnic or linguistic background; and the umbrella term "ethnic Mexican" to refer to members of the combined Mexican-heritage population of the United States without reference to their ethnic, linguistic, or citizenship status. Similarly, I use the terms "Latino," "Latina," "pan-Latino," "Hispanic," and "pan-Hispanic" as umbrella references to all persons of Latin American heritage or descent in the United States regardless of their ethnic or national origins. I hope that the text makes clear that these terms are used for rough descriptive purposes rather than as demarcations of immutable national and/or cultural essences.

2. Moises Sandoval, *Fronteras: A History of the Latin American Church in the USA since 1513* (San Antonio: Mexican American Cultural Center Press, 1983); Jay Dolan and Allan Figueroa Deck, eds., *Hispanic Catholic Culture in the U.S.: Issues and*

Concerns (Notre Dame, Ind.: University of Notre Dame Press, 1994); Jay Dolan and Gilberto M. Hinojosa, eds., *Mexican Americans and the Catholic Church* (Notre Dame, Ind.: University of Notre Dame Press, 1994); Jay Dolan and Jaime R. Vidal, eds., *Puerto Rican and Cuban Catholics in the U.S., 1900–1965* (Notre Dame, Ind.: University of Notre Dame Press, 1994).

3. Ramón A. Gutiérrez, *When Jesus Came, the Corn Mothers Went Away: Marriage, Sexuality, and Power in New Mexico, 1500–1846* (Stanford, Calif.: Stanford University Press, 1991); Jeanette Rodríguez, *Our Lady of Guadalupe: Faith and Empowerment among Mexican American Women* (Austin: University of Texas Press, 1994); Timothy Matovina, *Tejano Religion and Ethnicity: San Antonio, 1821–1860* (Austin: University of Texas Press, 1995); Albert L. Pulido, *The Sacred World of the Penitentes* (Washington, D.C.: Smithsonian Institution Press, 2000); Frederick John Dalton, *The Moral Vision of César Chávez* (Maryknoll, N.Y.: Orbis Books, 2003).

4. See, for example, Anthony M. Stevens-Arroyo and Gilbert Cadena, eds., *Old Masks, New Faces: Religion and Latino Identities* (New York: Bildner Center for Western Hemisphere Studies, 1995); Timothy Matovina and Gary Riebe-Estrella, eds., *Horizons of the Sacred: Mexican Traditions in U.S. Catholicism* (Ithaca, N.Y.: Cornell University Press, 2002); Miguel A. de la Torre and Gastón Espinosa, eds., *Rethinking Latino/a Religion and Identity* (Cleveland: Pilgrim Press, 2006); Hector Avalos, ed., *Introduction to the U.S. Latina and Latino Religious Experience* (Boston: Brill Academic Publishers, 2004); and Gastón Espinosa and Mario T. García, eds., *Mexican American Religions: Spirituality, Activism, and Culture* (Durham, N.C.: Duke University Press, 2008).

5. Space limitations preclude more than a glancing discussion of the larger field of Latino studies scholarship, but comparisons will be made in the analysis when warranted.

6. Roberto R. Treviño, *The Church in the Barrio: Mexican American Ethno-Catholicism in Houston* (Chapel Hill: University of North Carolina Press, 2006). It should be noted that Treviño's critique was not meant to suggest that the subject of religion has been completely absent from the historiography of ethnic Mexicans in the United States. Obviously, from the first major historical studies of Mexicans and Mexican Americans produced by pioneering scholars such as Paul S. Taylor, Manuel Gamio, Carlos Castañeda, and Emory S. Bogardus in the 1920s and 1930s and Carey McWilliams and others in the 1940s and beyond, religion was treated as an important cultural component of the nascent field of Mexican American history. Later, with the advent of modern Chicano history after the civil rights revolution of the 1960s, religious tradition was also often put to instrumental use as contextual background for the study of the Mexican American past, particularly with reference to religiously tinged historical events. This was seen most clearly in analyses of Cesar Chavez and the rise of the farmworkers' movement and of Reies López Tijerina and the emergence of his irredentist crusade in New Mexico. Still, it can be argued that for most secular Chicano/Latino scholars trained since the 1970s, attention to religion and religiosity and systematic engagement with Latino Christian and non-Christian metaphysics remain ancillary pursuits rather than central analytical concerns.

7. For recent discussion of some of these lacunae with reference to the intersection of social history, cultural history, and the history of human "sensibility," see

Daniel Wickberg, "What Is the History of Sensibilities? On Cultural Histories Old and New," *American Historical Review* 112, no. 3 (2007): 661–84.

8. See, for example, Donald Wiebe, *The Politics of Religious Studies: The Continuing Conflict with Theology in the Academy* (New York: St. Martin's Press, 1999); and Robert Orsi, "Everyday Miracles: The Study of Lived Religion," in *Lived Religion in America: Toward a History of Practice*, ed. David D. Hall (Princeton, N.J.: Princeton University Press, 1997), 3–21.

9. See Bill Maher, *Religulous*, directed by Larry Charles (Lions Gate Films, 2008); Richard Dawkins, *The God Delusion* (Boston: Houghton Mifflin, 2006); Sam Harris, *The End of Faith: Religion, Terror, and the Future of Reason* (New York: W. W. Norton & Co., 2004); Christopher Hitchens, *God Is Not Great: How Religion Poisons Everything* (New York: Twelve, 2007).

10. See Walter D. Mignolo, *Local Histories / Global Designs: Coloniality, Subaltern Knowledges, and Border Thinking* (Princeton, N.J.: Princeton University Press, 2000), 75; and Manu Goswami, "Remembering the Future," *American Historical Review* 113, no. 2 (April 2008): 422.

11. Historian Rodolfo Acuña was particularly strident in his assessment of the role of the church in Chicano history. Consistent with his adherence to the internal colonial model that was in vogue among Chicano intellectuals at the time, Acuña noted of Chicanos' relationship to Catholicism, "Although Mexicans comprised the majority of Catholics in the Southwest, they had no power within the institution. Few Mexicans became priests, and until recently, no Mexicans were bishops. The church in the United States was greatly influenced by an oligarchy of wealthy laymen who contributed heavily to the church coffers. In contrast, the Chicanos had little to give in material terms. . . . The church thus abetted the bigotry of its wealthy parishioners. The abandonment of the church was especially noticeable in rural areas where the rich parishioners employed Mexicans. There, the clergy knew that if they supported the Chicanos' rights, they would lose generous contributions. As a consequence, the church sided with the rich." Acuña, *Occupied America: The Chicano's Struggle toward Liberation* (London: Canfield Press, 1972), 148.

12. The Chicano challenge to constituted church authority in the 1960s and 1970s has been explored by a number of scholars. See, for example, primary documents generated by dissident groups such as Católicos por la Raza, PADRES (Padres Asociados para Derechos Religiosos, Educativos, y Sociales—Priests Associated for Religious, Education, and Social Rights), and Las Hermanas in *Presente! U.S. Latino Catholics from Colonial Origins to the Present*, ed. Timothy Matovina and Gerald E. Poyo (Maryknoll, N.Y.: Orbis Books, 2000), 209–218. See also Ana María Díaz-Stevens, "The Hispanic Challenge to U.S. Catholicism, Colonialism, Migration, and Religious Adaptation," in *El Cuerpo de Cristo: The Hispanic Presence in the U.S. Catholic Church*, ed. Peter Casarella and Raúl Gómez (New York: Crossroad Publishing, 1998), 157–79; and Gastón Espinosa, Virgilio Elizondo, and Jesse Miranda, eds., *Latino Religions and Civic Activism in the United States* (New York: Oxford University Press, 2005).

13. For more detailed discussion of these developments, see David G. Gutiérrez, "Sin Fronteras? Chicanos, Mexican Americans, and the Emergence of the Contemporary Mexican Immigration Debate, 1968–1978," *Journal of American Ethnic*

History 10, no. 4 (Summer 1991): 5–37; and Gutierrez, "Globalization, Labor Migration, and the Demographic Revolution: Ethnic Mexicans in the Late Twentieth Century," in *The Columbia History of Latinos in the United States since 1960*, ed. David G. Gutiérrez (New York: Columbia University Press, 2004), 43–86.

14. See table 8.1, "United States Mexican-Origin Population by Region and Foreign Birth, 1930–1990," in *North to Aztlán: A History of Mexican Americans in the United States*, by Arnoldo de León and Richard Griswold del Castillo, 2nd ed. (Wheeling, Ill.: Harlan Davidson, 2006), 160.

15. Ibid.; and Seth Motel, Statistical Portrait of Hispanics in the United States, 2010 (Washington, D.C.: Pew Hispanic Center, 2012), table 7, http://www.pe whispanic.org/2012/02/21/statistical-potrait-of-hispanics-in-the-united-states -2010/.

16. Of course, the growth of the pan-Latino population has been even more explosive. In 1960 there were fewer than 7 million Latinos of all backgrounds in the United States. By the turn of the twenty-first century that number had grown to 38 million, and the Pew Hispanic Center estimates that the population had reached almost 51 million by 2010. See Ibid., table 1. For a recent overview of the religious profile of the pan-Latino population, see Anthony M. Stevens-Arroyo, "From Barrios to Barricades: Religion and Religiosity in Latino Life," in Gutiérrez, *Columbia History of Latinos in the United States since 1960*, 303–54.

17. Indeed, the trajectory of Chicano history as it developed at the time was commonly conceived in terms of "generations," with the early twentieth century tagged as the "creation generation," the period between the 1940s and the mid-1960s as the "GI generation," and the post-1965 era as the "Chicano generation." For early iterations of this schematic view of Mexican American historical development, see Rodolfo Alvarez, "The Psycho-historical and Socioeconomic Development of the Chicano Community of the United States," *Social Science Quarterly* 53 (March 1973): 920–42; and Mario T. García, *Mexican Americans: Leadership, Ideology, and Identity, 1930–1960* (New Haven, Conn.: Yale University Press, 1989). For various critiques of this kind of conceptualization, see Alex M. Saragoza, "Recent Chicano Historiography: An Interpretive Essay," *Aztlán* 19, no. 1 (1988–90): 1–78; Gilbert G. González and Raul A. Fernández, *A Century of Chicano History: Empire, Nations, and Migration* (New York: Routledge, 2003); David G. Gutierrez, "The Third Generation: Reflections on Recent Chicano Historiography," *Mexican Studies/Estudios Mexicanos* 5, no. 1 (Summer 1989): 281–96, and Gutierrez, "An Ethnic Consensus? Mexican American Political Activism since the Great Depression," *Reviews in American History* 19 (June 1991): 289–95.

18. Although a few scholars continue to adhere to conceptual paradigms associated with the period in which Chicano studies first emerged, others have raised questions about the viability of these models in the twenty-first century. For examples of contemporary interpreters who have advocated for the continuation of lines of analysis and categorization that originated during the Chicano civil rights movement, see Ignacio M. García, "Chicano Studies since 'El Plan de Sánta Bárbara,'" in *Chicanas/Chicanos at the Crossroads: Social, Economic, and Political Change* (Tucson: University of Arizona Press, 1996), 181–204; and García, *Chicanismo: The Forging of a Militant Ethos among Mexican Americans* (Tucson: University of Arizona

Press, 1998); Armando Navarro, *La Raza Unida Party: A Chicano Challenge to the U.S. Two-Party Dictatorship* (Philadelphia: Temple University Press, 2000); and Jorge Mariscal, *Brown-Eyed Children of the Sun: Lessons from the Chicano Movement, 1965–1975* (Albuquerque: University of New Mexico Press, 2005). For skeptical views of this type of approach, see, for example, Juan Gómez-Quiñones, "Outside Inside—The Immigrant Workers: Creating Popular Myths, Cultural Expression, and Personal Politics in Borderlands Southern California," in *Chicano Renaissance: Contemporary Cultural Trends*, ed. David R. Maciel, Isidro D. Ortiz, and María Herrera-Sobek (Tucson: University of Arizona Press, 2000), 49–91; David G. Gutiérrez, "Demography and the Shifting Boundaries of 'Community': Reflections on 'U.S. Latinos' and the Evolution of Latino Studies," in Gutiérrez, *Columbia History of Latinos in the United States*, 1–42; and Gilda Ochoa, *Becoming Neighbors in a Mexican American Community: Power, Conflict, and Solidarity* (Austin: University of Texas Press, 2004).

19. See Nestor Rodríguez, "Theoretical and Methodological Issues of Latina/o Research," in *Latina/os in the United States: Changing the Face of América*, ed. Havidán Rodríguez, Rogelio Sáenz, and Cecilia Menjívar (New York: Springer, 2008), 3–18.

20. Guillermo Bonfil Batalla, *México Profundo: Reclaiming a Civilization*, trans. Phillip A. Dennis (Austin: University of Texas Press, 1996).

21. See Yolanda Broyles-González, "Indianizing Catholicism: Chicana/Mexicana Indigenous Spiritual Practices in Our Image," in *Chicana Traditions: Continuity and Change*, ed. Norma E. Cantú and Olga Nájera-Ramírez (Urbana: University of Illinois Press, 2000), 122.

22. For an excellent overview of the status of this ongoing debate, see "AHR Forum: Geoff Eley's *A Crooked Line*," *American Historical Review* 113, no. 2 (April 2008): 391–437.

23. Robert Orsi, "Everyday Miracles: The Study of Lived Religion," in *Lived Religion in America: Toward a History of Practice*, ed. David D. Hall (Princeton, N.J.: Princeton University Press, 1997), 7.

24. Robert Orsi, *Between Heaven and Earth: The Religious Worlds People Make and the Scholars Who Study Them* (Princeton, N.J.: Princeton University Press, 2005), 170, 171.

25. Ibid., 156.

26. Virginia Garrard-Burnett, introduction to *Earth as It Is in Heaven: Religion in Modern Latin America*, ed. Virginia Garrard-Burnett (Wilmington, Del.: Scholarly Resources), xv.

27. Luis D. León, *La Llorona's Children: Religion, Life, and Death in the U.S.-Mexican Borderlands* (Berkeley: University of California Press, 2004). See also an earlier iteration of his research agenda in León, "Metaphor and Place—The United States–Mexico Border as Center and Periphery in the Interpretation of Religion: 'Poetic' Formulation and Performance in Latino Religion," *Journal of the American Academy of Religion* 67, no. 3 (September 1999): 541–71.

28. León, *La Llorona's Children*, 15.

29. Ibid., esp. 5, 243.

30. See Tomás Ybarra-Frausto, "Rasquachismo: A Chicano Sensibility," in *Chicano Art: Resistance and Affirmation; An Interpretive Exhibition of the Chicano Art Move-*

ment, 1965–1985, ed. Richard Griswold del Castillo, Teresa McKenna, and Yvonne Yarbro-Bejarano (Los Angeles: Wright Art Gallery, UCLA, 1991), 155–62.

31. Gastón Espinosa, Virgilio Elizondo, and Jesse Miranda, eds., *Hispanic Churches in American Public Life: Summary of Findings* (South Bend, Ind.: Institute for Latino Studies, University of Notre Dame, 2003); Pew Forum on Religion and Public Life and the Pew Hispanic Center, *Changing Faiths: Latinos and the Transformation of American Religion* (Washington, D.C.: Pew Forum on Religion and Public Life and the Pew Hispanic Center, 2007). For comparison with an earlier period, see Leo Grebler, Joan W. Moore, and Ralph C. Guzmán, *The Mexican American People: The Nation's Second Largest Minority* (New York: Free Press, 1970), esp. pt. 5; and Patrick McNamara, "Assumptions, Theories and Methods in the Study of Latino Religion after 25 Years," in Stevens-Arroyo and Cadena, *Old Masks, New Faces,* 23–32.

32. Espinosa, Elizondo, and Miranda, *Hispanic Churches in American Public Life,* 86–87; Pew Forum, *Changing Faiths,* 6.

33. Rodolfo O. de la Garza and Jeronimo Cortina, "Are Latinos Republican and Just Don't Know It? The Latino Vote in the 2000 and 2004 Presidential Elections," *American Politics Research* 35, no. 2 (March 2007): 202–23.

34. For examples of these skeptical arguments, see Nathan J. Kelly and Jane Kelly, "Latino Religion and Partisanship in the United States," *Political Research Quarterly* 58 (2005): 87–95; Jongho Lee and Harry P. Pachón, "Leading the Way: An Analysis of the Effect of Religion on the Latino Vote," *American Politics Research* 35, no. 2 (March 2007): 252–72; George E. Schultze, *Strangers in a Foreign Land: The Organizing of Catholic Latinos in the United States* (Lanham, Md.: Lexington Books, 2007); and Nathan J. Kelly and Jane Morgan, "Latino Religious Traditionalism and Latino Politics in the United States," *American Politics Research* 36, no. 2 (March 2008): 236–63.

35. Edward E. Telles and Vilma Ortiz, *Generations of Exclusion: Mexican Americans, Assimilation, and Race* (New York: Russell Sage Foundation, 2008), esp. 199–202.

36. But again, it is also clear that such work may well help both refine the historical record on these key questions and provide deeper understanding of contemporary trends. For studies that are beginning to entertain such questions, see, for example, David Hayes-Bautista Werner O. Shink, and Jorge Chapa, *The Burden of Support: Young Latinos in an Aging Society* (Stanford, Calif.: Stanford University Press, 1988); David Hayes-Bautista, *La Nueva California: Latinos in the Golden State* (Berkeley: University of California Press, 2004); and Dowell Myers, *Immigrants and Boomers: Forging a New Social Contract for the Future of America* (New York: Russell Sage Foundation, 2007).

37. Ramón A. Gutiérrez, "Honor Ideology, Marriage Negotiation, and Class-Gender Domination in New Mexico, 1690–1846," *Latin American Perspectives* 12, no. 1 (Winter 1985): 81–104.

38. Robert A. Orsi, *Thank You, St. Jude: Women's Devotion to the Patron Saint of Hopeless Causes* (New Haven, Conn.: Yale University Press, 1996), 75.

39. Orlando S. Espín, *The Faith of the People: Theological Reflections on Popular Catholicism* (Maryknoll, N.Y.: Orbis Books, 1997), 4–5.

40. See, for example, Martha P.Cotera, *Diosa y Hembra: The History and Heritage of Chicanas in the U.S.* (Austin, Tex.: Information Systems Publications, 1976); Ad-

elaida del Castillo, "Malintzín Tenépal: A Preliminary Look into a New Perspective," in *Essays on la Mujer*, ed. Rosaura Sánchez and Rosa Martínez Cruz (Los Angeles: UCLA Chicano Studies Research Center Publications, 1977), 124–49; Sonya López, "The Role of the Chicana within the Student Movement," ibid., 16–29; Gloria Anzaldúa and Cherríe Moraga, eds., *This Bridge Called My Back: Writings by Radical Women of Color* (Watertown, Mass.: Persephone Press, 1981); Cherríe Moraga, *Loving in the War Years: Lo que nunca pasó por sus labios* (Boston: South End Press, 1983); and Gloria Anzaldúa, *Borderlands/La Frontera: The New Mestiza* (San Francisco: Aunt Lute Press, 1987).

41. For insightful analyses of the unfolding of this process, see Ramón A. Gutiérrez, "Community, Patriarchy and Individualism: The Politics of Chicano History and the Dream of Equality," *American Quarterly* 54, no. 1 (1993): 44–72; Alma M. García, introduction to *Chicana Feminist Thought: The Basic Historical Writings*, ed. Alma M. García (New York: Routledge, 1997), 1–19; and Paula Moya, "Postmodernism, 'Realism' and the Politics of Identity: Cherríe Moraga and Chicana Feminism," in *Feminist Genealogies, Colonial Legacies, Democratic Futures*, ed. Jacqui Alexander and Chandra Tapalde Mohanty (New York: Routledge, 1997), 125–50.

42. For excellent historical case studies of this kind of activism in action, see Mary S. Pardo, *Mexican American Women Activists: Identity and Resistance in Two Los Angeles Communities* (Philadelphia: Temple University Press, 1998); and Gina Marie Pitti, "'To 'Hear about God in Spanish': Ethnicity, Church, and Community Activism in the San Francisco Archdiocese's Mexican American *Colonias*, 1942–1965" (Ph.D. diss., Stanford University, 2003). In addition, while many Chicano militants attacked the Catholic Church for its patronizing attitudes toward Latinos, many others continued to advocate for church reform, used Catholicism as a foundation for their political activities, and established religious revivalist/renewal movements such as the Cursillo and the Encuentro. For discussion of the significance of these developments, see Stevens-Arroyo, "From Barrios to Barricades," esp. 313–33.

43. Lara Medina, *Las Hermanas: Chicana/Latina Religious-Political Activism in the U.S. Catholic Church* (Philadelphia: Temple University Press, 2004).

44. For further discussion of the evolution and significance of mujerista theology, see Ada María Isasi-Díaz and Yolanda Tarango, *Hispanic Women: Prophetic Voice in the Church* (Minneapolis: Fortress Press, 1992); Ada María Isasi-Díaz, *En La Lucha/In the Struggle: Elaborating a Mujerista Theology* (Minneapolis: Fortress Press, 1993); and Isasi-Díaz, *Mujerista Theology* (Maryknoll, N.Y.: Orbis Books, 1996).

45. Kristy Nablan-Warren, *The Virgin of El Barrio: Marian Apparitions, Catholic Evangelizing, and Mexican American Activism* (New York: NYU Press, 2005).

46. Peggy Levitt, *God Needs No Passport: Immigrants and the Changing American Religious Landscape* (New York: New Press, 2007), esp. 9–26.

47. There is a significant and growing literature on these types of links. Some representative examples are Elizabeth G. Ferris, "The Churches, Refugees, and Politics," in *Refugees and International Relations*, ed. Gil Loescher and Laila Monahan (New York: Oxford University Press, 1989), 159–78; Renny Golden and Michael McConnell, *Sanctuary: The New Underground Railroad* (Maryknoll, N.Y.: Orbis Books, 1986); Jacqueline María Hagan, *Deciding to Be Legal: A Maya Community in Houston* (Philadelphia: Temple University Press, 1994); María Cristina García, *Seeking Refuge:*

Central American Migration to Mexico, the United States, and Canada (Berkeley: University of California Press, 2006); Jeanne Petit, "Our Immigrant Coreligionists: The National Catholic Welfare Conference as an Advocate for Immigrants in the 1920s," in *Immigrant Rights in the Shadows of Citizenship*, ed. Rachel Ida Buff (New York: New York University Press, 2008): 315–28; and Pierrette Hondagneu Sotelo, *God's Heart Has No Borders: How Religious Activists Are Working for Immigrant Rights* (Berkeley: University of California Press, 2008).

48. León, *La Llorona's Children*, 244.

49. See Jorge Durand and Douglas S. Massey, *Miracles on the Border: Retablos of Mexican Migrants to the United States* (Tucson: University of Arizona Press, 1995).

50. Manuel A. Vásquez and Marie Friedman Marquardt, *Globalizing the Sacred: Religion across the Americas* (New Brunswick, N.J.: Rutgers University Press, 2003), 55.

51. Ibid., 59.

52. Robert Courtney Smith, *Mexican New York: Transnational Lives of New Immigrants* (Berkeley: University of California Press, 2006); Lynn Stephen, *Zapotec Women: Gender, Class, and Ethnicity in Globalized Oaxaca*, rev. ed. (Durham, N.C.: Duke University Press, 2005); and Stephen, *Transborder Lives: Indigenous Oaxacans in Mexico, California, and Oregon* (Durham, N.C.: Duke University Press, 2007). See also R. Stephen Warner and Judith G. Wittner, eds., *Gatherings in Diaspora: Religious Communities and the New Immigration* (Philadelphia: Temple University Press, 1998); Helen Rose Ebaugh and Janet Saltzman Chafetz, eds., *Religion across Borders: Transnational Immigrant Networks* (Walnut Creek, Calif.: Altimira Press, 2002); Jacqueline Hagan and Helen Rose Ebaugh, "Calling upon the Sacred: Migrants' Use of Religion in the Migration Process," *International Migration Review* 37, no. 4 (Winter 2003): 1145–62; and David A. Badillo, *Latinos and the New Immigrant Church* (Baltimore: Johns Hopkins University Press, 2006).

53. See, for example, Stephen R. Lloyd-Moffett, "The Mysticism and Social Action of César Chávez," in Espinosa, Elizondo, and Miranda, *Latino Religions and Civic Activism*, 35–52; and Luis D. León, "César Chávez and Mexican American Civil Religion," ibid., 53–64. Interestingly, one of León's later articles on Chavez offers a more nuanced reading of Chavez the symbol and Chavez the man. See Luis D. León, "César Chávez in American Religious Politics: Mapping the New Spiritual Line," in "Religion and Politics in the Contemporary United States," special issue, *American Quarterly* 59, no. 3 (September 2007): 857–81.

54. Given the veneration of figures like Tijerina and especially Chavez among ordinary Mexican Americans, until recently, most scholars have avoided looking critically at some of their less savory personal traits and activities. However, since these behaviors often had direct and material impacts on the movements they led, scholars and critics have begun to explore more critically some of the less salutary dimensions of their activities. See, for example, Miriam Pawel, "UFW: A Broken Contract," four-part series, *Los Angeles Times*, January 8–11, 2006; Pawel, *The Union of their Dreams: Power, Hope, and Struggle in Cesar Chavez's Farm Worker Movement* (New York: Bloomsbury, 2010); and Lorena Oropeza and Dionne Espinosa, eds., *Enriqueta Vasquez and the Chicano Movement: Writings from El Grito del Norte* (Houston: Arte Público Press, 2006). Historians Stephen Pitti at Yale and Matt García at Brown

are at work on book-length critical studies. In addition, the late Paul Henggeler at the University of Texas, Pan American, also produced an incomplete and as yet unpublished revisionist history of Chavez and the union before his untimely death.

55. Orsi, *Between Heaven and Earth*, 7.

56. See Richard White, "Round Table: Self and Subject," *Journal of American History* 89, no. 1 (2002): 7, http://www.historycooperative.org/journals/jah/89.1/white.html (accessed February 10, 2009).

Chapter 6

1. Lester J. Cappon, ed., *The Adams-Jefferson Letters* (Chapel Hill: University of North Carolina Press, 1988), 2:571.

2. On the negative reference group, see Robert K. Merton, *Social Theory and Social Structure* (New York: Free Press, 1968), 279–440.

3. Philip Hamburger, *Separation of Church and State* (Cambridge, Mass.: Harvard University Press, 2002), especially 479–92; see also Daniel Dreisbach, *Thomas Jefferson and the Wall of Separation between Church and State* (New York: New York University Press, 2002); and Evelyn Savidge Sterne, *Ballots and Bibles: Ethnic Politics and the Catholic Church in Providence* (Ithaca, N.Y.: Cornell University Press, 2004).

4. Louis Hartz, *The Founding of New Societies* (Chicago: University of Chicago Press, 1964).

5. Richard John Neuhaus, *The Catholic Moment: The Paradox of the Church in the Postmodern World* (New York: Harper and Row, 1987), 283.

6. J. G. A. Pocock, *The Machiavellian Moment: Florentine Political Thought and the Atlantic Republican Tradition* (Princeton, N.J.: Princeton University Press, 1975).

7. Michael J. Gerson, *Heroic Conservatism: Why Republicans Need to Embrace America's Ideals (and Why They Deserve to Fail If They Don't)* (New York: HarperOne, 2007), 160–63. See also his column "Open-Arms Conservatism," *Washington Post*, October 31, 2007, A21; and his Pew Forum talk, "Heroic Conservatism: A Conversation with Michael J. Gerson," including Michael Cromartie and E.J. Dionne, http://pewforum.org/events/?EventID=160 (accessed December 1, 2009).

8. Gerson, *Heroic Conservatism*, 161.

9. Gerson, "Heroic Conservatism: A Conversation."

10. Of course, the classic texts here are too many to enumerate, but two of the most important are Louis Hartz, *The Liberal Tradition in America* (New York: Harcourt, Brace and World, 1955); and Ernest Lee Tuveson, *Redeemer Nation: The Idea of America's Millennial Role* (Chicago: University of Chicago Press, 1968). See also Neil Jumonville, *Henry Steele Commager: Midcentury Liberalism and the History of the Present* (Chapel Hill: University of North Carolina Press, 1999).

11. John Ibson, "Virgin Land or Virgin Mary? Studying the Ethnicity of White Americans," *American Quarterly* 33, Bibliography Issue (1981): 284–308; reprinted as chapter 9 in *Ethnicity, Ethnic Identity, and Language Maintenance*, ed. George E. Pozzetti (New York: Garland Publishing, 1991), 160–84.

12. Henry Adams, *Mont-Saint-Michel and Chartres* (Boston: Houghton Mifflin, 1905); Adams, *The Education of Henry Adams: An Autobiography* (Boston: Massachusetts

Historical Society, 1918). See also the insightful treatment of Adams in T. J. Jackson Leare, *No Place of Grace: Antimodernism and the Transformation of American Culture* (New York: Pantheon, 1983), 262–97.

13. Barry Alan Shain, *The Myth of American Individualism: The Protestant Origins of American Political Thought* (Princeton, N.J.: Princeton University Press, 1994).

14. Michael J. Sandel, *Liberalism and the Limits of Justice* (Cambridge: Cambridge University Press, 1982); William Novak, *The People's Welfare: Law and Regulation in Nineteenth-Century America* (Chapel Hill: University of North Carolina Press, 1996).

15. Ralph Waldo Emerson, "Self-Reliance," in *The Collected Works of Ralph Waldo Emerson*, ed. Albert R. Ferguson, Joseph Slater, and Jean Ferguson Carr (Cambridge, Mass.: Belknap Press of Harvard University Press, 1971), 2:29–30.

16. Walt Whitman, *Walt Whitman: Poetry and Prose*, ed. Justin Kaplan (New York: Library of America, 1982), 84, 475.

17. Daniel Walker Howe, *Making the American Self: Jonathan Edwards to Abraham Lincoln* (New York: Oxford University Press, 1997), 50.

18. Ibid., 115.

19. Wilfred M. McClay, *The Masterless: Self and Society in Modern America* (Chapel Hill: University of North Carolina Press, 1994), 74–104; John L. Thomas, *Alternative America: Henry George, Edward Bellamy, Henry Demarest Lloyd, and the Adversary Tradition* (Cambridge, Mass.: Harvard University Press, 1983).

20. John Dewey, *Individualism—Old and New* (New York: Capricorn Books, 1962); McClay, *Masterless*, 149–88.

21. David Riesman, with Revel Denne and Nathan Glazor, *The Lonely Crowd: A Scholarly Study of the Changing American Character* (New Haven: Yale University Press, 1950); William H. Whyte, *The Organization Man* (New York: Simon and Schuster, 1956).

22. Cf. the extensive and magisterial work of philosopher Charles Taylor, including *The Ethics of Authenticity* (Cambridge, Mass.: Harvard University Press, 1992); *Sources of the Self: The Making of the Modern Identity* (Cambridge, Mass.: Harvard University Press, 1992); and *A Secular Age* (Cambridge, Mass.: Harvard University Press, 2007).

23. John McGreevy, *Catholicism and American Freedom: A History* (New York: W. W. Norton, 2003), 167. Paul Blanshard, *American Freedom and Catholic Power* (Boston: Beacon Press, 1949).

24. John Courtney Murray, SJ, *We Hold These Truths: Catholic Reflections on the American Proposition* (New York: Sheed and Ward, 1960); Keith J. Pavlischek, *John Courtney Murray and the Dilemma of Religious Toleration* (Kirksville, Mo.: Truman State University Press, 1994); Kenneth L. Grasso, " 'Building Better Than They Knew': John Courtney Murray on Catholicism, Modernity, and the American Proposition," *Journal of Catholic Social Thought* 4, no. 1 (2007): 163–98; McGreevy, *Catholicism and American Freedom*, 189–215.

25. John Courtney Murray, SJ, "The Construction of a Christian Culture," in *Bridging the Sacred and the Secular: Selected Writings of John Courtney Murray, SJ*, ed. J. Leon Hooper, SJ (Washington, D.C.: Georgetown University Press, 1994), 102.

26. John Courtney Murray, "Freedom, Responsibility, and the Law," *Catholic Lawyer* 2 (July 1956): 218; and Murray, "Construction of a Christian Culture," 103.

27. Kenneth L. Grasso, "Beyond Liberalism: Human Dignity, the Free Society, and the Second Vatican Council," in *Catholicism, Liberalism, and Communitarianism: The Catholic Intellectual Tradition and the Moral Foundations of Democracy*, ed. Kenneth L. Grasso, Gerard V. Bradley, and Robert P. Hunt (Lanham, Md.: Rowman and Littlefield, 1995), 55; and Grasso, "Saving Modernity from Itself: John Paul II on Human Dignity, 'the Whole Truth about Man', and the Modern Quest for Freedom," in *In Defense of Human Dignity: Essays for Our Times*, ed. Robert P. Kraynak and Glenn Tinder (Notre Dame, Ind.: University of Notre Dame Press, 2003), 207–36.

28. John Paul II, *Centesimus Annus*, ¶39, http://www.vatican.va/holy_father/john_paul_ii/encyclicals/documents/hf_jp-ii_enc_01051991_centesimus-annus_en.html (accessed December 1, 2009); *Pacem in Terris*, ¶16, http://www.vatican.va/holy_father/john_xxiii/encyclicals/documents/hf_j-xxiii_enc_11041963_pacem_en.html (accessed December 1, 2009). Some useful sources relating to the larger structure of Catholic social thought, including the way in which this body of thought has been communicated to the laity, include Kenneth R. Himes, ed., *Modern Catholic Social Teaching: Commentaries and Interpretations* (Washington, D.C.: Georgetown University Press, 2005); Charles E. Curran, *Catholic Social Teaching, 1891 Present: A Historical, Theological, and Ethical Analysis* (Washington, D.C.: Georgetown University Press, 2002); Edward P. DeBerri and James E. Hug, *Catholic Social Teaching: Our Best Kept Secret* (Maryknoll, N.Y.: Orbis Books, 2005); David J. O'Brien and Thomas A. Shannon, eds., *Catholic Social Thought: The Documentary Heritage* (Maryknoll, N.Y.: Orbis Books, 2005); George Weigel and Robert Royal, eds., *A Century of Catholic Social Thought: Essays on "Rerum Novarum" and Nine Other Key Documents* (Washington, D.C.: Ethics and Public Policy Center, 1991); Kevin E. McKenna, *A Concise Guide to Catholic Social Teaching* (Notre Dame, Ind.: Ave Maria Press, 2002); and Kenneth R. Himes, *Responses to 101 Questions on Catholic Social Teaching* (New York: Paulist Press, 2001). Reading through the sources, which range from the scholarly to the popular and didactic, one cannot help but be impressed by the fluidity of Catholic social teaching and the sometimes confusing variety of ways in which it has been conceptualized and presented.

29. Curran, *Catholic Social Teaching*, 250.

30. Ibid., 251.

Conclusion

1. At this writing there are twenty-five Roman Catholics serving in the United States Senate—sixteen Democrats and nine Republicans, together accounting for one-quarter of the total—and 134 Catholics serving in the United States House of Representatives, accounting for 31 percent of the total of 435, including House Speaker John Boehner. Former U.S. senator Joseph Biden is the first Catholic ever elected vice president.

2. Irish American males constituted only 7.5 percent of the labor force in 1900 but accounted for one-sixth of the teamsters, metalworkers, and masons, and nearly a third of plumbers, steamfitters, and boilermakers," writes historian Bruce Nelson. "Their position of dominance in the ranks of organized labor was even

more remarkable. By the early twentieth century, Irish Catholics headed 'more than fifty' of the 110 affiliated national unions of the American Federation of Labor (AFL) and were a major component of the unions' second-level and shop-floor leadership." Bruce Nelson, "Irish Americans, Irish Nationalism, and the 'Social' Question, 1916–1923," *Boundary 2* 31, no. 1 (2004): 147–78. Much of the coverage of Catholics in the twentieth-century U.S. labor force and labor unions focuses on the period from 1900 to 1925 and on Irish Catholics; the primary historiographical debate centers on their presumed antisocialist political conservatism, which is sometimes traced to their religion. Nelson notes a shift in the historiography of Irish Americans' relationship to the American working class from the work of David Montgomery, Sean Wilentz, Eric Foner, and David Brundage (among others), which emphasized the deep involvement of the Irish in the labor reform movements of the 1870s and 1880s, to that of Kerby Miller and David Emmons, which has portrayed the Irish American ethos as largely incompatible with socialism and other forms of labor radicalism that flourished in the early twentieth century. See especially Eric Foner, "Class, Ethnicity, and Radicalism in the Gilded Age: The Land League and Irish-America," in Foner, *Politics and Ideology in the Age of the Civil War* (New York: Oxford University Press, 1980), 150–200; Kerby A. Miller, *Emigrants and Exiles: Ireland and the Irish Exodus to North America* (New York: Oxford University Press, 1985); and David M. Emmons, *The Butte Irish: Class and Ethnicity in an American Mining Town, 1875–1925* (Urbana: University of Illinois Press, 1987). For a general statement of the (understudied) importance of Catholics in labor unions, see Charles R. Morris, *American Catholic: The Saints and Sinners Who Built America's Most Powerful Church* (New York: Times Books, 1997), 89, 111, 116–17, 133. In his study of Worcester, Massachusetts, Timothy Meagher argues persuasively that the persistent identification of Irish Catholics as conservative is an oversimplification. While highlighting the church's hostility to socialism, Meagher notes the development of an Irish Catholic outlook that had crystallized into a prototype of "urban liberalism" by the second decade of the twentieth century. Mary Lethert Wingerd makes the same point in her study of St. Paul, Minnesota, another "Irish town." Meagher, *Inventing Irish America* (Notre Dame, Ind.: University of Notre Dame Press, 2001), 10–13, 324; Mary Lethert Wingerd, *Claiming the City: Politics, Faith, and the Power of Place in St. Paul* (Ithaca, N.Y.: Cornell University Press, 2001), 101–6, 144–45.

3. In following the common usage of most historians of North America and/or the United States, I have retained the use of the word "America" as a synonym, given the context, for North America or the United States despite the understandable objections of scholars of Central America, the Caribbean, and South America.

4. Rosemary Haughton, *The Catholic Thing* (1980) (Springfield, Ill.: Templegate Publishers, 1997).

5. James Davidson, *Catholicism in Motion: The Church in American Society* (Ligouri, Mo.: Ligouri Publications, 1999).

6. David O'Brien, *Public Catholicism* (New York: Macmillan, 1989), 247.

7. R. Scott Appleby and John Haas, "The Last Supernaturalists: Fenton, Connell, and the Threat of Catholic Indifferentism," *U.S. Catholic Historian* 13 (Winter 1995): 23–48.

8. Robert Wuthnow, *The Restructuring of American Religion* (Princeton, N.J.: Princeton University Press, 1988).

9. David A. Hollinger, *Postethnic America: Beyond Multiculturalism* (New York: Basic Books, 1995), 54.

10. What Jon Butler said of American religious history is also more broadly applicable to American history: "Catholicism seems foreign rather than native, institutional rather than individual, hierarchical rather than democratic, and liturgical rather than evangelical. Yet it is the very richness and complexity of Catholicism that advances its promise as a model for understanding the American religious experience." Jon Butler, "Historiographical Heresy: Catholicism as a Model for American Religious History," in *Belief in History: Innovative Approaches to European and American Religion*, ed. Thomas Kselman (Notre Dame, Ind.: University of Notre Dame Press, 1991), 287–88.

11. Robert A. Orsi, *The Madonna of 115th Street: Faith and Community in Italian Harlem, 1880–1950* (New Haven, Conn.: Yale University Press, 1985); Orsi, *Thank You, St. Jude: Women's Devotion to the Patron Saint of Hopeless Causes* (New Haven, Conn.: Yale University Press, 1996); Timothy Matovina and Gary Riebe-Estrella, eds., *Horizons of the Sacred: Mexican Traditions in U.S. Catholicism* (Ithaca, N.Y.: Cornell University Press, 2002); Jay P. Dolan, *The Immigrant Church: New York's Irish and German Catholic, 1815–1865* (Baltimore: Johns Hopkins University Press, 1975); Margaret M. McGuinness, "Let Us Go to the Altar: American Catholics and the Eucharist, 1926–1976," in *Habits of Devotion: Catholic Religious Practice in Twentieth-Century America,* ed. James M. O'Toole (Ithaca, N.Y.: Cornell University Press, 2004), 9–88; James P. McCartin, *Prayers of the Faithful: The Shifting Spiritual Life of American Catholics* (Cambridge, Mass.: Harvard University Press, 2010); John T. McGreevy, *Catholicism and American Freedom: A History* (New York: W. W. Norton, 2003); Patrick Allitt, *Catholic Intellectuals and Conservative Politics in America, 1950–1985* (Ithaca, N.Y.: Cornell University Press, 1993); Evelyn Savidge Sterne, *Ballots and Bibles: Ethnic Politics and the Catholic Church in Providence* (Ithaca, N.Y.: Cornell University Press, 2003); Wingerd, *Claiming the City*; Paula M. Kane, *Separatism and Subculture: Boston Catholicism, 1900–1920* (Chapel Hill: University of North Carolina Press, 1994); James T. Fisher, *On the Irish Waterfront: The Crusader, the Movie, and the Soul of the Port of New York* (New York: Cornell University Press, 2009); Timothy Kelly. "Pittsburgh Catholicism," *U.S. Catholic Historian*, 18.4 (2000): 64–75; David J. O'Brien, *Public Catholicism* (New York: Macmillan; London: Collier Macmillan Publishers, 1989); Kathleen Sprows Cummings, *New Women of the Old Faith: Gender and American Catholicism in the Progressive Era* (Chapel Hill: University of North Carolina Press, 2009); Carol Coburn, *Spirited Lives: How Nuns Shaped Catholic Culture and American Life, 1836–1920* (Chapel Hill: University of North Carolina Press, 1999); Suellen Hoy, *Good Hearts: Catholic Sisters in Chicago's Past* (Urbana: University of Illinois Press, 2006); Amy Koehlinger, *The New Nuns: Racial Justice and Religious Reform in the 1960s* (Cambridge, Mass.: Harvard University Press, 2007); Joseph P. Chinnici, OFM., "The Catholic Community of Prayer, 1926–1976," in O'Toole, *Habits of Devotion*, 187–236; Leslie Woodcock Tentler, *Catholics and Contraception: An American History* (Ithaca, N.Y.: Cornell University Press, 2004); Una Cadegan, *All Good Books Are Catholic Books* (Ithaca, N.Y.: Cornell University Press, forthcoming);

Paul Elie, *The Life You Save May Be Your Own: An American Pilgrimage* (New York: Farrar, Straus and Giroux, 2003); James M. O'Toole, *The Faithful: A History of Catholics in America* (Cambridge, Mass.: Belknap Press of Harvard University Press, 2008); Philip Gleason, *Contending with Modernity: Catholic Higher Education in the United States* (Notre Dame, Ind.: University of Notre Dame Press, 1995).

⊂⊙ ACKNOWLEDGMENTS

This volume emerged in the context of the Catholicism in Twentieth-Century America project of the Cushwa Center for the Study of American Catholicism, University of Notre Dame. Funded by a generous grant from the Lilly Foundation, developed in conversation with Jeanne Knoerle, SP, Fred Hofheinz, Chris Coble, and Craig Dykstra, the project featured a series of conferences at Notre Dame that brought together an extraordinary company of scholars of American religion over several years. *Catholics in the American Century* is the seventh book produced as a result of that collaboration, and we are grateful to our editor at Cornell University Press, Michael McGandy, who has chaperoned most of the manuscripts through the publication process (and is working now on the eighth). Our friend and colleague Timothy Matovina was director of the Cushwa Center when the conference leading to this volume was held, and we thank him for hosting that seminal event, which provided the occasion for Joseph Chinnici, OFM, James T. Fisher, Philip Gleason, Amy Koehlinger, James McCartin, and Leslie Tentler to provide invaluable critical feedback to the authors. Not least, we stand in debt to the redoubtable Paula Brach of the Cushwa Center and the resilient Barbara Lockwood of the Kroc Institute for International Peace Studies for their administrative support, and to Dixie Dillon and Josh Kercsmar of Notre Dame's Department of History for their editorial assistance.

Scott Appleby
Kathleen Sprows Cummings
March 2012

ᐯ Contributors

R. Scott Appleby is Professor of History at the University of Notre Dame, director of the Kroc Institute for International Peace Studies, and former director of the Cushwa Center for the Study of American Catholicism. Author or editor of books on Catholic history and theology, global fundamentalisms and religious peacebuilding, he is the recipient of three honorary doctorates and a fellow of the American Academy of Arts and Sciences.

Lizabeth Cohen is the Howard Mumford Jones Professor of American Studies and chair of the History Department at Harvard University. She is the author of *Making a New Deal: Industrial Workers in Chicago, 1919–1939* (1990) and *A Consumers' Republic: The Politics of Mass Consumption in Postwar America* (2004).

Kathleen Sprows Cummings is an associate professor of American Studies and associate director of the Cushwa Center for the Study of American Catholicism at the University of Notre Dame. She is the author of *New Women of the Old Faith: Gender and American Catholicism in the Progressive Era* (2009).

R. Marie Griffith is the John C. Danforth Distinguished Professor in the Humanities and director of the John C. Danforth Center on Religion and Politics at Washington University in St. Louis. Her major publications include *God's Daughters: Evangelical Women and the Power of Submission* (1997), *Born Again Bodies: Flesh and Spirit in American Christianity* (2004), *Women and Religion in the African Diaspora: Knowledge, Power, and Performance* (coedited with Barbara Dianne Savage, 2006), *American Religions: A Documentary History* (2007), and *Religion and Politics in the Contemporary United States* (coedited with Melani McAlister, 2008).

David G. Gutiérrez is an associate professor in the Department of History at the University of California at San Diego. He is the author of *Walls and Mirrors: Mexican Americans, Mexican Immigrants, and the Politics of Ethnicity* (1995) and the editor of *Between Two Worlds: Mexican Immigrants in the United States* (1996) and *The Columbia History of Latinos in the United States since 1960* (2004).

Wilfred M. McClay holds the SunTrust Bank Chair of Excellence in Humanities at the University of Tennessee at Chattanooga. His major publications include *The Masterless: Self and Society in Modern America* (1994),

The Student's Guide to U.S. History (2001), and *Religion Returns to the Public Square: Faith and Policy in America* (2003).

JOHN T. McGREEVY is I. A. O'Shaughnessy Dean of the College of Arts and Letters and Professor of History at the University of Notre Dame. He is the author *Parish Boundaries: The Catholic Encounter with Race in the Twentieth Century Urban North*, (1996) and *Catholicism and American Freedom: A History* (2003).

ROBERT A. ORSI holds the Grace Craddock Nagle Chair in Catholic Studies at Northwestern University. His major publications include *The Madonna of 115th Street: Faith and Community in Italian Harlem, 1880–1950* (1985), *Thank You, St. Jude: Women's Devotion to the Patron Saint of Hopeless Causes* (1998), *Gods of the City: Religion and the American Urban Landscape* (editor) (1999), and *Between Heaven and Earth: The Religious Worlds People Make and the Scholars Who Study Them* (2004).

THOMAS J. SUGRUE is the David Boies Professor of History and Sociology at the University of Pennsylvania. He is the author of *The Origins of the Urban Crisis: Race and Inequality in Postwar Detroit* (1996), *Sweet Land of Liberty: The Forgotten Struggle for Civil Rights in the North* (2008), and *Not Even Past: Barack Obama and the Burden of Race* (2010),

∞ INDEX